The Art of Effective Facilitation

D1562696

ACPA Books and Media Contact Information

The Art of Effective Facilitation

Reflections From Social Justice Educators

Edited by

LISA M. LANDREMAN

STERLING, VIRGINIA

Published by Stylus Publishing, LLC
22883 Quicksilver Drive
Sterling, Virginia 20166-2102

Library of Congress Cataloging-in-Publication Data
The art of effective facilitation : reflections from social
justice educators / edited by Lisa M. Landreman.
     pages cm
Includes bibliographical references and index.
ISBN 978-1-57922-973-3 (cloth : alk. paper)
ISBN 978-1-57922-974-0 (pbk. : alk. paper)
ISBN 978-1-57922-978-8 (library networkable e-edition)
ISBN 978-1-57922-979-5 (consumer e-edition)
1. Social justice—Study and teaching.   2. Multicultural
education.   3. Critical pedagogy.   I. Landreman, Lisa M.,
1965– editor of compilation.
LC192.2.A78   2013
370.11'5—dc23   2012047150

13-digit ISBN: 978-1-57922-973-3 (cloth)
13-digit ISBN: 978-1-57922-974-0 (paper)
13-digit ISBN: 978-1-57922-978-8 (library networkable
e-edition)
13-digit ISBN: 978-1-57922-979-5 (consumer e-edition)

Printed in the United States of America

All first editions printed on acid-free paper
that meets the American National Standards Institute
Z39-48 Standard.

Bulk Purchases

Quantity discounts are available for use in workshops
and for staff development.
Call 1-800-232-0223

First Edition, 2013

10   9   8   7   6   5   4   3   2   1

Contents

Acknowledgments

To the many contributors, I offer a big thank-you for sharing their time, energy, patience, and best thinking to the process of developing this book. Their willingness to share their authentic, personal stories—missteps, challenges, and all—has moved me to become a better social justice educator, as I trust it will the readers.

The editorial board members of the ACPA–College Student Educators International Commission for Social Justice Educators played an important role in shaping the direction of this book from the call for submissions to many hours reading and rereading chapters and providing thoughtful feedback. This was a learning experience for all of us, and their willingness to take part in this collaborative process was invaluable.

Larry Mrozek served as a helpful and supportive editorial assistant. Together we worked through the construction of the initial chapters—compiling feedback, corresponding with authors and editorial board members, and discussing the nuances of social justice facilitation. I will forever be indebted to Larry's willingness to attend to the details of APA style.

A special appreciation goes to those at ACPA Books and Media for their enthusiasm for and feedback on this publication. In particular, Paul Shang from the University of Oregon, Books and Media associate editor, has been a wonderful source of support and counsel as we worked through this process together. His willingness to ask honest questions and provide feedback have been useful in clarifying my values and thinking and helped push this work forward, particularly as a book that is more accessible to a wide audience of educators.

Finally, I am very grateful to the ACPA Commission for Social Justice Educators. The existence and growth of this commission is a testament to what a small group of visionary leaders with an eye to justice can accomplish. The commission's continued commitment to social justice education in the spirit of learning and connection is an inspiration to me and educators everywhere.

Preface

WHETHER NEW to the field of student affairs or a seasoned administrator, you have likely attended a well-intentioned multicultural workshop that was unsuccessful. Perhaps the workshop was too advanced or too remedial for the participants. It may have been too complex a topic for the time allowed or for the capabilities of the presenter. At best it was ineffective. At worst, however, it decreased the likelihood that the participants would explore multicultural topics in the future, or it even caused harm. Becoming an effective facilitator for social justice educational efforts requires more than good intentions. Topics such as race, sexual orientation, gender, socioeconomic class, ethnicity, or ability are enmeshed in our own cultural traditions, our identities, our hurts, our joys, and our ways of seeing and being in the world. Workshops, trainings, or discussions that explore these topics require the facilitator to apply unique kinds of awareness and skills for these experiences to be truly transformative and, in some cases, healing.

Social justice facilitation is an art that comes from understanding oneself, designing optimal learning environments, developing authentic relationships, and articulating multicultural concepts, but also from practice—practice that includes ongoing reflection, action, and relearning as facilitators. The contributors to this book offer their experiences to help the reader transform social justice theory to practice. These authors have varied levels of facilitation experience, social identities, educational backgrounds, and positions within higher education and have been engaged in social justice education in and out of the classroom. These educators share their successes, reflections, challenges, mistakes, learning, and strategies that are helping them become more effective facilitators (as it is a lifelong journey).

Whether you identify as a teacher, trainer, educator, student affairs practitioner, higher education administrator, or facilitator, increasing students' multicultural understanding and graduating responsible global citizens who can make positive change in the world are likely aims for your institution.

More and more faculty and student affairs administrators are asked to become social justice educators who are responsible for preparing students to live successfully in and contribute to a multicultural society in ways that are equitable for all. However, too many educators' efforts reflect approaches to multicultural education that fall short of what could be called social justice. These programs provide "'exposure' or cosmetic efforts that fail to address the culpability of the dominant culture in perpetuating inequity and do not provide students with the knowledge and skills necessary to work for a more just society" (Jenks, Lee, & Kanpol, 2001, p. 88). The contributors to this book discuss how they address this concern. This book will benefit educators from a variety of contexts and from a range of experience levels by illuminating the art and complexity of facilitation and the ongoing reflection required to be successful in achieving the aspirations we set for ourselves in educating students toward social justice goals.

The journey to develop this book went through several transitions before arriving at its final destination. Discussions began at a Commission for Social Justice Educators directorate body meeting during the 2009 ACPA convention. Earlier, an e-mail was sent to the Commission for Social Justice Educators Listserv requesting a how-to manual for implementing the Tunnel of Oppression, a popular experiential exercise that illustrates multiple forms of oppression for participants. The directorate body began to discuss an ongoing question that has perplexed members since its inception in 2006: What is our role and responsibility to respond to these numerous how-to requests?

As an ACPA commission, our mission is to provide a place for college student educators committed to a broad range of social justice issues to network; share knowledge, tools, and resources; collaborate across institutions and identities; and provide support to social justice educators. Certainly gathering and sharing best practices in social justice education is consistent with these roles. Yet many of us were uncomfortable sharing exercises or how-to advice without knowing more of the context. Our response was dependent on the skill level of the facilitator, the developmental readiness of the participants, the particular issues and historical context of the campus, and the answers to myriad other questions that should be considered prior to designing and facilitating a social justice training session. We worried about the potential impact on learners resulting from the uncritical use of exercises and the lack of facilitators' personal reflection that is crucial to effective social justice education. Too many of us had experienced the negative consequences of social justice workshops gone wrong, understanding fully that "the magic is almost never in the exercise or the handout but, instead, is in the facilitation" (Landreman, Edwards, Balón, & Anderson, 2008, p. 2). This last point was illuminated in a 2008 *About Campus* article, "Wait! It Takes Time to Develop Rich and Relevant Social Justice Curriculum," and encouraged readers to think more complexly about social justice education. How could we convey comprehensive information such as this in an e-mail response?

Several quality publications have served as foundational texts for many of the contributors to this book and other social justice educators. These indispensible works provide frameworks to help readers understand and critically analyze multiple forms of oppression and issues in social justice education. Examples include *Teaching for Diversity and Social Justice* (Adams, Bell, & Griffin, 2007), *Readings for Diversity and Social Justice* (Adams et al., 2010), *Privilege, Power, and Difference* (Johnson, 2001), and *Developing Social Justice Allies* (Reason, Broido, Davis, & Evans, 2005). In addition, in the popular book *Teaching for Diversity and Social Justice*, interactive, experiential, and pedagogical principles are presented that can help learners understand the meaning of social difference and oppression in society and in their personal lives.

Two other important contributions to the literature include, first, *Multiculturalism on Campus: Theories, Models, and Practices for Understanding Diversity and Creating Inclusion* (Cuyjet, Howard-Hamilton, & Cooper, 2011), which explores models and theories that have historically informed our understanding of the development of college students and offers new interpretations for understanding historically marginalized students. The book introduces the problems, concerns, issues, and perspectives of various cultural groups on a college campus and offers suggestions for faculty and student affairs practitioners' development of cultural competence. Second, *Facilitating Intergroup Dialogues: Bridging Differences, Catalyzing Change* (Maxwell, Nagda, & Thompson, 2011) provides guidance on how to facilitate a particular kind of social justice program: intergroup dialogues. The important role facilitators played in the intergroup dialogue participants' experiences is shown throughout the book. Facilitators were identified as key to contributing to the participants' gains in a variety of characteristics essential to social justice learning. These dialogue groups employ an explicit pedagogy that features a particular kind of sustained content, group structure, and facilitator-guided process. While certainly *Facilitating Intergroup Dialogues* provides guidance that is transferable to other kinds of social justice education efforts, the book's primary focus is specifically on the intergroup dialogue program model used at many colleges and universities throughout the country.

These publications serve as foundational works that are important in informing educators' social justice facilitation efforts. However, few prior works specifically addressed the art of social justice facilitation in the depth of personal narratives offered by facilitators faced with challenges and how they overcame them. This book was developed to complement the afore-mentioned texts by communicating a personal voice that explores a particular kind of social justice practice—social justice facilitation—and the multiple approaches to executing successful facilitation.

While many of us used the previously mentioned resources to begin our work as social justice educators, some questions remained unanswered: How do I best apply the social justice theory and scholarship I am reading to prepare myself for social justice facilitation? How do I respond when things aren't going as planned? How can I apply what I have read to become a better facilitator? Should I prepare differently for workshops around specific identities? Our learning as educators committed to creating inclusive campuses and engaging in socially just practices can be accelerated when we take the risk to make our learning transparent to other educators.

All of us who have engaged in social justice facilitation have had incidents in our classes or workshops that challenged our thinking and our ability to facilitate. These challenges came despite our educational backgrounds, understandings, or years of experience. As the societal landscape changes, the tools, strategies, and ways of connecting with one another need to change. In recalling the aftermaths of our own facilitations gone wrong, we recognize that we may have had a negative impact on our participants. Strong facilitators understand that facilitation must be a thoughtful, intentional act and that even the best of facilitators struggle and make mistakes. What has enhanced our facilitation is being committed to doing our own personal work, continuing to be engaged in our own learning, and having the support of a community of social justice educators who can listen to our stories and help us reflect and acquire greater understanding and skills. What we offer in this book are personal stories from facilitators that illuminate the art and complexity of social justice facilitation.

We have taken a different approach to creating this book, one that mirrors our commitment to ensuring a collaborative process that allows for a diversity of perspectives to be heard. An open invitation was issued to any member of the Commission for Social Justice Educators directorate body to serve on the editorial board. This board of seven members is diverse in terms of their multiple social identities (i.e., race, class, gender identity, sexual orientation, age); experiences with teaching, training, writing, and research on social justice topics; and positions in higher education (i.e., faculty, doctoral students, entry-level professionals, mid- and senior-level administrators). The editorial board assisted in the development of the open call to authors and the evaluation rubric used to review submissions. The call for submissions was shared on listservs, in newsletters, and at ACPA convention programs. Each chapter submission was reviewed by two or three reviewers in addition to a review by me, the editor. Although it is not possible to address all critical facilitation issues or voices in one book, I invited authors with particular expertise to submit chapters in some key omitted areas identified by the editorial board.

SOCIAL JUSTICE CONCEPTS AND LANGUAGE

The concepts and discourse surrounding social justice education can be found in a wide range of communities and ideological beliefs from religious traditions (e.g., Catholic social teachings, Judaism, Islam) to academic discourses (e.g., Rawls, 1971; critical theorists) to political activists (e.g., Freire, 1970; the Green Party) and, therefore, come with a range of nuances and meanings. Words and phrases such as *success for all, inclusion, empowerment,* and *equity* may be popular rhetoric among people from diverse political positions, yet strong disagreements remain concerning the strategies for obtaining these seemingly lofty goals. For some, just the words *social justice* can conjure up a set of social and political beliefs that arouse fear for the loss of a shared American culture. For others, social justice represents an acknowledgment of the existence of a system of unequal distribution of resources that has provided unfair advantage to some members of society and a commitment toward changing this system.

The concern that social justice education moves us away from a common culture can be found in the comments of multicultural education critic Schlesinger (1991), who stated,

> What happens when people of different ethnic origins, speaking different languages and professing different religions, settle in the same geographical locality and live under the same political sovereignty? Unless a common purpose binds them together, tribal antagonisms will drive them apart. (p. 13)

Conservative critiques such as these are primarily concerned that schools and universities are responding to diversity in an "increasingly harmful manner" (Sleeter, 1995, p. 83) and that these damaging ideas increasingly drive educational efforts. Approaches that drive educational efforts primarily toward our "common purpose," often referred to as *assimilation,* is in conflict with the strategies, theories, and concepts of contemporary social justice efforts (Jenks et al., 2001) and with the approach we take in this book. Assimilation efforts have resulted in specific cultures' being ignored and excluded, negatively affecting educational attainment for many.

As social justice educators, we aim to help educators identify and analyze dehumanizing processes on our campuses and in the larger society, reflect on our own socialization, and engage in proactive strategies to dismantle oppression. Our concept of social justice within education includes elements such as giving voice to particular groups' experiences, incorporating sociopolitical perspectives into dialogue (i.e., more than dates and facts), reflecting upon and asking critical questions to motivate students to become culturally competent and critical thinkers, and creating classrooms and educational environments where students feel intellectually and emotionally able to explore issues and topics. To incorporate these elements into effective facilitation, facilitators must come to these processes having done their own work. We believe that multicultural and social justice education efforts cannot afford to divorce a focus on theoretical issues from the lived experiences of oppressed groups (McLaren, 1995). "The problem of multiculturalism must not be reduced to simply one of attitudes and temperament or, in the case of the academy, textual disagreement and discourse wars" (McLaren, 1995, p. 203). *Multiculturalism* (and, we would contend, *social justice*) has too often been transformed into a code word in contemporary political jargon that has been grossly invoked in order to divert attention from the racism and social injustice in this country and the ways differences are demonized (McLaren, 1995).

It is important to note that the philosophical and political critiques and ideological conflicts surrounding notions of social justice and strategies to remedy societal disparities have been going on for centuries. Unfortunately in many cases, both liberal and conservative views of multiculturalism have contributed to an aversion to rather than a respect for difference. Analyzing these debates is beyond the scope of this book, but it is important to acknowledge the existence of these conflicts and their impact on educational reform efforts.

In the first chapter Christopher MacDonald-Dennis and I briefly recount the multicultural and social justice movement and the conceptions of theory and language that followed. Critics and advocates of social justice education have identified the language of social justice education as problematic, but for different reasons. Critics find the language of social justice educators divisive, elitist, and political. The authors of *Readings for Diversity and Social Justice* acknowledged their difficulty with social justice terminology when they stated,

> The binary terms "oppressor" and "oppressed," for example, do not reflect the intersections of privilege or disadvantage across different identities and different social locations or positions. We continue to struggle to frame language that doesn't trivialize the power or the damage from the oppressive system we want to expose. (Adams et al., 2010, p. xxix)

The introductory chapter provides a framework for understanding social justice theory that informs such language as *social identity, target, agent* or *privileged,* and *marginalized*—terms that attempt to capture the positions of groups of people within a system of oppression based on social hierarchy. Social justice education strives to bring these social structures into the consciousness of our everyday lives so that we can then begin to identify strategies to dismantle them. However, these labels can initially feel uncomfortable for people new to social justice education and the perspective that the "either/or" categorizing, often referred to as a binary framework, can discount the complexity of the intersections of our identities. The struggle we face is to teach and communicate social justice goals in a language and manner that can be embraced by the general public, not only by members of the academy. The task is to connect the necessary structural and contextual analyses with real issues of educational practice, inside and outside the classroom.

The contributors were not asked to subscribe to particular word choices but rather to define terms as appropriate for their topic, although shared understandings of social justice theory and concepts are evident between chapters. We recognize that having common language and shared meaning is important in reaching understanding and that not defining language can be confusing. However, language is fluid, ever evolving, and difficult to reconcile. We ask readers to continue to work within this discomfort as this is the place where new understandings and transformative learning happens.

The mission of the ACPA Commission for Social Justice Educators is to provide a collaborative home for college student educators who are committed to integrating social justice education in their practice. We believe this book is an important contribution to this mission. All those involved with this project hope this book serves as a catalyst for continued collaboration and learning across institutions, experiences, and identities, toward improving our educational efforts aimed at equity and justice for all.

—Lisa M. Landreman

REFERENCES

Adams, M., Bell, L. A., & Griffin, P. (Eds.) (2007). *Teaching for diversity and social justice* (2nd ed.). New York, NY: Routledge.

Adams, M., Blumenfeld, W. J., Castañeda, C. R., Hackman, H. W., Peters, M. L., & Zuñiga, X. (Eds.). (2010). *Readings for diversity and social justice* (2nd ed.). New York, NY: Routledge.

Cuyjet, M. J., Howard-Hamilton, M. F., & Cooper, D. L. (Eds.). (2011). *Multiculturalism on campus: Theories, models, and practices for understanding diversity and creating inclusion.* Sterling, VA: Stylus.

Freire, P. (1970). *Pedagogy of the oppressed.* New York, NY: Continuum.

Jenks, C., Lee, J., & Kanpol, B. (2001). Approaches to multicultural education in pre-service teacher education: Philosophical frameworks and models for teaching. *Urban Review, 33*(2), 87–105.

Johnson, A. G. (2001). *Privilege, power, and difference* (2nd ed.). Mountain View, CA: Mayfield.

Landreman, L. M., Edwards, K. E., Balón, D. G., & Anderson, G. (2008, September/October). Wait! It takes time to develop rich and relevant social justice curriculum. *About Campus, 13*(4), 2–10.

Maxwell, K. E., Nagda, B. A., & Thompson, M. C. (2011). *Facilitating intergroup dialogue.* Sterling, VA: Stylus.

McLaren, P. (1995). *Critical pedagogy and predatory culture: Oppositional politics in a postmodern era.* London, UK: Routledge.

Rawls, J. (1971). *A theory of justice.* Cambridge, MA: Harvard University Press.

Reason, R. D., Broido, E. M., Davis, T. L., & Evans, N. J. (Eds.). (2005). *Developing social justice allies.* San Francisco, CA: Jossey-Bass.

Schlesinger, A. M. (1991). *The disuniting of America: Reflections on a multicultural society.* Knoxville, TN: Whittle Direct Books.

Sleeter, C. (1995). An analysis of the critique of multicultural education. In J. Banks & C. Banks (Eds.), *Handbook of research on multicultural education* (pp. 81–94). New York, NY: Macmillan.

Part One

Frameworks From Theory to Practice

THE CHAPTERS IN THIS SECTION provide a brief overview of the conceptual and theoretical foundations that inform the social justice facilitation practices of many educators, particularly those shared in this book. They also demonstrate that social justice educators can have shared philosophical grounding but approach their work in different ways. The introductory chapter by Lisa M. Landreman and Christopher MacDonald-Dennis provides an overview of conceptualizations of diversity, multicultural, and social justice education and, more specifically, social justice facilitation within the context of higher education and student affairs. We discuss how college and university educators' responsibilities toward social justice moved from recruiting and retaining historically disenfranchised students to consciousness-raising and social action. The chapter ends with a summary of some overarching core competencies of social justice facilitation.

Grounded in her 15 years of experience as a social justice educator, in Chapter 2 Annemarie Vaccaro shares her working framework for social justice education, the essential factors of facilitation, and her journey as a social justice educator.

In Chapter 3, Kelly Carter Merrill shares her reflections on her own struggle to identify as a social justice educator that involves merging her multiple professional identities and their accompanying discourse communities into a unified approach. This story reminds us of the importance of situating social justice within a broad body of theory and practice grounded in an anti-oppression framework.

1

The Evolution of Social Justice Education and Facilitation

Lisa M. Landreman and Christopher MacDonald-Dennis

IN PROPOSING THIS BOOK, we set out to create a publication that would communicate the complexity of social justice facilitation and the multiple ways successful facilitation can transform learning for students. We would be remiss, however, to discuss facilitation without an understanding of what we mean by social justice education. Social justice is a concept that has entered many discourses throughout higher education in recent decades and, for many, is a critical aspect of educating college students and student affairs practice. Despite its priority, social justice education remains a concept and a practice that is often widely misunderstood. Many use it interchangeably with terms such as *diversity, multiculturalism,* and *inclusion.* We hold that while having roots in conceptions of diversity and multiculturalism, social justice education is distinct from these earlier terms. It is important to understand social justice education's evolution from early goals aimed at diversifying American education systems (i.e., representation in and access to education) to the multicultural education movement. This movement began the process of challenging monocultural assumptions and efforts to understand the histories, traditions, and experiences of marginalized people toward creation of a heterogeneous society. These efforts evolved into contemporary social justice efforts aimed at more directly identifying and remedying institutionalized systemic privilege and discrimination in higher education. This chapter serves as a brief overview of conceptualizations of diversity, multicultural and social justice education, and, more specifically, social justice facilitation in the context of higher education and student affairs.

EVOLUTION OF INCLUSION, MULTICULTURALISM, AND SOCIAL JUSTICE IN EDUCATION

Challenges experienced today surrounding notions of social justice in education are not new. Tensions such as respecting cultural differences and maintaining one's culture versus creating a common culture, and notions of race and the existence of a racial hierarchy have existed since the start of the common school system (Tyack, 1993). Initially, whiteness was a diversified category, with western and northern European immigrants enjoying privileges southern and eastern European immigrants did not have. By the turn of the twentieth century whiteness became synonymous with *American citizen* for all European immigrants willing to forfeit the culture and language of their culture of origin (Williamson, Rhodes, & Dunson, 2007). "However, forfeiting culture and language and assimilating into White American Society was not an option for non-White groups" (Williamson et al., 2007, p. 196). Long before *Brown v. Board of Education* (1954), people of color understood that an education

> is required in the performance of our most basic public responsibilities. . . . It is the very foundation of good citizenship. . . . To see them from others of similar age and qualifications solely because of their race generates a feeling of inferiority as to their status in the community. (Davis & Graham, 1995, p. 165)

This racial hierarchy affected generations of students, with the effects of this legacy still felt by college and university students.

Early work on what some may now term *social justice* in higher education began as efforts to admit groups other than White Anglo-Saxon Protestant men, such as White women and African Americans. Between 1790 and 1850 these access goals resulted in a noticeable growth in female schooling. This increase was driven by a number of economic, political, and sociocultural factors, not withstanding the idea of "republican motherhood" that called for raising "virtuous citizens in the new nation" (Miller Solomon, 1985,

p. 14); as a result, notions of collegiate study for women began to become more common. In 1835 Oberlin College became the first American institution of higher education to adopt a policy to admit students of color, and in 1841 was the first college to award bachelor's degrees to women in a coeducational program.

Although these early examples of access for women and people of color exist, true systematic efforts at *representation* for women and people of color did not occur until the mid-1960s civil rights movements (Levine, 1991). These efforts to provide equal access to education, regardless of race and sex, forever changed higher education as it had been conceived for centuries. Institutions that formerly had been the exclusive educational home for upper-class, White, Protestant men were forced to reconsider their missions and the makeup of their student bodies. Although access to education for women can be accounted for in these early movements, the early definition of *diversity* in education was promoted by educators who believed people of color could acquire the benefits White people had through desegregated schools.

As students from more ethnically diverse backgrounds emerged on campuses (i.e., diversity increased), the movement to increase educational access for diverse populations of students grew to include *support*. Diversity efforts that encompassed support focused on the retention of underrepresented students, primarily through specific programs such as the Federal TRIO programs, aimed at helping them navigate the educational system. Notions of *integration* soon followed, trying to assimilate these new populations of students into existing campus communities. As Williamson et al. (2007) pointed out, "Scholars who subscribe to the notion of assimilation and individual advancement as social justice confuse the battle to acquire the privileges of Whiteness with the desire to assimilate" (p. 198). Critics of these early assimilation efforts contended that instead of examining the ways racism and sexism were institutionalized to maintain an unwelcome environment for its new members (primarily people of color and women), educational efforts attempted to understand the histories, traditions, and experiences of people who had formerly been excluded and marginalized. These approaches toward access, retention, and understanding began as radical approaches to education, but over time educators saw that they were ineffective at challenging deeply embedded systems that disenfranchise people of color and women. Educators began to see there were limitations to framing these early multicultural education efforts primarily around learning

about "other" cultures, displacing stereotypes, and changing prejudicial attitudes. Without examining the larger structural issues, educators gave the
illusion of doing something constructive, when in fact little transformative
education took place. Understanding cultural differences was an important
project in a segregated society, but understanding alone does not transform
the academy or end oppression. Even when students of color and other
marginalized students conformed to traditional norms of behavior and
attended historically White institutions, they did not reap the benefits assimilation promised (Williamson et al., 2007).

Therefore, many progressive educators argued that discussions concerning
diversity needed to move beyond access and assimilation (or diversity, support, and integration; Manuel & Marin, 1997) and that retention efforts
needed to include a transformation of cultural norms that privileged some
students over others. Efforts moved from developing awareness or expertise
about a particular culture toward raising one's consciousness about the ways
educational systems continued to marginalize the very students institution
administrators declared they wanted to admit, welcome, and retain. This
evolution, developed in the mid- to late 1980s, was the notion of multiculturalism. Multicultural education theorists and educators such as Banks
(1991), Banks and Banks (1995), Nieto (2004), Grant (1992), and Sleeter
and Grant (1993) introduced democratic classroom processes that integrated
experiential pedagogy; an analysis of social inequality and institutional
power; and students' and educators' personal narratives that enriched educational practice. These contemporary notions of multiculturalism moved
beyond diversity and challenged the assimilationist idea of monocultural-
ism—the fairly unchallenged assumption that we all lead our lives by a
shared understanding of common sense as members of a homogeneous society (Goldberg, 1994). Multiculturalism rests upon ideals and principles of
equity that challenge monocultural assumptions. Reich (2002) asserted that
multiculturalism "represents a theory or position that emphasizes diversity
over sameness, recognition of difference over homogenizing similarity, the
particular over the universal, the group over the individual . . . and cultural
identification rather than cultural affiliation" (p. 12). This form of multiculturalism promotes social and political change and constitutes social critique.
The emphasis is on creating a shared community that maintains the integrity
of various groups and involves general education and experiences for all
students.

Multiculturalism in higher education increasingly represented a desire to
rethink academic canons and to search for knowledge production and cultural and political norms that support heterogeneous societies. However, it

was soon realized that the introduction of the multicultural movement did not necessarily challenge established cultural norms as was envisioned. At a major meeting of proponents of social change in higher education, it was stated, "Multiculturalism is proving to be fluid enough to describe very different styles of cultural relations, and corporate multiculturalism is proving that the concept need not have any critical content" (Chicago Cultural Studies Group, 1994, p. 115). The term *multiculturalism*, referring to the variety of strategies institutions and leaders had developed to address the consequences of exclusion in higher education, still did not address the issues that created the unequal social conditions that existed in society based on social identity (Smith & Associates, 1997).

In summary, a movement for social change in higher education should be more than the representation of many cultures in our institutions. Instead, educators committed to justice are searching for a pedagogical strategy and movement that challenges the assumptions, practices, and norms embedded in the notion that we live in a homogeneous society. What brought this need to the forefront was the inability of even the recent multicultural movement to reduce racial tensions in communities and on campuses; these tensions led to a national concern for promoting the knowledge and skills needed to work through differences created by historical legacies of discrimination and social identity differences (Bidell, Lee, Bouchie, Ward, & Brass, 1994). True social justice had come to be understood as the development of a community that allowed for those who had traditionally been marginalized the ability to prosper without having to forfeit their cultural heritage (Williamson et al., 2007).

SOCIAL JUSTICE EDUCATION
IN HIGHER EDUCATION

As stated previously, initial educational reforms aimed at including marginalized students in the academy did not change the nature of teaching and scholarship. As new scholarship entered the curriculum, questions arose about pedagogy, cultural histories, and authority in the classroom. In short, educators realized that previous educational efforts did not go far enough to challenge the ways society marginalized particular social identity groups while privileging others. They contended that even though the multicultural movement ostensibly wanted other cultures to be included on college campuses, its proponents did not recognize that the foundations of college campuses benefited certain groups while the exclusion of others went unexamined.

Although ethnic studies and other efforts to diversify the curriculum are recognized as important components of educational reform, additional changes were required to address educational equity for low-income students, students of color, and other historically marginalized groups. An educational movement was needed to address structural changes in the educational environment to benefit all students, regardless of social identity. Inspired by the earlier call for ethnic studies and the inclusion of people of color, other groups (e.g., women, people with disabilities) also pushed for curricular changes and program inclusion in colleges and universities (Banks & Banks, 1995; Gollnick & Chinn, 2002). This broader concept focused on individuals' memberships in different social identity groups, particularly race, ethnicity, socioeconomic class, and gender (Gollnick & Chinn, 2002). It also called for the recognition of the ways society dispensed benefits and power based on race, ethnicity, class, gender, sexual orientation, age, and ability.

THEORY OF SOCIAL JUSTICE EDUCATION

The movement that was created to build on the earlier strategies of inclusion and multiculturalism was the field of social justice education. Social justice education, based on the writings of Fanon (1952, 1961), Freire (1970), Memmi (1965), and Young (1990), among others, arose from the Black Power, New Left, and women's liberation movements of the late 1960s and early 1970s. Many definitions of *social justice* are also grounded in political philosopher John Rawls's (1971) book, *A Theory of Justice*. His theory has two underlying principles: fair treatment (i.e., liberty) and a just share of society's benefits for all (i.e., equity). Theorists held that the models earlier inclusion practices rested upon were incomplete to understand the experience of racialized minorities and women.

Paulo Freire (1970) is considered by many to be the most influential educational philosopher in the development of critical pedagogical thought and practice. His writings and teaching provided a theoretical philosophy and pedagogy that served as an impetus for consciousness-raising, liberation movements, critical educational work, and social justice action. Freire believed that the goal of attaining critical consciousness is to understand how relationships among social groups can be changed and become more equitable (Freire, 1970, 1973; Gutierrez, 1989). He believed that if people were to become critical (e.g., approach the interpretation of problems with depth, openness, and dialogue), increase their capacity to make choices, and reject the prescriptions of others, progress could be made toward dismantling systems of oppression. Good education, Freire (1970) contended, connects theory, reflection, and action. Good multicultural education asks students to critically examine social practices, reflect on what they learn, and put that learning into action. Therefore, we believe that this type of critical multicultural education *is* social justice education.

In the foundational text *Teaching for Diversity and Social Justice Sourcebook* (Adams, Bell, & Griffin, 1997), Bell articulated her vision of social justice:

> Social justice includes a vision of society in which the distribution of resources is equitable and all members are physically and psychologically safe and secure. We envision a society in which individuals are both self-determining (able to develop their full capacities) and interdependent (capable of interacting democratically with others). Social justice involves social actors who have a sense of their own agency as well as a sense of social responsibility toward and with others and the society as a whole. (p. 3)

Bell's (1997) philosophy on social justice education is grounded in a long historical legacy of radical social thought and progressive educational movements to link education to democracy, and transformative social action to the liberation of oppressed people (Darder, Baltodano, & Torres, 2003). Tensions lie, of course, in how these principles and concepts are defined, how inequality is believed to have originated, and how to address inequity (Lechuga, Clerc, & Howell 2009).

Theory of oppression. Changes in the conceptualization of the role of oppression in society marked a critical shift from earlier multicultural movements to social justice education. Bell's (1997) vision of social justice, informed by previously mentioned scholars and a theory of oppression, has shaped many social justice educators' practice. We offer the following model and summary of the theoretical and conceptual foundations for social justice education discussed by Bell and Hardiman and Jackson (1997) as the foundation for our thinking about social justice. These educators contended that social oppression is different from isolated acts of mistreatment. Instead, social oppression refers to

a system of ideological control as well as domination and control of the social
institutions and resources of the society, resulting in a condition of privilege
for the agent group relative to the disenfranchisement and exploitation of the
target group. (Hardiman & Jackson, 1997, p. 17)

Bell (1997) explained that "the term *oppression* is used rather than discrimination, bias, prejudice, or bigotry to emphasize the pervasive nature of
social inequality woven throughout social institutions as well as embedded
within individual consciousness" (p. 4). According to this model, oppression
is not simply ideology or random violence and discrimination. The relationship between members of the dominant group (also referred to as *agents* or
those with privilege) and members of marginalized (or *target*) groups keeps
the system of domination in place. By controlling social institutions, ideology, language, culture, and the history of marginalized people, dominance
by agent group members over target group members is established over time.
This process is often unconscious, and when institutionalized, the conscious
intent to oppress others is no longer needed to maintain power and privilege
by the dominant group (Hardiman & Jackson, 1997).

The social oppression matrix. Although reproduced within institutions and
societal structures, oppression is operated and maintained by individuals at
three levels, as shown in Figure 1.1, Hardiman and Jackson's (1997) oppression model. This matrix illustrates the complex dynamics of oppression.

The context. At the individual level, the beliefs and behaviors, conscious
and unconscious, of individuals are the focus. Examples include an employer
believing that his female employee is too emotional, a White person choosing a White physician over an African American physician because the White
person believes Whites are naturally more intelligent than people of color,
or a transgender person being the target of hate speech.

Individuals work and live in social institutions, and these institutions
regulate how individuals are rewarded, socialized, punished, or guided to
maintain and perpetuate oppressive structures. At the institutional level,
institutions such as schools, government, industry, family, and religious
organizations influence and are influenced by the other two levels. Institutional policies, practices, and procedures, and the individuals who support
and collude with oppression can have adverse consequences on people who
are not members of dominant groups in society. Examples include unequal
treatment of people of color by the judicial system; housing and employment
discrimination for lesbian, gay, bisexual, or transgender people; unequal
access to quality education for the poor and working classes; and limited
inclusion in the military for women.

Figure 1.1 The Oppression Model

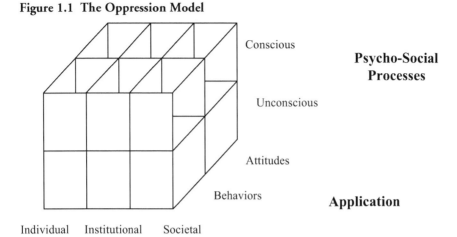

Conscious

**Psycho-Social
Processes**

Unconscious

Attitudes

Behaviors   **Application**

Individual   Institutional   Societal

Context

From "Conceptual Foundations for Social Justice Courses," by R. Hardiman and R. Griffin, in *Teaching for Diversity and Social Justice: A Sourcebook*, p. 18, by M. Adams, L. A. Bell, & P. Griffin, 1997, New York, NY: Routledge. Reproduced with permission of TAYLOR & FRANCIS GROUP LLC-BOOKS in the format Trade Book via Copyright Clearance Center.

At the societal level, society's norms, also referred to as *cultural norms*, "perpetuate implicit and explicit values that bind institutions and individuals" (Hardiman & Jackson, 1997, p. 19). The cultural norms of the dominant group are imposed on society through and by institutions and individuals. These norms include beliefs that guide how we lead our lives—definitions of good, normal, health, deviance, family, community, and success. These norms, then, provide individuals and institutions with justification for the perpetuation of social oppression. Examples include beliefs about homosexuality as sick or evil, legal definitions of rape and its causes, and assumptions perpetuated in the media and society about physical beauty and attractiveness. Although the boundaries among the individual, institutional, and societal dimensions are more fluid than may be implied by the matrix, according to the Hardiman and Jackson model they are mutually reinforcing.

The psychosocial processes. Psychosocial processes refer to the nature of individuals' involvement in the system of social oppression. These processes are conscious (explicit and "knowingly supporting the maintenance of social oppression" [Hardiman & Jackson, 1997, p. 19]) or unconscious ("unknow-ing or naïve collusion" or acceptance of the "dominant logic system that justifies social oppression as normal or part of the natural order" [Hardi-man & Jackson, 1997, p. 19]). Other scholars have referred to these pro-cesses as *dominative* or *aversive* (e.g., Kovel, 1970) or *active* or *passive acceptance* (Hardiman, 1982; Jackson, 1976). Examples of the unconscious process include members of ethnic groups Anglicizing their names to dimin-ish their connection to their ethnic heritage, Asian Americans having eyelid surgery (Hardiman & Jackson, 1997), and women spending exorbitant amounts of money on cosmetic products and procedures.

The application. The application dimension illustrates that oppression appears in attitudes and behaviors at the individual and systemic levels. The attitudinal level describes the individual and systemic values, beliefs, philoso-phies, and stereotypes that justify oppression within the other dimensions. Examples include the stereotypes that members of certain ethnic groups are lazy, that women are weak, or that poor and working-class people are igno-rant. The behavioral level describes the actions individuals and systems take to support and maintain social oppression. Examples include banking prac-tices that deny people of color loans to live in certain neighborhoods (i.e., "redlining") or pressuring girls not to receive an education.

Roles in the system of oppression. Foundational to understanding how oppression operates is the concept of social identity. As Maxwell, Chesler, and Nagda (2011) stated, "We use social identities to refer to group mem-berships based on physical or social characteristics ascribed by self or others that locate people within societal structures that confer advantage/privilege or disadvantage/oppression" (p. 163). Therefore, our social identities can include our ethnicity, gender, sexual orientation, socioeconomic status, abil-ity, age, national origin, and religion and the intersection of these character-istics. As introduced earlier, the language used by Hardiman and Jackson (1997) and many social justice educators to describe members of oppressed and oppressor groups is target and agent of oppression. Targets are members of social identity groups who are disenfranchised, exploited, and victimized in a variety of ways by individuals, institutions, and systems. Agents are members of dominant social groups who reap unfair advantage over mem-bers of target groups. Because of their roles in society, agent group members define the rules, customs, and values for what is considered acceptable, responsible, or appropriate and, therefore, see themselves and are seen by others as "normal." Conversely, targets are likely to be labeled deviant, evil, abnormal, or defective in some way. Unlike target group members, agent members are frequently unaware they are members of the dominant group.

Most, if not all, people have both agent and target identities. This adds a level of complexity in understanding the dynamics of oppression. For example, a Latino man with a professional occupation who is a member of the owning socioeconomic class may enjoy economic privileges not available to people who don't identify as male yet also experience limitations not presented to White coworkers, despite his gender privilege. He may, however, experience greater acceptance in his work environment as compared to his gay coworker, despite the gay coworker's White male identity. It is important that we capture the complexity of oppression as a social phenomenon in clear and understandable terms that neither oversimplify nor reify processes and experiences that are lived by diverse human beings in historically specific and individual ways (Bell, 1997).

Educators who employ critical pedagogical practices (which we contend are akin to critical multiculturalism or working toward social justice) reject the notion that education is a value-neutral process and instead attempt to make the political dimensions of education transparent through examining the ways schools and other institutions have operated that reproduce discourse, values, and privileges of existing elites (McLaren & Giroux, 1995). However, according to McLaren and Giroux (1995), "Many current trends in critical pedagogy are embedded in the endemic weaknesses of a theoretical project overly concerned with developing a language of critique" (p. 32). Although critical educators express their moral indignation toward the injustices that continue to be reproduced in our educational systems and the larger society, the lack of practical discourse has resulted in a lack of vision for critical praxis that leads to social justice (McLaren & Giroux, 1995). In general, critical educators have not provided a theoretical basis for alternative approaches to the organization of schools, curricula, pedagogy, social relations, or day-to-day practice.

In addition to the moral imperative to create accessible and inclusive educational opportunities and systems, numerous researchers have confirmed that students receive many individual educational benefits from engaging in interactions with peers different from themselves, which further forwards the social justice movement. Examples of these gains include an appreciation of differences (Baxter Magolda, 2001, 2004; Chang, Witt, Jones, & Hakuta, 2003); active thinking, engagement with learning, engaged citizenship, and social self-confidence (Gurin, Dey, Hurtado, & Gurin, 2002); and reduced stereotypes (Allport, 1954). Early diversity and multicultural education efforts in higher education set the vision for institutions to be a model for an equitable and democratic society. Intentionally structured opportunities for students to have meaningful interactions and relationships across differences are important initiatives to move this vision forward, clearly indicating the importance of adequately prepared social justice facilitators.

SUMMARY OF THE EVOLUTION
OF SOCIAL JUSTICE EFFORTS

In these few pages, we have provided a broad and brief overview of the evolution of the field of multicultural education in the United States from early understandings of diversity (or representation) and higher education access to its political roots in U.S. civil rights movements to contemporary notions of social justice education pedagogy. Because conflicting political paradigms influence definitions of *multicultural* and *social justice education*, it is critical to continue to clarify what we mean by the use of the term *social justice education* and its subsequent application in educational settings.

Our approach to social justice education attempts to challenge assumptions that all members of society share a universally common culture that ensures equal access to resources and opportunity. Instead, it is vital for us to challenge the assumption that we live or strive to live in a homogeneous society and the norms (conscious and unconscious) that privilege members of some social identity groups over others. Although initially focused on curriculum reform and access, educators who are truly interested in fairness and equity are calling for a transformation of the whole educational environment. Early perspectives that limited diversity to issues of race are being challenged by social justice educators to include the multiple and intersecting identities students bring to the educational environment and to members of other historically targeted groups, such as people with disabilities; people who identify as lesbian, gay, bisexual, or transgender; people who are members of the poor and working classes; and people who don't speak English or identify as Christian. Finally, we understand social justice education to be a lifelong process of development (Wurzel, 1988).

This chapter points to the need for social justice education efforts to explore power, privilege, and oppression to create truly just campuses. The challenge is to move the theoretical discourse to an examination of effective educational practices that lead to the development of students' critical consciousness and institutional and societal change. Multicultural education began as a radical approach to education toward greater equity and is now seen by social justice educators as an approach that was ineffective at challenging oppression and inequality. To these critics, key components of a social justice approach include a movement away from becoming an expert of a particular culture but instead toward raising one's own and others' critical consciousness. This process involves gaining complex knowledge of history, contemporary issues, cultures and experiences, and engaging in relationship building, reflection, and action.

FACILITATING SOCIAL JUSTICE EDUCATION

While many educators may understand and support the theory of oppression and social justice education, more is needed to be a good facilitator of social justice learning. A few years ago Lisa cowrote an article for *About Campus* (Landreman, Edwards, Balón, & Anderson, 2008) that offered the authors' thinking about the core competencies necessary for effective social justice education. These thoughts were grounded in the authors' collective experiences and the writings of scholars and educators in the field. The primary premise was that many well-intentioned educators remember and rely on "that great activity" they experienced at a conference that raised their critical consciousness but caused them to lose sight of the complexities of why or how that transformative learning occurred. In reality, the magic is not in the exercise alone but, instead, in the facilitation—not any facilitation, but facilitation that is informed by an understanding of the aforementioned social justice issues and the content and components of transformative learning.

Educators who aspire to engage in social justice education have an obligation to be aware of how well-intentioned work could do harm if good intentions and seemingly powerful exercises are assumed to be all it takes to be effective educators. "Social justice education requires awareness of content and process, and ability to simultaneously participate in the process and step outside of it to assess and mediate interactions in the group" (Griffin & Ouellett, 2007, p. 90).

Social justice facilitation competence includes having skills in managing group dynamics, communication and empathy, an awareness of oneself and historical and contemporary social justice issues, and knowing how to apply this knowledge to optimize learning for participants. It does not mean that skilled facilitators won't make some mistakes but that they approach facilitation with an awareness and humility that developing effective facilitation skills is a lifelong process.

Adams (2007) wrote that the general goals of social justice facilitation are to help participants "develop credible sources of information, honest personal reflection, comfort with questioning their prior beliefs and assumptions, and sustained critical thinking, as the bases for a larger and more adequate view of their social roles and responsibilities as social agents" (p. 32).

The goal of any facilitation is to build a bridge from participants' current experiences to a new more critically conscious awareness, or as Baxter Magolda (2009) has discussed, to be a good guide for this learning journey. Being a good guide includes setting up the physical space, designing developmentally appropriate training, and working with students to create opportunities to reflect on their salient learning experiences. A good guide also helps students explore who they are and what matters to them and provides opportunities to practice their new learning in the process.

A variety of frameworks exist for facilitating social justice education, and a more thorough review is beyond the scope of this chapter. We do, however, offer a few here and encourage those readers interested in social justice facilitation to explore these in more detail as well as the other works on the topic referred to throughout this book.

The framework for approaching social justice facilitation that I and my colleagues suggested encompassed four competencies for social justice educators: knowing ourselves, knowing learners, designing outcomes-based activities, and cocreating facilitation (Landreman et al., 2008). We believe that when combined, these competencies allow educators to create transformative learning experiences through an integrative process that incorporates cognitive, affective, interpersonal, and intrapersonal domains of learning—all necessary for holistic growth. Quaye (2012) confirmed similar results in his research that explored how educators engage in constructive race dialogues. Based on his analysis, he identified several strategies educators used to plan for racial dialogues in their courses, including knowing oneself as a facilitator, partnering with learners to create a space for dialogue via setting ground rules, and understanding learners' developmental readiness.

In King and Baxter Magolda's (2005) developmental model of intercultural maturity, they emphasize the importance of this idea of understanding learners' developmental readiness and the complexity of learning. They contend that intercultural educators must understand that holistic learning goals (which include cognitive, intrapersonal, and interpersonal dimensions) and developmentally appropriate curriculum are necessary for what they term the achievement of intercultural learning, the development of intercultural maturity. The authors propose a three-level framework (initial, intermediate, and mature levels of development) that can assist educators in program design, again reinforcing that effective social justice facilitators must know and become partners with their learners.

In the second edition of *Teaching for Diversity and Social Justice* (2007), Adams synthesized the body of social justice education traditions into what she identified as the following core principles for social justice education practice:

1. Establish an equilibrium between the emotional and cognitive components of the learning process.
2. Acknowledge and support the personal and individual dimensions of experience; while making connections to and illuminating the systemic dimensions of social group interactions.
3. Pay explicit attention to social relations within the classroom.
4. Make conscious use of reflection and experience as tools for student-centered learning.
5. Reward changes in awareness, personal growth, and efforts to work toward change, understood as outcomes of the learning process. (p. 15)

With these principles in mind, facilitators can guide participants to take responsibility for their own learning and their interactions with other participants, and to give themselves and others permission to make some mistakes as part of the learning process (Adams, 2007).

In their article on facilitating experiential social justice learning, Lechuga et al. (2009) identified three key components facilitators should remember to address the developmental level of students and to ensure that learning occurs: (a) provide preactivity reflection and discussion about the social justice issue being addressed, (b) engage in an activity that allows participants to apply their experiences and previous knowledge to current events or familiar acts of social injustice (i.e., allow them to engage in reflective action), and (c) evaluate the outcomes of their actions to determine if any other actions should follow, and allow for introspection on the experience. In addition to these three key components, the authors discussed the importance of facilitators' providing the appropriate amounts of challenge and support to participants, identifying clear learning objectives and activities that are theoretically grounded, forming partnerships with learners in the design of activities, maximizing intergroup contact and dialogue opportunities, preparing for and effectively working with the emotional content that is likely to arise, and providing ongoing opportunities for critical self-reflection and practice.

Two articles discussed essential components of the content and process of social justice education. In their study on social justice outcomes, Mayhew and DeLuca Fernández (2007) explored the pedagogical components that were most conducive to social justice learning. They found that content that exposed students to systemic oppression and to the societal structures and inequalities that cause and sustain this oppression, and also content that provided insight into how individuals perpetuate or discourage its reproduction, was more likely to facilitate social justice learning. In her framework of components for social justice education, Hackman (2005) listed (a) tools for content mastery, (b) tools for critical thinking, (c) tools for action and social change, (d) tools for personal reflection, and (e) tools for awareness of multicultural group dynamics as essential.

Another popular framework for social justice facilitation is the intergroup dialogue model used by colleges and universities throughout the country. Intergroup dialogue involves sustained and guided contact and uses an explicit pedagogy for dialogue that involves content learning, structured interaction, and facilitative guidance (Maxwell, Nagda, & Thompson, 2011). Students are involved in content learning in specific ways in dialogue groups that are intentionally structured with equal numbers of students from each identity group. The curriculum is designed with four stages: (a) group beginnings, (b) exploring differences and commonalities of experience across and within social identity groups, (c) exploring and discussing controversial issues, and (d) action planning and alliance building for creating change (Zúñiga, Nagda, Chesler, & Cytron-Walker, 2007). These groups use peer facilitators who have been carefully trained to recognize group dynamics that reinforce oppressive patterns and to "model dialogic communication and equal relationships between themselves as a team" (Zúñiga et al., 2007, p. xvi). Intergroup dialogue requires students to engage in critical self-reflection, an exploration of difference, and alliance building to achieve social justice outcomes (Zúñiga et al., 2007).

Again, this is not an exhaustive list of the effective frameworks, principles, or competencies needed for social justice facilitation, although upon review, the consistency of these scholars' and social justice educators' approaches does become apparent. The appropriateness of any framework is dependent on the context and learning goals of any particular training or educational setting. Our goal in introducing these frameworks is to prompt readers to consider how they approach social justice facilitation and to engage in reflection about the complexity and necessary competencies for facilitation. The contributors to this book have spent time reflecting on their experiences with social justice facilitation and offer detailed accounts of their learning concerning many of these specific practices.

CONCLUSION

Engaging in effective social justice education facilitation is more than applying techniques. It is a way of being in our day-to-day lives that is grounded in an understanding of the history and legacy of exclusion, discrimination, and oppression and a vision for systemic social change. Social justice education facilitation is a complex task that should be undertaken with full knowledge of the elements that foster learning, social justice, and a commitment to building authentic relationships. As we make connections between our personal experiences and those of our students, local communities, and the larger world, we must make this learning transparent in our practice. It is in the spirit of this transparency that our colleagues offer their facilitation experiences on their journeys toward creating socially just communities.

REFERENCES

Adams, M. (2007). Pedagogical framework for social justice education. In M. Adams, L. Bell, & P. Griffin (Eds.), *Teaching for diversity and social justice: A Sourcebook* (2nd ed., pp. 15–33). New York, NY: Routledge.

Adams, M., Bell, L., & Griffin, P. (Eds.). (1997). *Teaching for diversity and social justice: A Sourcebook.* New York, NY: Routledge.

Allport, G. W. (1954). *The nature of prejudice.* Reading, MA: Addison-Wesley.

Banks, J. (1991). *Teaching strategies for ethnic studies* (5th ed.). Boston: Allyn & Bacon.

Banks, J., & Banks, C. M. (Eds.). (1995). *Handbook of research on multicultural education.* New York, NY: Macmillan.

Baxter Magolda, M. B. (2001). *Making their own way: Narratives for transforming higher education to promote self-development.* Sterling, VA: Stylus.

Baxter Magolda, M. B. (2004). Learning partnerships model: A framework for promoting self-authorship. In M. B. Baxter Magolda & P. M. King (Eds.), *Learning partnerships: Theory and models of practice to educate for self-authorship* (pp. 37–62). Sterling, VA: Stylus.

Baxter Magolda, M. B. (2009). *Authoring your life: Developing an internal voice to navigate life's challenges.* Sterling, VA: Stylus.

Bell, L. A. (1997). Theoretical foundations for social justice education. In M. Adams, L. Bell, & P. Griffin (Eds.), *Teaching for diversity and social justice: A sourcebook* (pp. 3–15). New York, NY: Routledge.

Bidell, T., Lee, E. M., Bouchie, N., Ward, C., & Brass, D. (1994). Developing conceptions of racism among young White adults in the context of cultural diversity coursework. *Journal of Adult Development, 1*(3), 185–200.

Brown v. Board of Educ., 347 U.S. 483 (1954).

Chang, M. J., Witt, D., Jones, J., & Hakuta, K. (Eds.). (2003). *Compelling interest: Examining the evidence on racial dynamics in colleges and universities.* Stanford, CA: Stanford University Press.

Chicago Cultural Studies Group. (1994). Critical multiculturalism. In D. T. Goldberg (Ed.), *Multiculturalism: A critical reader* (pp. 114–139). Oxford, UK: Blackford.

Darder, A., Baltodano, M., & Torres, R. (Eds.). (2003). *The critical pedagogy reader.* New York, NY: RoutledgeFalmer.

Davis, A., & Graham, B. (1995). *The Supreme Court, race, and civil rights: From Marshall to Rehnquist.* Thousand Oaks, CA: Sage.

Fanon, F. (1952). *Peau noire, masques blancs* (Black skin, White masks). Paris, France: Éditions du Seuil.

Fanon, F. (1961). *Les damnés de la terre* (Wretched of the earth). Paris, France: François Maspero.

Freire, P. (1970). *Pedagogy of the oppressed.* New York, NY: Continuum.

Freire, P. (1973). *Education for critical consciousness.* New York, NY: Continuum.

Goldberg, D. T. (Ed.). (1994). *Multiculturalism: A critical reader.* Oxford, UK: Blackford.

Gollnick, D., & Chinn, P. (2002). *Multicultural education in a pluralistic society* (6th ed.). Upper Saddle River, NJ: Merrill Prentice Hall.

Grant, C. A. (Ed.). (1992). *Research and multicultural education.* London, UK: Falmer.

Griffin, P., & Ouellett, M. L. (2007). Facilitating social justice education courses. In M. Adams, L. A. Bell, & P. Griffin (Eds.), *Teaching for diversity and social justice* (2nd ed., pp. 89–113). New York, NY: Routledge.

Gurin, P., Dey, E., Hurtado, S., & Gurin, G. (2002). Diversity and higher education: Theory and impact on educational outcomes. *Harvard Educational Review, 72,* 330–366.

Gutierrez, L. (1989). *Ethnic consciousness, consciousness raising and the empowerment process of Latinos* (Doctoral dissertation). Available from ProQuest Dissertations and Theses database. (UMI No. 9013915).

Hackman, H. (2005). Five essential components for social justice education. *Equity & Excellence in Education, 38,* 103–109.

Hardiman, R., & Jackson, B. W. (1997). Conceptual foundations for social justice courses. In M. Adams, L. A. Bell, & P. Griffin (Eds.), *Teaching for diversity and social justice: A sourcebook* (pp. 16–29). New York: Routledge.

Jackson, B. (1976). Black identity development. In L. Golubschick & B. Persky (Eds.), *Urban social and educational issues* (pp. 158–164). Dubuque, IA: Kendall/ Hunt.

King, P. M., & Baxter Magolda, M. B. (2005). A developmental model of intercultural maturity. *Journal of College Student Development, 46*(6), 571–592.

Kovel, J. (1970). *White racism: A psychohistory.* New York. NY: Pantheon Books.

Landreman, L., Edwards, K., Balón, D. G., & Anderson, G. (2008, September/ October). Wait! It takes time to develop rich and relevant social justice curriculum. *About Campus, 13*(4), 2–10.

Lechuga, V. M., Clerc, L. N., & Howell, A. K. (2009). Power, privilege, and learning: Facilitating encountered situations to promote social justice. *Journal of College Student Development, 50*(2), 222–244.

Levine, A. (1991, September/October). The meaning of diversity. *Change, 23*(5), 4–5.

Manuel, R., & Marin, P. (1997, June 30). *Diversity, affirmative action and higher education: Coordination, collaboration and dissemination of information.* Washington, DC: U.S. Department of Education, National Institute on Postsecondary Education, Libraries, and Lifelong Learning. Retrieved from http://www2 .ed.gov/offices/OERI/PLLI/June30_web_version.html

Maxwell, K. E., Chesler, M., & Nagda, B. A. (2011). Identity matters: Facilitators' struggles and empowered use of social identities in intergroup dialogue. In K. E. Maxwell, B. A. Nagda, & M. C. Thompson (Eds.), *Facilitating intergroup dialogues: Bridging differences, catalyzing change* (pp. 163–177). Sterling, VA: Stylus.

Maxwell, K. E., Nagda, B. A., & Thompson, M. C. (2011). *Facilitating intergroup dialogues: Bridging differences, catalyzing change.* Sterling, VA: Stylus.

Mayhew, M., & DeLuca Fernández, S. (2007). Pedagogical practices that contribute to social justice outcomes. *Review of Higher Education, 31*(1), 55–80.

Memmi, A. (1965). *The colonizer and the colonized.* New York, NY: Orion Press.

McLaren, P., & Giroux, H. (1995). Radical pedagogy as cultural politics: Beyond the discourse of critique and anti-utopianism. In P. McLaren (Ed.), *Critical pedagogy and predatory culture: Oppositional politics in a postmodern era* (pp. 29–57). New York, NY: Routledge.

Miller Solomon, B. (1985). *In the company of educated women.* New Haven, CT: Yale University Press.

Nieto, S. (2004). *Affirming diversity: The sociopolitical context for multicultural education* (4th ed.). New York: Longman.

Quaye, S. J. (2012). Think before you teach: Preparing for dialogues about racial realities. *Journal of College Student Development, 53*(4), 542–562.

Rawls, J. (1971). *A theory of justice.* Cambridge, MA: Harvard University Press.

Reich, R. (2002). *Bridging liberalism and multiculturalism in American education.* Chicago, IL: The University of Chicago Press.

Sleeter, C. E., & Grant, C. A. (1993). *Making choices for multicultural education: Five approaches to race, class, and gender* (2nd ed.). New York, NY: Macmillan.

Smith, D. G., & Associates. (1997). *Diversity works: The emerging picture of how students benefit.* Washington, DC: Association of American Colleges and Universities.

Tyack, D. B. (1993). Constructing difference: Historical reflections on schooling and social diversity. *Teachers College Record, 95*(1), 8–34.

Williamson, J. A., Rhodes, L., & Dunson, M. (2007). A selected history of social justice education. *Review of Research in Education, 31*(1), 195–224.

Wurzel, J. (1988). Multiculturalism and multicultural education. In J. Wurzel (Ed.), *Toward multiculturalism: A reader in multicultural education* (pp. 1–13). Yarmouth, ME: Intercultural Press.

Young, I. M. (1990). *Justice and the politics of difference.* Princeton, NJ: Princeton University Press.

Zúñiga, X., Nagda, B. (R.) A., Chesler, M., & Cytron-Walker, A. (2007). Intergroup dialogue in higher education: Meaningful learning about social justice. *ASHE Higher Education Report, 32*(4).

2

Building a Framework for Social Justice Education

One Educator's Journey

Annemarie Vaccaro

REFLECT UPON YOUR EXPERIENCES as a participant in social justice education (SJE). What did you learn? Were you stretched to consider new perspectives? Did you engage in activities that evoked emotion? Were you inspired to take action, or were you unchallenged and disappointed by the experience? As a participant, I have had a range of social justice experiences—from highly inspirational to utterly underwhelming. As a facilitator, this spectrum of experiences was troubling. I certainly did not want to deliver SJE that was uninformative, disengaging, or inconsequential. So I embarked on a journey to find effective conceptual frameworks and facilitation strategies.

While there is no recipe for successful SJE, I have found that my most effective SJE sessions include a number of essential factors. In this chapter, I present those factors in the form of a working SJE framework. The framework, comprising theoretical concepts and facilitation strategies, has helped ground my practice in more effective design. That is not to say the framework is perfect. In fact, as I have grown as an educator, my framework has too. In this chapter, I share my successes and challenges using the framework. It is not enough, however, to offer personal accounts of my effectiveness; evidence of success must come from learners. As such, reflections and evaluations from former SJE participants are included throughout the chapter. Pseudonyms have been used for all students.

My SJE journey, framework, and facilitation style are all informed by critical theory, which has roots in a variety of disciplines, including politics, economics, sociology, anthropology, cultural theory, and philosophy. Critical perspectives inspire individuals to question why society is structured in a way that privileges some and oppresses others. Beyond a mere intellectual perspective, critical theorists strive to incite social change and end all forms of marginalization (Bronner & Kellner, 1989). More specifically, critical pedagogy exposes educational inequalities and aspires to end them. Critical educators value equity, inclusion, self-reflection, and educational reform (Brookfield, 1995; Irving, 2006; Tuitt, 2006). Tenets of critical theory and critical pedagogy are embedded throughout this chapter as they inform how I craft and deliver SJE.

A FRAMEWORK OF SJE

A visual image of my working SJE framework is shown in Figure 2.1. The outside layers of the framework represent contextual factors for facilitators to consider before and throughout the SJE process. The outer contextual layer of the framework represents self-awareness and continued facilitator growth, while the inner contextual layer denotes the creation of an inclusive learning environment. As outside layers, they are not peripheral factors; in fact, they are essential. Without these contextual factors to envelope the learning process, social justice sessions are likely to be ineffective. At the center (or core) of the framework is a tripartite process that includes a theoretical model of oppression, engaging participants in self-reflection, and calling participants to action. The three-part process represents what I attempt to accomplish in social justice sessions. In the following pages, I offer details about the framework and use participant narratives to provide a snapshot of how the framework can have an impact on learners.

Facilitator Self-Awareness and Growth

SJE is not just about participant learning; facilitators must also be willing to learn, grow, and change. Critical scholars argue that effective educators are those who engage in critical reflective practice (Brookfield, 1995) or cultural paradigms of practice (Irving, 2006) whereby they interrogate their own

Figure 2.1 SJE Framework

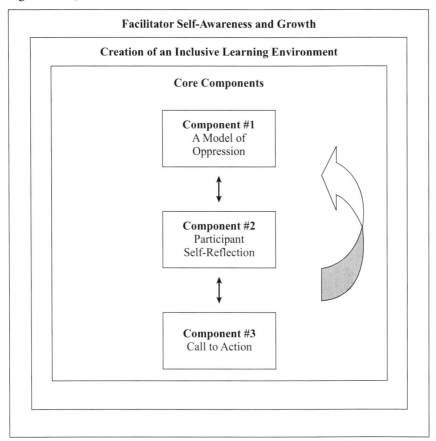

assumptions, biases, beliefs, and practices. Because of the significance of facilitator development, it serves as the outermost contextual layer of the SJE framework. Visually, it encompasses the other components of the model representing its significance. As a critical scholar, I believe that continuous growth, rooted in self-awareness, helps facilitators create inclusive learning environments and deliver the core components most effectively.

Facilitator self-awareness and growth can result from formal education or informal learning opportunities such as interpersonal dialogue and guided self-reflection. My growth and development was inspired by social justice courses, professional development opportunities, interpersonal dialogue, and feedback from SJE participants. In the following paragraphs, I share highlights from my social justice journey, including key turning points in my self-awareness and growth as an educator that were especially influential in the development of the framework.

I have always been interested in issues of diversity. As a teenager, I took advantage of opportunities to make contact with people from a variety of racial, religious, and social classes. In high school and college I served as a student leader (i.e., student government, resident assistant (RA), orientation leader), where I was involved in many diversity trainings. I also spent three college summers working in a community center that provided services to African American and Latino/Latina youth. Student leader training and the community center experiences allowed me to focus on appreciation and support of others who were different from me. However, much was missing from those educational experiences, including an examination of social inequalities embedded in U.S. society, an understanding of my own social identities, and an awareness that the conception of diversity as "the Other" is incredibly problematic.

In college I studied to be a high school social studies teacher. My favorite and most life-altering class was about the development of multicultural education for K–12 learners. In this class, I was forever changed by Sleeter and Grant's (1993) notion of education as multicultural and social reconstructionist. Their work was my first exposure to a social justice lens. Even though I had always been someone who fought against overt prejudice and discrimination, I never considered how society was structured in a way that privileged some and oppressed others. This new perspective changed my worldview in ways that years of diversity training had not. It offered me a theoretical framework within which I could understand larger societal forces that shaped my personal experiences as a White middle-class, bisexual woman.

My life journey led me away from teaching high school to the profession of student affairs. During my first graduate school experience, I had the good fortune of working in a student affairs department with many social justice activists. In particular, a number of influential women in the residence life department challenged me to explore the notion of oppression in U.S. society. One of my many epiphanies in graduate school was realizing how my privileged identities affected my ability to be a socially just student affairs professional. I will never forget when the judicial coordinator asked me how my identity as a White woman influenced the way I managed a particular incident in my residence hall. This question stopped me in my tracks. Until then, I had not considered the significance of my identities to my professional life. With the help of great mentors, I began to understand that such a perspective was naive and potentially harmful. I also started to more deeply explore my marginalized and privileged identities.

After earning my master's degree in student affairs, I facilitated diversity trainings for RAs, service-learning students, student leaders, and entry-level professionals. Through successful and unsuccessful SJE sessions, I realized that although my awareness was growing, my knowledge of societal oppression and facilitation skills was insufficient. I could talk about institutional oppression on a theoretical level, but I could rarely address probing questions by workshop participants. Although no one can be an expert on oppression, I needed to enhance my multicultural competence (Pope, Reynolds, & Mueller, 2004) to become a more effective social justice educator. One strategy to increase my competence was to engage in formal education through a doctoral program in higher education and a second master's degree in sociology. A sociological lens combined with critical race and feminist perspectives gave me the much-needed depth of learning about social inequalities. Moreover, my doctoral program allowed me to craft a curricular plan where I learned pedagogical issues and facilitation techniques related to teaching social justice to college learners. I explored critical educational perspectives such as inclusive pedagogy (Tuitt, 2006), feminist pedagogy (Maher & Tetreault, 1994, 2006; Tisdell, 1995), transgressive education (hooks, 1994), and transformative learning (Dirkx, 1998; Mezirow, 1991), all of which influence my perspectives on SJE.

Another way I increased my multicultural competence was through professional workshops and conferences. Programs like the Social Justice Training Institute (SJTI) and the National Coalition Building Institute (NCBI) helped me build my facilitation skills and connect the academic knowledge of oppression with the much-needed affective realm. Through those professional experiences I also learned to harness my emotions of guilt, anger, sadness, and fear and turn them into something positive.

For much of my early career, I facilitated short-term SJE trainings that often lasted only a few hours. During those trainings, I imagined that the passion I witnessed from participants could be monumentally more powerful in longer SJE sessions. In 1999 I was given the opportunity to teach a social justice course in a service-learning program. Soon after, I instructed a first-year experience class on social justice issues. In these long-term educational settings, I witnessed much more than a spark of interest in social justice. I was able to see miraculous development and perspective transformation.

Today, I continue my social justice work as a faculty member in a student affairs program where I have the responsibility and joy of educating student affairs professionals who go on to lead diversity trainings for RAs, orientation staff, and other student leaders.

Creating an Inclusive Learning Environment

The second contextual layer of the SJE framework represents the creation of an inclusive learning environment rooted in trust and respect. Amstutz (1999) argued that meaningful engagement can only happen in supportive and inclusive learning environments where trusting interpersonal relationships are fostered between students and facilitators. One of the ways facilitators create inclusive environments is through positive social interactions between themselves and learners (Tuitt, 2006). Another way to engender trust is to show participants that we care about them as learners, we value their experiences and perspectives (Amstutz, 1999).

Educators can begin to build inclusive learning environments before a social justice session begins. Whenever possible, I collect data from participants prior to a class or workshop. Sometimes I do this electronically (e.g., questionnaires, reflection questions), while other times I ask participants to tell me about themselves at the start of the session. This knowledge allows me to craft (or adapt) the session to best meet participant needs. It also sends a powerful message that I respect and care about the perspectives and experiences they bring to the session.

Creating an inclusive environment continues by ensuring that all participants are physically able to access the space and participate fully in the activities. Beyond physical inclusion, the environment should convey a feeling of community and a shared responsibility. For instance, organizing seating in a circle allows participants to engage directly with one another. Once the session begins, facilitators can situate themselves in the circle to show participants they are partners in the learning process.

A central tenet of inclusive pedagogy is that educators share the power of knowledge construction with learners (Freire, 1970; hooks, 1994; Tuitt, 2006). By doing so, they coconstruct not only knowledge but also an inclusive and affirming learning environment. Such a paradigm contrasts with traditional frameworks of education where the facilitator is assumed to hold all the knowledge and power. Facilitators can share power in a number of ways. By inviting participants to determine their own ground rules for the session, facilitators can help participants gain a sense of ownership in the learning environment. In my SJE sessions, students almost always craft

lengthy lists of ground rules, such as using "I" statements, reserving judgment, and not talking over others. On the rare occasion when participants
have not mentioned key ground rules (e.g., confidentiality), I ask the group
members' permission to add additional rules.

Another method for sharing the power of knowledge construction is for
facilitators to invite participants to discuss personal experiences. Beyond
mere acknowledgement of participant comments, inclusive educators respect
and affirm participant experiences. Showing students openness, compassion,
and empathy is essential to an environment where participants feel they can
take risks. On a course evaluation, one student wrote, "The facilitation of
this class encouraged discussion from a personal perspective." Another said
that the class "provided an accepting space to talk about some very sensitive
issues." Even when facilitators must offer constructive feedback to participants, they do so in a manner that is respectful and compassionate. If a
participant engages in behavior or shares comments that may be offensive, I
try to model patience and care in my response. On a course evaluation, one
student described me as "patient and flexible." The specific words I use vary
by situation, but the tone is always consistent: gracious and respectful.
Another student wrote the following on a course evaluation: "She was very
respectful to all students and allowed us to voice our opinions." Admittedly,
this is not always easy, but respecting and validating all participants is a
foundation for creating an inclusive learning environment.

A third way to share the power of knowledge construction is to be a
transparent and self-actualized facilitator. Tuitt (2006) argued that inclusive
educators should "be willing to demonstrate their humanity by identifying
weaknesses and sharing personal accounts" (p. 255). Inclusive educators are
willing to learn from participants and admit their challenges (e.g., unseen
weaknesses, unconscious fears, shortcomings). I have experienced success in
sharing my social justice fears, mistakes, and successes. Through this openness, I signal to participants that I trust them with my story. Facilitator
candor also models that taking risks and making mistakes are part of the
educational process. Of course, if facilitators share too much information, it
can be detrimental to the learning process. Facilitator stories should merely
augment the learning process, not dominate it.

THREE CORE COMPONENTS

In this section, I focus on the core components of the SJE framework, which
include using a model of oppression, engaging students in self-reflection,

and calling participants to action. I envision the core processes as an inter-connected and somewhat hierarchical cycle. The three-stage process begins with teaching models or theories of oppression. I teach these models because I believe it is difficult for participants to effectively engage in social justice learning without a basic understanding of oppression. The second essential component, self-reflection, is most meaningful when participants situate their experiences in the context of oppression. Finally, the third component is a call to action. Merely thinking about social justice does little to change oppression. Hence, as a critical educator, it is important for me to call upon participants to engage in justice work. Although the cycle begins with Component 1, it is a reiterative and lifelong process. The large arrow located on the right side of the framework shows that social justice learning is not finished after Component 3 is complete. Throughout their lives, participants can learn more about oppression, engage in further self-reflection, or discover new venues for activism.

Core Component 1: Using a Model of Oppression

It is important for participants to understand what oppression is and the various forms it can take. Participants who are engaged in powerful activities and discussions must have a context for making meaning of those SJE exercises. Many resources are available that can help social justice educators convey the complexity of oppression to learners (Adams, Bell, & Griffin, 1997, 2007; Goodman, 2011; Johnson, 2006). Table 2.1 is an adaptation of the model (Hardiman & Jackson, 1997; Hardiman, Jackson, & Griffin, 2007) introduced in Chapter 1 that shows how oppression exists on three levels: institutional, cultural, and individual.

Institutional oppression is a foundation of many of our social institutions, including law, health care, media, the military, and higher education (Law, Phillips, & Turney, 2004; Vaccaro, 2011). Cultural oppression surrounds us. It manifests itself in societal norms, language, values, icons, and popular culture. Finally, individual oppression emerges through active or passive interpersonal interactions and stems from conscious or unconscious prejudices (Adams et al., 2007; Constantine, 2007; Solórzano, Ceja, & Yosso, 2000; Sue, 2010).

During SJE sessions, I talk about the three-level model of oppression and offer examples of what oppression looks like in everyday life. Examples can come from a variety of sources, such as video clips, news stories, campus

Table 2.1
THREE-LEVEL MODEL OF OPPRESSION

Level of Oppression	Manifests In
Institutional	Social institutions such as education, politics, healthcare, economy, media, religion, family, and the military, etc.
Cultural	Societal norms, values, icons, ideologies, aesthetics, lore, jokes, music, popular culture, shared beliefs.
Individual	Personal beliefs and behaviors. Interpersonal interactions.

Adapted from Hardiman and Jackson (1997) and Hardiman, Jackson, and Griffin (2007).

incidents, or personal narratives. I ask participants to apply their new knowledge by brainstorming their own examples of institutional, cultural, and individual oppression. To maintain an inclusive learning environment, I offer positive reinforcement when participants come up with good examples. I also use redirecting or context sharing when they struggle. For instance, when participants use examples of reverse racism or special treatment for oppressed groups, I reframe their examples to situate them within the framework of oppression. In the instance of reverse racism, I offer an explanation of affirmative action and how cultural and institutional oppression limits contemporary education and employment opportunities for women and people of color. Many students have some knowledge of historical oppression in the United States, but few understand the depth and complexity of contemporary inequality. Once Tara, a student in one of my classes, learned how cultural and institutional oppression manifested itself in modern society, her reality shifted. She said,

> I used to think that racism and oppression had, for the most part, died out over the years since there is more diversity on television and due to the existence of things like affirmative action. I thought most oppression took place more on an individual basis and I ceased to look at the whole picture and really analyze the cultural and institutional levels of oppression.

Another student, Nate, was also socialized to believe that institutional racism was no longer a reality in the United States. In fact, he wholeheartedly believed that reverse racism existed. After learning about the model of oppression, Nate's perspectives were transformed. He learned that as a White person he had many privileges that people of color did not. He admitted,

> How can I—a white, middleclass, heterosexual—even begin to say that every day of my life I have to deal with "reverse racism"? I look back on the statements that I made . . . and I see the ignorance in these statements.

Young social justice learners have also grown up being exposed to media that discounts people's experiences with inequality. Some commentators even argue that the existence of oppression is merely a matter of opinion. It is convenient for SJE participants to deny or minimize (Johnson, 2006; Watt, 2007) social inequality by dismissing it as opinion. I have found, however, that once students learn the three levels of oppression, they are less apt to dismiss examples of oppression as "mere opinion," "no big deal," or a topic that people are being "too sensitive about." As a facilitator, I invite students to consider this question: What if this *one* example you think is no big deal is *one of many* interconnected instances of oppression? During a social justice class, Patty began to see how things she had considered no big deal were connected to larger systems of oppression. She explained,

> I have learned so many invaluable things and honestly have adopted a new strategy for the way in which I look at the world. I feel as though I am seeing through new lenses and am able to identify so many ills and misfortunes occurring in and throughout the world because of my expanding knowledge of oppression.

Toward the end of my social justice sessions, it is not uncommon to hear students lament that they cannot enjoy media, politics, or song lyrics as casually as they once did. Students complain about no longer living in naive bliss because they now see institutional and cultural oppression happening all around them. After participants learn and apply the model of oppression, oppressive messages in music, on television, and on the Internet become hard to ignore. Kat admitted, "One of the hardest parts of becoming sensitized to all of the oppression issues has been my inability to watch TV, read magazines and laugh at jokes the same way I used to."

In addition to learning about oppression in our social institutions and culture, I encourage SJE participants to explore individual oppression. In some ways, this can be the easiest level to teach, as most people believe that "isms" are the product of individual prejudice and discrimination. Yet, I have found few participants are ready to explore how interpersonal oppression can happen covertly or unconsciously (Sue, 2010). Many young people arrive at my social justice sessions with the belief that individual oppression is conscious and intentional. Such a perspective allows participants to argue that "it doesn't count if you don't mean it" (Johnson, 2006, p. 114). By exploring the concept of intent versus impact (Cullen, 2008), participants learn that a belief or behavior can be oppressive even though it is not intended to be. When asking students to think about the impact of their behaviors and perspectives, I invite them to begin the process of self-reflection.

Core Component 2: Participant Self-Reflection

The model of oppression is merely something to be learned until participants place themselves within it. Once participants have had an introduction to the model of oppression, I encourage them to reflect upon their social identities (i.e., race, class, gender, sexual orientation, or ability). Every participant has a race, gender, sexual orientation, social class, and ability, and those identities can be privileged (e.g., White, male, middle to upper class, heterosexual, or able bodied) or marginalized (e.g., people of color; women; people with disabilities; lesbian, gay, bisexual, transgender, intersex, queer, questioning people; or those who identify as poor or working class). Through self-reflection on their privileged and marginalized identities, participants begin to see how they are connected to the model of oppression.

Self-reflection can be done privately or publicly. For instance, reflection can take place publicly when it is embedded into cultural sharing activities, typically used in diversity education, such as step-ins, privilege walks, or small dialogue groups. However, in some SJE settings, group reflection can be difficult. It is hard for participants to deal with privileges, biases, and emotions. It can be even more difficult for participants to publicly expose themselves to others. In some cases I find it helpful to ask students to privately document their thoughts and feelings. In classroom settings, I encourage self-reflection in the form of papers or journals. In shorter sessions, I often ask participants to write a three-minute reflection.

Whether self-reflection activities happen individually or with a group, it is important for facilitators to know where participants are emotionally and cognitively. I ask questions like, What immediate reactions do you have to the three levels of oppression? What are your marginal and privileged identities? How do you make meaning of those identities in your daily life? How does learning about these identities make you feel? What issues are you struggling with? If you could ask one question, what would it be? Answering questions like these is not always easy. Chad explained how reflection could be challenging:

> I'll be honest with you. . . . When I walked in through the door on the first day of class, I was hoping that this would be an easy elective that would take care of my [general education] requirement. Boy, was I in for a surprise! This class required of me something that none of my other classes ever did . . . to reach deep down inside and deal with tough [stuff].

As Chad described it, self-reflection can be challenging work. Candid reflections often reveal issues that participants would rather not admit to themselves or others. For instance, Rachel admitted, "I learned that I am not as open minded as I had previously thought." Another student said,

> At times, I make pre-judgments before being aware of all the facts. I would never have admitted this on the first day of class, . . . partly because I really didn't think that I had racist tendencies. Even if I were to recognize [it], I would never have had the guts to share it with people.

Self-reflection often leads participants to want to change their own perspectives or behaviors. Melissa explained, "I realize now just how racist I used to be. I have never thought of myself as racist before, but I definitely was and . . . I have [tried to] change." Similarly, Jake explained how self-reflection inspired him to engage in further personal growth. He said, "A change needs to be made within myself." Melissa's and Jake's comments show awareness that change is part of the educational process.

Core Component 3: Call to Action

SJE is more than merely learning about privilege and oppression and engaging in self-reflection. Working to change dominant ideologies, inequitable systems, and cultural oppression is at the heart of critical pedagogy and social justice work (Freire, 1970; Goodman, 2011). Adams et al. (2007) suggested that learners should be viewed as "social justice actors who have a sense of their own agency as well as a sense of social responsibility toward and with others, their society, and the broader world in which we live" (pp. 1–2). They also argued that social justice is a process and a goal. I agree. Encouraging students to act is a *process* embedded in my SJE framework, while social justice action by participants is an ultimate *goal*.

As Domingue and Neely discuss in their dialogue in Chapter 13 on why preparing students for social action engagement is so hard, action does not equate to changing the world singlehandedly. In fact, depending on participant readiness, action can come in all shapes and sizes. Through engaging in self-reflection exercises, writing letters to themselves, or brainstorming activities, participants consider small and large ways they might infuse action into their everyday lives. A newspaper editor could be moved to stop the use of offensive comic strips in the campus paper. Student leaders can engage their peers in discussions about how events such as date auctions objectify human beings. Any participant can question campus policies and practices that marginalize particular groups. The possibilities are endless. I sometimes share my own social justice efforts with participants to show how action can be taken in large commitments (teaching a semester-long class) or in brief instances (confronting offensive comments by loved ones).

When contemplating action, many SJE participants start with their innermost spheres of influence—family and friends. It is not uncommon for students to approach me at the end of a session with ideas for (and fears of) confronting oppressive family members. Kelly surprised herself when she found the courage to question her grandfather about his prejudicial attitudes. Since he was a man whom she deeply respected and admired, merely asking why was a big action step for Kelly. She explained,

> Last night at dinner, my grandpa told the table how he was afraid of Arabs. I asked him, "Why?" He really could not give me a good reason. It showed me how as a little girl I was influenced by opinions that really had no credibility.

Participants can engage in social justice action by becoming educators themselves. By sharing their transformed worldviews, students can educate roommates, friends, and classmates to see the world through the lens of oppression. Rachel talked about how she shared her newfound passion for social justice with her closest friends and roommates:

> Every day after getting home from class I would tell my roommates what we had discussed in class. This was enlightening for me to see their reactions as well as my own passions for something I had no clue existed inside of me.

Grace explained how learning about the theoretical and structural view of oppression inspired her to action. She always thought that her experiences with racism were the result of interactions with closed-minded individuals, and thus she rarely spoke out. Once she learned about the pervasiveness of cultural and institutional oppression, she was inspired to act. She said, "I discovered how much stronger and louder I am [especially in] voicing my outrage [about] race discrimination."

Beyond personalized forms of action, continued growth and development are a perfect form of action for everyone. Becoming an effective social justice activist requires much learning and self-reflection. Thus, I always encourage participants to continue their educational journeys. One SJE participant said, "If I took one thing only from this class, it is . . . the value of educating oneself." Similarly, at the end of her social justice class, Rachel said, "I learned that I have much learning and growing to do." Students in search of learning opportunities often approach student affairs professionals for suggestions. Student affairs professionals should be familiar with their campuses and local communities so they can refer students to workshops, organizations, classes (e.g., women's studies, critical theory, queer studies, or ethnic studies) and other social justice opportunities where learners can continue their education.

SJE CHALLENGES

Social justice facilitation can be incredibly rewarding. Student narratives from the previous sections show how moving SJE can be. Yet, to share only success stories is to show only part of the educational picture. There are many challenges associated with the facilitation of SJE, some of which become roadblocks to SJE success. In this section, I explore some of these potential difficulties, which include challenges of assessing developmental readiness, overintellectualization, managing emotions, and navigating resistance.

Assessing Developmental Readiness

One of the foundations of the student affairs profession is using developmental theory to assess appropriate levels of challenge and support (Sanford, 1966). Social justice facilitation is no different. Humans are complex beings who inhabit a variety of cognitive-structural and psychosocial developmental locations. Understanding and applying models of college student development to SJE is at the heart of assessing readiness. Facilitators should be familiar with classic models of identity development (e.g., Cross, 1971; Gilligan, 1993; Helms, 1993) and keep abreast of emerging ones (e.g., Abes,

Jones, & McEwen, 2007; Jones, 2009; Savin-Williams, 2005; Stevens, 2004; Stewart, 2008). Armed with an understanding of these theories, facilitators can determine how best to appropriately challenge and support participants. An excess of challenge can make individuals shut down, while too much support may prohibit participants from attaining their full potential.

SJE facilitators have the difficult task of developing SJE content and activities that are appropriate for particular audiences. There are dangers in using high-risk activities with students who are not ready for such risks. Similarly, it is problematic to require (or even suggest) that participants engage in action they are not developmentally ready for (Jones, 2002; Vaccaro, 2009). Inclusive educators have the responsibility to encourage SJE participants to engage in action that is appropriate for their developmental readiness. Otherwise, unprepared but well-intentioned participants can do harm when they intend to make a positive difference. Participants who are struggling with believing that oppression exists can enhance their awareness and knowledge by registering for a social justice class or participating in a dialogue group. For participants who have a firm understanding of their own privileged and oppressed identities, I might encourage engagement in direct forms of activism around their social justice passions.

Overintellectualization

Oppression is a powerful system that touches people's lives in complicated and deeply emotional ways. Learning about oppression should never happen in a fashion that removes these lived realities from an intellectual framework. Unfortunately, any time educators share models or theories, there is a danger of overintellectualization. Incorporating affective components into the learning process helps avoid this problem.

Painful, challenging, and inspirational stories of social justice are common ways to infuse affect into the learning process. Stories alone, however, often have no context. Students hear people's individual stories every day through news, social media, informal conversations, and literature. It is the responsibility of a social justice educator to help participants understand how stories exist against the backdrop of oppression. If we do not help students make these connections, stories lose their social justice significance.

June, a young White woman, talked about how she had taken many classes that incorporated diversity topics. Yet, to June, diversity topics were like mathematical formulas or historical dates: Diversity content was merely something she needed to learn to pass a class. In one of my courses about race, class, and gender, June read very moving stories from a young Asian

American woman who documented her experiences with individual, cultural, and institutional oppression. June was so moved by the stories that she was inspired to talk candidly with a friend who identified as Asian American. After that conversation, June reflected,

> What I learned in this book has been invaluable. And I will remember its messages with me forever. One of my best friends is an Asian American woman, and I had no idea that these facts and these statistics were *real* until I talked to her about them personally. Her stories lay side by side with the [book]. Everything became real, not just words on a page. It opened my eyes to realize that these oppressions are happening right in front of my face, without my knowledge or understanding. Making something real is what it often takes for people to see and realize that something is wrong!

June's experience shows how powerful the combination of cognitive and affective learning can be.

Managing Emotions

While incorporation of affective components is essential, the emergence of deeply emotional responses can be challenging for SJE facilitators. A study with social justice educators found that most felt unprepared to deal with sadness, anger, fear, or other powerful emotions associated with SJE (Sue, Torino, Capodilupo, Rivera, & Lin, 2009). Study participants feared the emergence of deep emotions from their students and a corresponding loss of classroom control. Emotional responses in SJE, however, are inevitable. Learning about individual, cultural, and institutional oppression and reflecting on social identities can bring about intense emotions. Participants who are coming to terms with their privilege may feel frustration, shame, guilt, or fear (Lawrence & Bunche, 1996; Sue & Constantine, 2007; Tatum, 1994), while those who experience marginalization can exhibit anger, resentment, frustration, or sadness (Hardiman & Jackson, 1992; Sue, 2010). Social justice educators must be prepared for the emotional responses of not only participants but also themselves. Developing tactics for managing emergent emotions during SJE sessions is no easy task, but it is an essential one.

To be effective, facilitators must be prepared for the emotional work of SJE. Ineffectively addressing emotional responses such as sadness, anger, resistance, and sarcasm can be detrimental to the learning process. In an attempt to address emergent emotions, I incorporate a discussion of emotions into my SJE sessions. I have had some amazing success with assuring students that a wide range of emotions is normal. When students learn that anger, shame, guilt, or frustration is a natural part of the learning process, they become more comfortable acknowledging and dealing with those emotions. In classroom dialogues or reflection papers, I ask students to name and reflect upon their emotions. Karen said, "I learned a lot about myself and was truthfully ashamed of what I found out." Farah admitted, "I have overcome [my] guilt. . . . and am no longer comfortable denying the fact that as a white, middle class individual, I carry my own backpack of white privilege." When students like Farah and Karen name their feelings, they can expose the roots of their emotions and work through them.

There have been many occasions where I used a social justice story or activity that evoked more emotions than I expected. The reality is that we do not know who will be in our workshops, trainings, and classrooms. People are complex beings with a lifetime of triumphs and trials. It is impossible to know how deeply people will be affected by learning about oppression. Facilitators must be prepared to support and challenge participants as emotions emerge. Unfortunately, there is no formula for how to do this effectively. Each situation requires appropriate levels of attentiveness, eye contact, and empathy. Timing is also important. Sometimes I take a significant amount of time to address emergent emotions with a group. Other times I acknowledge and validate emotions (e.g., "Thank you for sharing that difficult story; I appreciate your willingness to share your feelings") and move on with the session. In all instances, I check in with participants who display deep emotions during a break or after the SJE session concludes.

Navigating Resistance

Learning about oppression and privilege is often difficult work and sometimes shows up as resistance. In her privileged identity exploration model, Watt (2007) detailed a variety of typical defense mechanisms associated with learning about privilege, such as denial, deflection, rationalization, intellectualization, false envy, benevolence, and minimization. Other social justice scholars have documented resistance in the form of silence (Jones, 2008), or denying, minimizing, and focusing on good intentions (Johnson, 2006). In an effort to explain why individuals resist diversity initiatives, Goodman

(2011) summarized some key psychological, sociological, identity, cognitive-structural, and cultural factors. Finally, Jones (2008) examined student resistance in the context of student affairs settings such as residence halls, service-learning, and leadership development. All of these resources are useful for social justice educators.

Because resistance is inevitable, I discuss it in my sessions instead of allowing it to become the proverbial elephant in the room. There is something very powerful about teaching participants that resistance can be a natural developmental response to learning about oppression and privilege. When students learn that denying, minimizing, and avoiding are common reactions, they can spend time reflecting on why they are resisting. Often I take the opportunity to share my journey of resistance. When participants hear that at points in my life I avoided, denied, or minimized my privileges, they realize that resistance is something everyone must work through.

Much of the resistance literature focuses on privilege (Goodman, 2011; Johnson, 2006; Jones, 2008; Watt, 2007), but any participant can engage in resistance. Most people from marginalized backgrounds already know they are members of an oppressed group. Lesbian, gay, and bisexual students experience heterosexism, students of color live through racism, and students from poor and working-class socioeconomic backgrounds know what it is like to struggle to afford what they need. Hence, many participants from marginalized backgrounds feel they do not need a facilitator (especially someone from a privileged background) to explain their oppression to them. People from marginalized groups may resist SJE for this or a host of other reasons. For instance, they may not want the responsibility of being educators for their peers or to be spokespeople for their social identities (Martínez Alemán, 2000).

Although resistance may happen, some participants from marginalized backgrounds can also find it validating to learn how their personal experiences are part of a larger and well-documented system of oppression. Charlie, a woman of color, said, "It was not until [this class] that I became more aware of the existence of [all forms of] oppression—even though I had always experienced prejudice and discrimination based on my race and ethnicity." Charlie's quote shows that even students who have experienced a lifetime of oppression may not have an understanding of the cultural and institutional contexts of their experiences. The class was also the first time Charlie considered her multiple identities. Although she had experienced racism, she had never recognized her privileges related to social class, sexual orientation, or ability. Luckily, resistance did not keep Charlie from engaging in self-reflection on the complexity of her identities.

CONCLUSION

SJE is challenging but incredibly rewarding work. Over the past 15 years, I have learned that my most effective social justice sessions result from a combination of factors. In this chapter, I discuss those factors in the form of a working SJE framework. The outer layers of the framework represent contextual factors for effective SJE. They surround the model and highlight their significance. The first contextual layer is facilitator self-awareness and growth—a hallmark of an inclusive educator. The second contextual layer includes setting the stage for SJE by creating an inclusive learning environment. Finally, the framework contains three core components: teaching a model of oppression, self-reflection, and a call to action. The framework presented in this chapter has served me well when facilitating short- and long-term SJE sessions. Yet, as a working framework, I expect it to evolve as I grow as a facilitator.

REFERENCES

Abes, E. S., Jones, S. R., & McEwen, M. K. (2007). Reconceptualizing the model of multiple dimensions of identity: The role of meaning-making capacity in the construction of multiple identities. *Journal of College Student Development, 48*(1), 1–22.

Adams, M., Bell, L. A., & Griffin, P. (Eds.). (1997). *Teaching for diversity and social justice: A sourcebook.* New York, NY: Routledge.

Adams, M., Bell, L. A., & Griffin, P. (Eds.). (2007). *Teaching for diversity and social justice: A sourcebook* (2nd ed.). New York, NY: Routledge.

Amstutz, D. D. (1999). Adult learning: Moving toward more inclusive theories and practices. *New Directions for Continuing and Adult Education, 1999*(82), 19–32. doi: 10.1002/ace.8202

Bronner, S. E., & Kellner, D. M. (1989). Introduction. In M. Horkheimer, E. Fromm, L. Lowenthal, H. Marcuse, F. Pollock, T. W. Adorno, . . . W. Benjamin (Eds.), *Critical theory and society: A reader* (pp. 1–21). New York, NY: Routledge.

Brookfield, S. D. (1995). *Becoming a critically reflective teacher.* San Francisco, CA; Jossey-Bass.

Constantine, M. G. (2007). Racial microaggressions against African American clients in cross-racial counseling relationships. *Journal of Counseling Psychology, 54*(1), 1–16. doi:10.1037/0022–0167.54.1.1

Cross, W. E., Jr. (1971). The Negro-to-Black conversion experience: Toward a psychology of Black liberation. *Black World, 20*(9), 13–27.

Cullen, M. (2008). *35 dumb things well-intentioned people say: Surprising things we say that widen the diversity gap.* Garden City, NY: Morgan James.

Dirkx, J. M. (1998). Transformative learning theory in the practice of adult education: An overview. *PAACE Journal of Lifelong Learning, 7*, 1–14. Retrieved from http://www.iup.edu/page.aspx?id=17475

Freire, P. (1970). *Pedagogy of the oppressed.* New York, NY: Continuum.

Gilligan, C. (1993). *In a different voice: Psychological theory and women's development.* Cambridge, MA: Harvard University Press.

Goodman, D. J. (2011). *Promoting diversity and social justice: Educating people from privileged groups.* New York: Routledge.

Hardiman, R., & Jackson, B. (1992). Racial identity development: Understanding racial dynamics in college classrooms and on campus. *New Directions for Teaching and Learning, 1992*(52), 21–37.

Hardiman, R., & Jackson, B. W. (1997). Conceptual foundations for social justice education. In M. Adams, L. A. Bell, & P. Griffin (Eds.), *Teaching for diversity and social justice: A sourcebook* (pp. 16–29). New York, NY: Routledge.

Hardiman, R., Jackson, B., & Griffin, P. (2007). Conceptual foundations for social justice education. In M. Adams, L. A. Bell, & P. Griffin (Eds.), *Teaching for diversity and social justice: A sourcebook* (2nd ed., pp. 35–66). New York, NY: Routledge.

Helms, J. E. (1993). *Black and White racial identity: Theory, research, and practice.* Westport, CT: Praeger.

hooks, b. (1994). *Teaching to transgress: Education as the practice of freedom.* New York, NY: Routledge.

Irving, M. A. (2006). Practicing what we teach: Experiences with reflective practice and critical engagement. In J. Landsman & C. H. Lewis (Eds.), *White teachers/diverse classrooms: A guide to building inclusive schools, promoting high expectations, and eliminating racism* (pp. 195–202). Sterling, VA: Stylus.

Johnson, A. G. (2006). *Privilege, power and difference* (2nd ed.). Boston, MA: McGraw-Hill.

Jones, S. R. (2002). The underside of service learning. *About Campus, 7*(4), 10–15. doi:10.1002/abc.74

Jones, S. R. (2008). Student resistance to cross-cultural engagement: Annoying distraction or site for transformative learning. In S. R. Harper (Ed.), *Creating inclusive campus environments for cross-cultural learning and student engagement* (pp. 67–85). Washington, DC: NASPA–Student Affairs Administrators in Higher Education.

Jones, S. R. (2009). Constructing identities at the intersections: An autoethnographic exploration of multiple dimensions of identity. *Journal of College Student Development, 50*(3), 287–304.

Law, I., Phillips, D., & Turney, L. (Eds.). (2004). *Institutional racism in higher education.* Stoke-on-Trent, UK: Trentham.

Lawrence, S. M., & Bunche, T. (1996). Feeling and dealing: Teaching White students about racial privilege. *Teaching and Teacher Education, 12*(5), 531–542. doi:10.1016/0742–051X(95)00054-N

Maher, F. E., & Tetreault, M. K. (1994). *The feminist classroom: An inside look at how professors and students are transforming higher education for a diverse society.* New York, NY: Basic.

Maher, F. E., & Tetreault, M. K. T. (2006). Learning in the dark: How assumptions of whiteness shape classroom knowledge. In A. Howell & F. Tuitt (Eds.), *Race and higher education: Rethinking pedagogy in diverse college classrooms* (pp. 69–96). Cambridge, MA: Harvard Educational Review.

Martínez Alemán, A. M. (2000). Race talks: Undergraduate women of color and female friendships. *Review of Higher Education, 23*(2), 133–152.

Mezirow, J. (1991). *Transformative dimensions of adult learning.* San Francisco, CA: Jossey-Bass.

Pope, R. L., Reynolds, A. L., & Mueller, J. A. (2004). *Multicultural competence in student affairs.* San Francisco, CA: Jossey-Bass.

Sanford, N. (1966). *Self & society: Social change and individual development.* New York, NY: Atherton Press.

Savin-Williams, R. C. (2005). *The new gay teenager.* Cambridge, MA: Harvard University Press.

Sleeter, C. E., & Grant, C. A. (1993). *Making choices for multicultural education: Five approaches to race, class, and gender* (2nd ed.). New York, NY: Macmillan.

Solórzano, D. J., Ceja, M., & Yosso, T. J. (2000). Critical race theory, racial microaggressions, and campus racial climate: The African American college students. *Journal of Negro Education, 69*(1/2), 60–73.

Stevens, R. A., Jr. (2004). Understanding gay identity development within the college environment. *Journal of College Student Development, 45*(2), 185–206.

Stewart, D. L. (2008). Being all of me: Black students negotiating multiple identities. *Journal of Higher Education, 79*(2), 183–207.

Sue, D. W. (2010). *Microaggressions in everyday life: Race, gender and sexual orientation.* Hoboken, NJ: Wiley.

Sue, D. W., & Constantine, M. G. (2007). Racial microaggressions as instigators of difficult dialogues on race: Implications for student affairs educators and students. *College Student Affairs Journal, 26*(2), 136–143.

Sue, D. W., Torino, G. C., Capodilupo, C. M., Rivera, D. P., & Lin, A. I. (2009). How White faculty perceive and react to difficult dialogues on race. *Counseling Psychologist, 37*(8), 1090–1115. doi:10.1177/0011000009340443

Tatum, B. D. (1994). Teaching White students about racism: The search for White allies and the restoration of hope. *Teacher's College Record, 95*(4), 462–476.

Tisdell, E. J. (1995). *Creating inclusive adult learning environments: Insights from multicultural education and feminist pedagogy.* Retrieved from ERIC database. (ERIC Information Series No. 361).

Tuitt, F. (2006). Afterword: Realizing a more inclusive pedagogy. In A. Howell & F. Tuitt (Eds.), *Race and higher education: Rethinking pedagogy in diverse college classrooms* (pp. 243–369). Cambridge, MA: Harvard Educational Review.

Vaccaro, A. (2009). Racial identity and the ethics of service learning as pedagogy. In S. Evans, C. Taylor, M. Dunlap, & D. Miller (Eds.), *African Americans and community engagement in higher education* (pp. 119–134). Albany, NY: SUNY Press.

Vaccaro, A. (2011). The road to gender equality in higher education: Women's standpoints, successes, and continued marginalization. *Wagadu: Journal of Transnational Women's and Gender Studies, 9,* 25–53.

Watt, S. K. (2007). Difficult dialogues, privilege, and social justice: Uses of privileged identity exploration framework in student affairs practice. *College Student Affairs Journal, 26*(2), 114–126.

3

The Evolution of a Social Justice Educator's Professional Identity

Impacts of Professional Maturation and Multiple Discourse Perspectives on Personal Practice

Kelly Carter Merrill

S OCIAL JUSTICE EDUCATORS arrive at their professional identities as social justice educators from a variety of paths. One could arrive at an identity as a social justice educator through work with diversity education initiatives, power and privilege discourse, higher education access and success advocacy, multicultural education, intercultural communication competence, legal advocacy, or some combination of those perspectives. Many educators begin and maintain their identities rooted firmly in social justice theory and scholarship throughout their careers.

Lately I have reflected on my own struggle to identify (or not) with being a social justice educator. I believe I first identified as a diversity educator and later understood my work as social justice education. Nearly ten years later I began to understand myself as an intercultural communications educator. I became more critical and, consequently, less attached to my previous approach, so I believed I was no longer a social justice educator (for reasons that are explained later in more detail). Now, after reflecting on the motivations for my work, I see myself, fundamentally, as a social justice educator who employs various discourse perspectives. I have come to believe that understanding the various discourse communities that support social justice education work is important because such understanding allows us to better situate our own assumptions in a larger context. Broadening our scope can enhance our facilitation and assist in communicating with people from a broader spectrum of life experiences. The following is my story of merging my multiple professional identities, and their accompanying discourse communities, into my current approach to social justice education.

MY APPROACH AS A DIVERSITY EDUCATOR

When I first began my work as a diversity educator in the early 1990s, I modeled what I had been exposed to as a college student in the 1980s. During educational programs and training sessions I attended, oppression was named; participants expressed raw emotions and "oppressors" felt bad and confused about what they could do. The approach worked for me and drew me to work toward social equity. I assumed the best approach to achieving social justice would be to focus on helping individuals identify and struggle with the dynamics of power and privilege. *Privilege*, I tried to explain, is unearned advantages or benefits extended to certain groups of people, and the resulting social power provides access and resources toward the needs or desires of members of those groups (Hardiman & Jackson, 2007). At that time I thought that all people, according to their social identity groups, were classified as either privileged (also known as advantaged, agents of oppression, or dominant group members) or oppressed (also called disadvantaged, targets of oppression, or nondominant group members). This framework guided my view of social justice issues and consequently my workshop goals. At times I would even make the distinction visible by creating two large discussion groups, the privileged and the oppressed, for certain activities. I used a dualistic framework to organize my own thinking and practice.

At that time I viewed social justice only from a domestic cultural context. I restricted my exercises, examples, and main points to the ethnicities, cultures, and *isms* that were historically and contemporarily from the United States. For example, I facilitated White-on-White antiracism training workshops, in which the people of color were assumed to be African *American*, Hispanic/Latino/Latina (which is arguably a more meaningful identity within the United States than outside it), Asian *American*, and Native *American*. I also conducted a humorous, yet poignant, workshop called Homophobia: Get Over It Already, during which I presented a slide show of same-sex couples together in provocative, yet mildly intimate ways. My rationale was that people (assume Americans) are uncomfortable with seeing same-sex couples together because of their lack of visibility in mainstream culture (read American culture). If I included the experiences of people from other countries in my work, I viewed them as immigrants to the United States and not as singularly cultural beings in their own right. I did not view social justice from a global perspective. In my defense, at the time I might have argued that U.S. culture was all that I knew and, therefore, it was likely what most participants would know; in reality it was all that I could see from my worldview at that time.

Emotionally, it was hard work. With each workshop, I could count on participants from the dominant group becoming defensive. My strategies for becoming a better facilitator involved learning new ways to manage defensiveness through reflection for the participants and me. I had not thought of avoiding putting people on the defensive, because I felt this was a necessary step toward social justice: pushing people toward owning their part in social inequities. My mantra was that if people feel defensive, then my work is effective.

Besides the defensiveness, I noticed several outcomes of my workshops that left me feeling inappropriately self-righteous. My goal was to help non-dominant group members realize they are not inferior people nor are they responsible for their societal position—the result of not having power and privilege. I wanted to put the burden of social justice squarely on the shoulders of dominant group members, as if these were separate groups of people. Just as defensiveness was a sign to me that dominant group members were being appropriately challenged, I also celebrated moments when target group members would passionately voice their experiences and school others on power and privilege. I considered it an effective workshop when the discussion simulated the emotional responses seen in several social justice education films such as *The Color of Fear* (Mun Wah, 1994) and *Skin Deep* (Reid, 1995)—emotions such as anger, distrust, denial, vulnerability, guilt, and utter sadness acted out in raised voices, pointed fingers, rolled eyes, quiet crying, and downright sobbing. Looking back, I aimed to facilitate division through conflict with the hope that unity would soon follow. I believed this would work because I saw it modeled in popular social justice films, and I experienced it myself as a college student. The approach worked for me, not immediately, but over time.

MY EXPOSURE TO THE INTERCULTURAL
COMMUNICATIONS APPROACH

In the late 1990s I became exposed to the intercultural education movement. I relearned much of what I had learned about intergroup relations through the social justice movement from what was for me this new intercultural perspective (M. J. Bennett, 1998). The discourse of the intercultural perspective highlighted three new paradigm shifts for me that would fundamentally change how I approached my work. First, rather than viewing *culture* as synonymous with *identity* (e.g., my culture is European American), in this perspective it is defined as a system of values and resulting behaviors (e.g., it is my culture to value efficiency). Milton Bennett's (1998) definition of *culture* is "the learned and shared patterns of beliefs, behaviors, and values of groups of interacting people" (p. 3); the foundation of his definition rests on beliefs, behaviors, and values, not on the identities of the interacting people. Once I was able to define *culture* in this way, I was consequently able to see the importance of making educated and nonjudgmental generalizations of cultural systems. For example, to understand that Japanese people have a central tendency toward collectivism while U.S. Americans have a central tendency toward individualism is a meaningful distinction. I made a significant shift away from discouraging generalizations (because I had assumed all generalizations to be stereotypes, as similarly noted in Engle, 2007) toward training students to be better at making generalizations. Consequently, I saw cultural differences as meaningful, not as simple superficial stumbling blocks in the way of world unity.

Second, rather than assuming a singular domestic cultural context (i.e., U.S. culture from a national perspective)—where the dominant groups are assumed to be fixed in space and time, for example, the dominant ethnic group is White and the dominant religion is Protestant Christian (Hardiman & Jackson, 1997)—the intercultural perspective emphasizes diverse cultural contexts of the world where dominant groups are dependent on the context (e.g., the dominant religion of Italy is Catholicism, and the dominant religion of Israel is Judaism). Viewing cultural contexts from a worldview, however, does not mean limiting our vision to national perspectives.

The intercultural perspective also examines the intricacies of domestic cultures in the United States and abroad (J. M. Bennett & Bennett, 2004). Examples of more fine-tuned understandings of contemporary U.S. domestic cultures' contexts are that the dominant ethnic groups in Hawaii have come to include Japanese Americans (Matsu, Takeshita, Izutsu, & Hishinuma, 2011; Okamura, 2008) and the dominant gender in many African American family structures is female (Burton & Tucker, 2009; Collins, 2000; Landry, 2000).

Third, rather than putting the issues of power and privilege on center stage, the intercultural perspective focuses on the challenges of communicating across cultures, primarily on intergroup conflict resulting from cross-cultural communication breakdowns rather than focusing on the intentional or unintentional exertion of power from one group toward another. Hall (1976), who is largely considered a founding researcher of intercultural communication studies, revealed through rigorous studies that humans conduct themselves according to culture-specific rhythms through language and body movement, and with these communication patterns come cultural value systems associated with the behaviors. Hall described a "built-in tendency for all groups to interpret their own nonverbal communicative patterns as though they were universal" (p. 75). Such ethnocentrism assumed by parties on both sides of the oppression issue can lead to phenomena termed, for example, *racism*.

But Hall (1976) warned that "the subject of racism . . . is touchy, complex, often oversimplified, and frequently treated improperly" (p. 74). What makes racism so complex and often oversimplified is the confounding role structural differences play in cultural systems, not to be confused with deliberate racism. Hall explained that many White Americans use the only form of communication they know to function in, process, and make meaning of their world. As a dominant culture group, White American culture may seem less obvious to White Americans and may even be assumed to be the only worldview. Along the way, White people are bound to misinterpret the intentions of behaviors and corresponding values of others and occasionally judge the other accordingly. For example, a White American may judge an Arab as too pushy and interpersonally inappropriate when the Arab stands "too close for comfort" while they are engaged in a conversation (Nydell, 2006). Or a White American may judge a Navajo person as flighty and lacking intelligence when the White person fails to identify the point in the Navajo's circular story-telling patterns (Hall, 1976).

On the receiving end, people of color can also misread benign behaviors of White people. Hall (1976), a European American from the Midwest, provided an example:

> It is the practice of my regional sub-culture to avoid direct eye contact with strangers in public when they are closer than twelve to fourteen feet. A member of any group that is used to visual involvement inside that distance will automatically misread my behavior. When miscuing of this sort is added to feelings of rejection, prejudice, or discrimination on the conscious level, the results can be overwhelming. (p. 74)

Hall cautioned, "To categorize all behavior as racist sidesteps the issue that not every White [person] is consciously or even unconsciously racist but will, regardless of how he [or she] feels, use white forms of communication" (p. 75).

Milton Bennett (1998) cautioned that to view the challenges of intercultural communication from a power lens will impede progress toward intercultural understanding:

> When communication behavior is labeled as "Marxist," or "imperialist," or "racist," or "sexist," the human aspects of that behavior are overshadowed by the reifications of principle. Polarization usually supplants any hope of inclusivity, and further exploration of communication differences is drowned out by the political commotion. . . . The professional work of interculturalists is not primarily ideological. . . . Purely ideological analyses yield little light and much heat. (pp. 10–11)

This is not to say that the intercultural perspective dismisses the existence of oppression and social inequities. Indeed, it does not. Bennett clarified,

> I do not mean to say here that the abuse of power is inconsequential to communication. On the contrary, no improvement of intercultural relations is likely to occur in a climate of oppression and disrespect, and interculturalists have a role in changing that climate through their explication and facilitation of interaction. (p. 11)

Another perspective on social inequities provided from the intercultural perspective comes from Geert Hofstede's (1991) classic work on a phenomenon called *power distance*, defined as "the extent to which the less powerful members of institutions and organizations within a country expect and accept that power is distributed unequally" (p. 28). In other terms, some people, depending on their cultural context, may expect social inequities to persist, and the extent to which this expectation is held is measured by the power distance index. According to Hofstede's research, the United States provides a cultural context with a low power distance, with Scandinavian countries, among a few others, scoring even lower. To employ a singular U.S. cultural context, I might have assumed that all people seek the same type of participatory equality that people from the United States do and that individuals who do not are still struggling with the social validity of their identities. From the intercultural perspective, I learned to assume such things would be ethnocentric of me, not to mention wrong. My exposure to the basics of intercultural communication theory enhanced and expanded my view of social justice. I learned that culture is not the same as identity, there is room for generalization, and power and communication exist in multiple domestic and global contexts.

MY APPROACH AS AN INTERCULTURAL COMMUNICATIONS EDUCATOR

In essence, I experienced a paradigm shift that in the end honored a broader and more complex worldview than I had before. This paradigm shift has changed my teaching and facilitation. For the past eight years, I have been teaching a graduate course called Intercultural Interactions in Education in which I employ techniques inspired by lessons learned from the intercultural communications perspective and by my past as a diversity educator. I have taught the course in two distinct cultural contexts, in Chicago and Honolulu. In the course we define *culture* broadly, including not only national culture but also culture systems related to individuals' race, ethnicity, religion, language, sexual orientation, gender, sex, ability, political affiliation, region, urbanicity, and generation, among others. Very early in the course, with the goal of helping students identify influences on their cultural perspectives, I distribute an identity worksheet that lists 15 social categories students may have an expressed (or unexpressed) identity with. Next to each identity category the students are asked to name their identity and list one value they have that comes from that identity. It often takes students the experiences and reflections of the whole semester before they can complete the entire worksheet. Through this process I challenge students to view their cultural systems beyond just their identities.

I did not abandon discussions of power and privilege, but some of my methods and goals for those conversations have changed. My paradigm shift helped me see that power and privilege are extended to identity groups rather than to individuals, per se. Although identity groups can be so labeled (Hardiman & Jackson, 2007), individuals cannot. I do not believe I have ever had a participant who was a target of oppression in every sense (e.g., race, ethnicity, religion, sexual orientation, gender, sex), nor have I ever had a participant who was purely an agent of oppression in every sense. Nearly every individual is oppressed and oppressive. And as a matter of consequence, I developed a belief that we all have the responsibility to achieve social justice, although I am aware that many students may not see it that way. This understanding actually revealed a new, less divisive, opportunity in my work. Instead of dividing groups and separating responsibility and blame, I ask individuals to consider and reflect on the feelings they have when they act as agents and to use empathy (not anger or pity) gained from those reflections when experiencing oppression by people from an agent identity. Conversely, I ask them to reflect on their reaction to being a target of oppression and to use caution and empathy gained from those reflections when judging other targets' reactions to oppression. We get these conversations started by participating in cultural power simulation activities that I learned in the early 1990s, such as Archie Bunker's Neighborhood (Schingen, 2002)[1] or StarPower (Shirts, 1969). More discussion about facilitating these kinds of simulation activities can be found in Chapter 11. These exercises put students into simulative dichotomous roles of those in power and those without that are not immediately transparent to the participants. They then participate in a social experience that quickly turns competitive and often divisive, thus revealing the impacts of unequal distributions of power. I emphasize that each exercise is a metaphor for society, not a revealer of who participants truly are or would be as oppressors or the oppressed. In addition to asking students to see themselves as agents and targets of oppression, my debriefing goal is to demonstrate what oppression is, where it comes from, and what the range of responses may be to oppression.

Ironically, I realized my previous approach to social justice education viewed intergroup relations from a singular dominant-culture (U.S.) view of inequities in the world. I needed to view the dynamics of power and privilege from multiple perspectives all at once, not just from a national perspective but from the perspective of each of the participants' smaller cultural communities that have influenced them. I was humbled at the prospect of learning every participant's cultural contexts, which I realized would not be possible. Consequently, I was left more empathetic and forgiving toward participants who were feeling challenged on these issues for the first time, because I felt a similar challenge.

As a result, I learned to de-emphasize culture-specific lessons and move to more culture-general discussions (M. J. Bennett, 1998). Examples of culture-specific lessons I removed from my curriculum were that many African Americans do not like to have their hair touched, and Chicanos may not make eye contact with you out of respect. Focusing on culture-specific differences became too daunting, given the scope, complexity, and global span of culture. Besides, my culture-specific examples tended to maintain a domestic national perspective on cultural differences. Instead, I moved my curriculum toward making culture-general lessons, thus teaching students how to become better at making educated nonjudgmental generalizations. "*Culture-general* approaches to interaction describe general cultural contrast that are applicable in many cross-cultural situations" (M. J. Bennett, 1998, p. 9).

For example, three prominent intercultural scholars, in particular, have rigorously researched and described several dimensions of culture that can be measured or understood relative to other cultures. Hall (1976) contrasted high-context and low-context cultures, where more of the communicating is being done in the nonverbal context of the situation in the former type of culture than in the latter. Later, Hall (1983) also described differences in the way cultures conceptualize time along a continuum between monochronic and polychronic time structures. Hofstede (1991) identified six dimensions of culture: power distance (from small to large), collectivism versus individualism, femininity versus masculinity, uncertainty avoidance (from weak to strong), long-term orientation versus short-term orientation, and indulgence versus restraint. Anderson (2008) described an immediacy dimension, where cultures are described along a continuum from high contact (closeness, approach) to low contact (avoidance, distance). In my class, not only do we learn these cultural dimensions in detail, but I coach students toward becoming comfortable with interpreting intercultural moments with educated generalizations versus stereotypes. M. J. Bennett (1998) noted, "Culture-general skills are communication competencies that would be useful in any cross-cultural situation. They usually include cultural self-awareness, nonevaluative perception, cultural adaptation strategies, and cross-cultural empathy" (p. 9).

In my more recent educational efforts, I put cross-cultural communication at the center stage, and have reduced power and privilege discussions to just 2 weeks out of 16. Through various cross-cultural simulation strategies, I expose students to the challenges of cross-cultural communication and being understood in the way that we intend and, conversely, understanding others the way they intend. The classic intercultural simulation activities I use are Barnga (Thiagarajan & Thiagarajan, 2006), Bafa' Bafa' (Shirts, 1977), and the lesser-known Anthropologists (Intercultural Dynamics in European Education Through Online Simulation, 2001), which divides the group into two cultures, the visiting group and the host group, the latter of which has specific directions regarding how they will communicate with each other and their visitors. Participants feel the emotions of frustration, inadequacy, and ignorance that come with these challenges of intercultural communication. Many who felt they were already "down with diversity" and had little to learn became aware of their narrow view of others and became painfully aware of their own ignorance. They learned to extend the benefit of the doubt and be more forgiving of themselves and of others.

TALKING ABOUT INTERCULTURAL MOMENTS

Every interaction we have is an intercultural interaction, because so few people share our own cultural systems given all the influences on our identities. Consequently, cross-cultural communication challenges us every day. I have come to believe that many instances of social injustice are actually something I call *intercultural moments*. I begin each week's class meeting with an opportunity for students to share their intercultural moments for the week. Through these stories, as a class we help each other to interpret the people and interactions in our daily lives. As the semester begins, the students struggle to think of intercultural moments.

I have come to view the central learning outcome for my course to be to improve students' abilities to identify and analyze intercultural moments (Storti, 2001). Through the lessons of the semester I give students the affective and analytical tools they need to be more adept at identifying the intercultural moments of their lives. Any time they feel that someone is acting inappropriately—or they feel judgmental, offended, or misunderstood—the students learn to evaluate these moments through an intercultural lens. By the end of the term the students have become more aware and have several stories to share. Two of the students' stories are repeated here, along with an explanation of how I facilitated the discussion with the learning outcomes for the course in mind. In addition I have listed four other memorable intercultural moments my students have shared over the years in the appendix to this chapter (see p. 61). I have two purposes in mind: (a) to provide examples and (b) to provide case studies for further reflection and investigation for the reader. All names are pseudonyms.

Story 1: Talking About Skin

When I was teaching in Chicago, a biracial-identified student (African American and European American), Paige, described an experience she had in line at a FedEx store. The man behind her said, "Excuse me, I know what you are. You are half Black and half White, aren't you?!" Paige was disgusted by this man butting into her business, labeling her, and referring to her as a "what." Erin, an Irish American student in my class spoke up: "Why was that offensive? Granted, he didn't pick out the best words, but how do you know that he wasn't trying to connect with you?" Paige explained, "Because he commented on the color of my skin." Erin asked for more explanation: "Kelly asked me on the first day of class if I was Irish because I blushed bright red; she asked me about my ethnicity based on my skin color and I was not offended. I'm just trying to understand." Paige clarified, "But this man didn't know me." Other African American students in the class tried to help: "He was butting into her business; it's like a privilege he has as a White man, to claim to know you, when he doesn't." But the White students continued to look confused.

After some level of heated discussion, it occurred to me that in addition to the power dynamics the students were adept at identifying, there was also an intercultural communication issue at play. Kochman (1981) described an African American communication style that views personal information, such as the races of one's mother and father, as personal property and as such would be something that would be inappropriate to share with strangers. Conversely he described a White American communication style that views personal information seeking as a socially friendly strategy.

Before I gave the class this information I asked the group to spend some quiet time writing two lists: questions that are too personal to ask when you first meet someone and questions that are appropriate to ask. After the students had several items on each list, I asked them to pair up and discuss their lists. I asked if they noticed any patterns. Some students had noticed that one person's appropriate question was another's inappropriate question. I asked the students what that would mean if these two people met, and they agreed that there would be a miscommunication, and the relationship would likely not go much further.

I then explained in detail Kochman's (1981) cultural observation that many African Americans view personal information as property. We discussed likely origins of such a cultural characteristic given the context of social power. Kochman listed several origins with histories in power dynamics experienced by Black Americans, including a concern that personal information could be used as a *signifying* strategy. Kochman explained that within the African American community direct questions are often used to signify some underlying message; in the case of Paige, the concern was that the information asked is assumed to signify that her social status was of a lesser value than that of the stranger at the FedEx store. As a class we analyzed Paige's story from a power and an intercultural perspective.

Story 2: Tour Guide

When I was teaching in Hawaii, a local Hawaii graduate student, Linda, whose bicultural ethnicity was Japanese American and Chinese American, told our class of an advising session she had with an incoming international undergraduate student from Japan, Yuki. Yuki expressed some trepidation at learning to live in a new place. Linda offered to take Yuki on a tour of the area at Yuki's convenience. Yuki seemed not to hear or understand the offer; Yuki changed the subject. Linda made the offer again, this time as clearly as she could. Again Yuki changed the subject. Because of her exposure to intercultural analysis in the course, Linda assumed that something intercultural was going on but could not surmise what exactly it was. She had had similar experiences with Japanese, and sometimes Chinese, students in the past and had brushed them off. This time Linda wanted the assistance of the class to analyze the conversation from an intercultural perspective.

Immediately, it occurred to me that Yuki was practicing a high-context form of communication characteristic of Japanese culture and described in depth by Hall (1976). In high-context communication more is conveyed outside the spoken word and within the context than in low-context communication. For example, high-context communication occurs in pauses, eye contact or shifts, body positioning, person placement in a room, and even in the clothes people wear.

I asked Linda what her impressions had been of the Japanese students she had come into contact with in the past. "Sometimes I thought they didn't understand the language and that they weren't going to be very good students in the U.S." I asked other students in the class if they'd had similar experiences, and one student said, "They won't tell you no, they think it's rude, so they lie or ignore you." Another student chimed in, "And they won't tell you when they think you are inappropriate; they just smile and judge you."

I asked the students to shift their perspectives: "Let's extend benefit of the doubt. What if Yuki was communicating with Linda? How might she have communicated it?" The students agreed that it was not through anything she said. I reminded the students, "Aren't there other, nonverbal, ways of communicating?" Linda recalled, "Yuki did look away from me and shifted in her seat; she did appear uncomfortable." I asked Linda to think carefully about what message that body language conveys. Linda thought, "My offer made her uncomfortable; maybe it was inappropriate or undesirable given our different social roles." I clarified the point: "So Yuki did communicate, just not in a way that you were accustomed to receiving messages."

Together as a class we reviewed the characteristics of high- and low-context communication styles. Students pointed out that their low-context assumptions had yielded judgments of the Japanese students that were not accurate and, worse, distanced themselves from the Japanese students who needed them.

My hope is that these example stories, as well as those in the appendix, reveal the dual possibilities of viewing each of these scenarios as fundamentally an issue of power or as an issue of communication difference. Each perspective can yield different, yet equally compelling, insights.

MY PROFESSIONAL IDENTITY AS AN INTERCULTURAL COMMUNICATIONS AND SOCIAL JUSTICE EDUCATOR

When I first began practicing these new approaches in the first decade of this century, I felt I was no longer a social justice educator. I felt this way because I had shifted away from putting lessons of power and privilege on center stage and because I learned to view cultural differences as meaningful and generalizations as helpful. My identity shifted toward being an intercultural communications educator. I spent several years believing that I was an ex-social justice educator. It was a professional identity I did not share with my peers who were social justice educators because I felt it would be misunderstood. Would my peers believe I no longer cared for social justice? However, more recently I have reflected on the meaning of social justice. Bell (2007) defined *social justice* as a goal and a process. As a goal, social justice is "full and equal participation of all groups in a society that is mutually shaped to meet their needs" (Bell, 2007, p. 1), and I still believe in this very strongly. My educational efforts have always been focused on realizing social justice. As a process, social justice is attained through "democratic and participatory" (Bell, 2007, p. 2) strategies. And I believe my more recent strategies meet these criteria more successfully. What I have come to believe now is that the approaches I have taken toward social justice, early in my career and now, represent different processes toward the same goal—different means to the same end. Whether I put power and privilege on center stage or intercultural communication, both educational efforts, if successful, will yield social justice. So after a several-year hiatus of sorts, I identify, once again, as a social justice educator.

I do not believe I was successful in my initial approach as a power and privilege social justice educator. I intentionally put some participants on the defensive and others on the offensive. Participants learned to interpret events as unfair instead of different. I did not teach students how to extend benefit of the doubt regarding communication perception and intention. I exacerbated poor intercultural communication. I ignored cultural contexts. I valued healthy expressions of conflict and negatively judged those who were made uncomfortable by them, sadly, even when that discomfort was culturally driven. My fear is that my previous approach to social justice education may have inadvertently taught students to identify intercultural moments as moments of conflict instead of moments to give benefit of the doubt and use clarification communication. I fear I set up students to believe people are either targets or agents, when, in fact, most of us are both and much more.

But I believe my exposure to discourse on power and privilege was an appropriate first step in my preparation as a social justice educator before learning of intercultural communication nuances. With sensitivity and understanding of unequal power distributions socially and historically, I was better able to understand cultural differences. Understanding cultural differences without regard for social inequities does not honor the whole picture of culture. Indeed, many cultural differences are formed through groups' experiences with oppression.

I understand many of the changes in my practice are because of my personal development as an individual and as a professional, and that along with my own maturation, the field of social justice education has also evolved. I am aware the field has changed from the 1980s to the present, viewing cultural contexts from a global perspective and challenging the binary notion that people are oppressors or oppressed. My point here is not to advocate that social justice educators abandon the exploration of power and privilege but to reflect meaningfully on what they do, why, and with what result.

Social justice educators approach their work from a variety of perspectives, bringing with them the experiences of their own lives. This observation may seem obvious considering background characteristics such as ethnicity, gender, sexual orientation, able-bodiedness, and religion, among others. Of course, life experiences associated with identities will affect the approach we take with social justice education. But I have come to believe that the diversity of *how* we talk about social justice education can influence our work strongly. Said another way, the specific discourse communities that inform our practice can potentially represent a singular perspective, and like culture, when you are too close to the rhetoric of your discourse you cannot see it much less evaluate it. To talk about social justice differently and to view different perspectives on social justice as equally viable can broaden our ways of thinking, being, and understanding, thus facilitating connections with our learners.

NOTE

1. Schingen is not the author of the exercise, but she provides a thorough description. She cites Robert Gonyea and Michelle Tanaka, who presented Archie Bunker's Neighborhood to a National Association of College and University Residence Halls conference in 1989. They were not the authors of the exercise either. Gonyea learned of the activity as a graduate student at Michigan State University in 1986 through a handout titled "Unequal Resources Activity"; however, no original source or author was listed (R. M. Gonyea, personal communication, September 29, 2011).

REFERENCES

Anderson, P. A. (2008). *Nonverbal communication: Forms and functions* (2nd ed.). Long Grove, IL: Waveland Press.

Bell, L. A. (2007). Theoretical foundations for social justice education. In M. Adams, L. A. Bell, & P. Griffin (Eds.), *Teaching for diversity and social justice: A sourcebook* (2nd ed., pp. 1–14). New York, NY: Routledge.

Bennett, J. M. (1998). Transition shock: Putting culture shock in perspective. In M. J. Bennett (Ed.), *Basic concepts of intercultural communication* (pp. 215–223). Yarmouth, ME: Intercultural Press.

Bennett, J. M., & Bennett, M. J. (2004). Developing intercultural sensitivity: An integrative approach to global and domestic diversity. In D. Landis, J. M. Bennett, & M. J. Bennett (Eds.), *Handbook of intercultural training* (3rd ed., pp. 147–165). Thousand Oaks, CA: Sage.

Bennett, M. J. (1998). Intercultural communication: A current perspective. In M. J. Bennett (Ed.), *Basic concepts of intercultural communication* (pp. 1–34). Yarmouth, ME: Intercultural Press.

Burton, L. M., & Tucker, M. B. (2009). Romantic unions in an era of uncertainty: A post-Moynihan perspective on African American women and marriage. *ANNALS of the American Academy of Political and Social Science, 621*(1), 132–148. doi: 10.1177/0002716208324852

Collins, P. H. (2000). *Black feminist thought: Knowledge, consciousness, and the politics of empowerment* (2nd ed.). New York, NY: Routledge.

Engle, J. (2007, February 2). Culture's unacknowledged iron grip. *Chronicle of Higher Education, 53*(22), B16.

Hall, E. T. (1976). *Beyond culture.* New York, NY: Random House.

Hall, E. T. (1983). *The dance of life: The other dimensions of time.* New York, NY: Doubleday.

Hardiman, R., & Jackson, B. W. (1997). Conceptual foundations for social justice courses. In M. Adams, L. A. Bell, & P. Griffin (Eds.), *Teaching for diversity and social justice: A sourcebook* (pp. 16–29). New York, NY: Routledge.

Hardiman, R., & Jackson, B. W. (2007). Conceptual foundations for social justice education. In M. Adams, L. A. Bell, & P. Griffin (Eds.), *Teaching for diversity and social justice: A sourcebook* (2nd ed., pp. 35–66). New York, NY: Routledge.

Hofstede, G. (1991). *Cultures and organizations: Software of the mind.* London, UK: McGraw-Hill.

Intercultural Dynamics in European Education Through Online Simulation. (2001). *Cross-cultural activity: The anthropologists.* Retrieved from http://www.ideels.uni-bremen.de/anthropologists.html

Kochman, T. (1981). *Black and White styles in conflict.* Chicago: University of Chicago Press.

Landry, B. (2000). *Black working wives: Pioneers of the American family revolution.* Berkeley: University of California Press.

Matsu, C., Takeshita, J., Izutsu, S., & Hishinuma, E. (2011). The Japanese. In J. F. McDermott & N. N. Andrade (Eds.), *People and cultures of Hawaii: The evolution of culture and ethnicity* (pp. 107–130). Honolulu: University of Hawai'i Press.

Mun Wah, L. (Producer). (1994). *The color of fear* [Motion picture]. United States: StirFry Productions.

Nydell, M. K. (2006). *Understanding Arabs: A guide for modern times* (4th ed.). Boston, MA: Intercultural Press.

Okamura, J. Y. (2008). *Ethnicity and inequality in Hawai'i.* Philadelphia, PA: Temple University Press.

Reid, F. (Producer, director). (1995). *Skin deep: College students confront racism* [Documentary film]. United States: Iris Films.

Schingen, K. M. (2002, November). *Archie Bunker's neighborhood.* Workshop presented at the annual meeting of the Society of Intercultural Education Training and Research-USA, Portland, OR. Outline retrieved from http://islam-zwart.net/workstuff/Training/Diversity%20Training%20Material/ArchieBunkersNeighborhood.pdf

Shirts, R. G. (1969). *StarPower.* Delmar, CA: Simulation Training Systems.

Shirts, R. G. (1977). *Bafa' Bafa': A cross cultural simulation.* Delmar, CA: Simulation Training Systems.

Stewart, E. C., Danielian, J., & Foster, R. J. (1998). Cultural assumptions and values. In M. J. Bennett (Ed.), *Basic concepts of intercultural communication* (pp. 157–172). Yarmouth, ME: Intercultural Press.

Storti, C. (2001). *The art of crossing cultures* (2nd ed.). Yarmouth, ME: Intercultural Press.

Thiagarajan, S., & Thiagarajan, R. (2006). *Barnga: A simulation game on cultural clashes* (3rd ed.). Boston, MA: Intercultural Press.

APPENDIX

In addition to the two stories in the text, here I list four additional intercultural moments that can be discussed in terms of power and intercultural communication issues. Suggestions for additional reading are included for background on the intercultural issues that influence the scenario.

Story 3: No Culture?

On the first day of class, I ask students to sign up to take turns bringing in snack foods from their cultures to share with the class. When I was teaching this class in Chicago, one midwestern White student, Erica, came up to me at the break and said, "What if I don't have a culture? What food do I bring?" Erica, obviously, was not yet aware that she had a culture, and the implications of that lack of awareness likely went far beyond her snack selections. To help her make her decision, we had a careful conversation about some of her family traditions and any food associated with those traditions. Halfway through the term, after being immersed in the course materials, she presented this story to the class as her intercultural moment. Erica explained that as a dominant culture person, her culture had been too close for her to see, let alone to understand (see Stewart, Danielian, & Foster, 1998, for an analysis of American culture).

Story 4: Fish Out of Water

Suditta, a Bengali Indian international student who is Muslim, was new to the United States when she began her semester in our class. In fact, this was her first trip out of India, and it seemed fitting that the intercultural class was her first graduate course in this country. She reflected her stories of transition from the very beginning of the course. During our week on culture shock and transition shock, Suditta said that she grew up knowing what it meant to be Bengali and Muslim, because she did not have to travel far in India to be in Hindi and Punjabi communities. The comparison was available and made obvious. But not until she came to the United States at age 31 was she made aware of what it meant to be Indian. Similarly, Matthew, a European American from Chicago who had lived and traveled extensively in the Middle East during his early adult years, related that he knew what it meant to be an American only after returning to Chicago. Chris, an African American student from Detroit who had never traveled outside the United

States said, "But I bet you still do not know what it means to be White in America"; Matthew conceded. Chris explained, "I may not have international experiences and I may not have experienced what it means to be American, but I know intimately what it means to be Black in this country. I live it every day since the day I was born, like Suditta knew long ago what it meant to be Bengali." (See J. M. Bennett, 1998, for a description of transition shock, which emphasizes the utility of emotionally recalling other life transitions in order to comprehend culture shock.)

Story 5: Too Close!

Rayna, an Okinawan American woman local to Hawaii, worked as a program administrator for a Hawaii community college. She told a story of a student worker who had annoyed her for quite some time. He would sit very close to her when they reviewed his paperwork together, help himself to snacks in the shared office refrigerator, and interrupt her work to ask personal questions, such as how much money she made and who were the members of her family. The interactions were awkward enough for her that she decided there must be an intercultural issue. Rayna invited him to sit and talk with her and discovered that he was from American Samoa and grew up in a very small, tight-knit village in a three-bedroom house with his parents, grandparents, and five siblings. The more he talked, the more Rayna understood how strongly collectivist his values were. (See Hofstede, 1991, Chapter 3 for a discussion of collectivism versus individualism.)

Story 6: You Are Touching Me!

Della, a Hawaii-local, Filipino American woman who worked as a student life coordinator at a small baccalaureate regional college in Hawaii, told a story of one of her students being so grateful for her assistance that the student hugged her. Della panicked and was instantly uncomfortable. Her first thought from the intercultural perspective was, "What did I do to communicate that I wanted a hug?" She wondered, "Is this necessary? What is possessing her? Was I too nice?" After the hug was over, Della realized she had not hugged back. She wondered if her discomfort offended the student. Later, upon reflection, Della realized that the student was Samoan and likely from a cultural context where touching and affection are more easily shared. (See Chapter 8 in Anderson, 2008, for a more thorough discussion of immediacy and contact cultures.)

Part Two

Understanding Identities and Facilitation

THIS SECTION explores the importance of understanding specific and intersecting social identities in social justice education. It is, of course, impossible to address all the complexities and ever-emerging social identities in one book, much less one section. Salient social identities such as religion, ability, socioeconomic status, language, and national origin are not discussed at length in this section but are named in other examples throughout the book (e.g., in Chapter 3, numerous case studies are provided that illuminate differences resulting from culture and national origin, and in Chapter 11, the authors provide an example of an entire program that brings to light U.S. Christian privilege). It is important to acknowledge that the omission of these identities in this section does not make them less relevant. The chapters included here, however, do shed light on the importance of understanding how the history, context, nuances, and experiences of all our multiple and intersecting social identities can and should influence our facilitation.

In Chapter 4, Brent L. Bilodeau shares emerging theory and practice on gender identity and specifically the impact of the term *genderism*. As notions of gender fluidity and queer gender identity are relatively new to social justice education efforts, workshop participants and facilitators often find this work challenging. Bilodeau reflects on his journey to understand gender identity and provides strategies for ensuring greater gender inclusivity and dismantling the gender binary in courses and workshops aimed at eradicating racism, sexism, and all forms of systematic oppression.

In Chapter 5, Rebecca Ropers-Huilman reminds us that exploring our own and participants' dominant identities are a critical component to social justice work. Specifically she argues that exploring whiteness is an essential part of facilitating and promoting social justice in educational settings. Failing to explore whiteness, she contends, may perpetuate the very oppression that educators are attempting to dismantle through social justice facilitation. The chapter presents scholarship that can guide facilitators to disrupt unexamined whiteness and discusses some uncomfortable questions.

Chapter 6 offers reflections and insights from Tanya Williams and Elaine Brigham, two educators who have had a long-term cofacilitation relationship. Many educators choose to cofacilitate social justice workshops. The goals of this choice often include modeling collaboration and valuing multiple identities and diverse communication styles, and assisting in more effectively navigating difficult conversations. Challenges can arise, however, when facilitators have not done the personal and intergroup work with one another needed to successfully cofacilitate across social identity differences. In a dialogic format, Williams and Brigham reflect upon their experiences as cofacilitators of an intergroup dialogue course and make transparent the issues that can play out in cofacilitation as they work to navigate their multiple social identities.

In Chapter 7, Adam J. Ortiz urges educators to consider the importance of supporting multiracial students in social justice education by recognizing multiracial as a distinct social identity. Multiracial individuals are susceptible to experiencing inadequate facilitation because their racial experiences are so varied. In this chapter Ortiz shares his reflections and experience with racial affinity groups, a popular method of creating small-group discussions in larger training workshops. In addition, he discusses an example of a key strategy aimed at supporting multiracial students in facilitation.

4

Developing Gender-Inclusive Facilitation

Understanding Genderism

Brent L. Bilodeau

M Y FIRST SENSE that something might be wrong with my educational efforts related to transgender people and gender identity came in the spring of 2002. At that time, it was just a glimpse, a first moment when my comfortable, unconscious cocoon of cisgender privilege, the privilege that comes from having a gender identity consistent with my sex assignment, was challenged. In that year, I was serving as the coordinator of the Lesbian, Bisexual, Gay, and Transgender Concerns Program at Michigan State University. As a student group adviser, I worked with a Lebanese Armenian international student from Cyprus named TJ, who was emerging as a gifted student leader and activist with an unusual depth of perspective regarding social justice issues, their intersections, and systems of oppression.[1] I had known TJ as a proud lesbian. In one of our weekly meetings that spring, TJ disclosed a lifelong process of coming to understand personal gender identity, different from what I had known previously. Based on assigned sex at birth, TJ was labeled *female*. He had no choice in the matter. Because of this, he had been raised as a girl. Yet, he felt a deep, primary connection to a male gender identity. When he reflected on his childhood experience, he remembered feeling he was really a boy, but he "pushed it way down." TJ had come to an awareness that his identity was not lesbian, but transgender, female to male. This was the first of many conversations TJ and I would have regarding his identity process and journey.

From those initial discussions, I have profound memories of TJ talking about the ways he wanted to express gender and the related challenges. With great clarity, he explained that he didn't want to become the type of man who was an echo of male standards dictated by the social systems of Cyprus or the United States. He wanted to be his own man, on his own terms, yet he felt constrained and oppressed by the power of gender systems. What I heard in his voice was a call for liberation, and it hit me hard. As a social justice educator, I had done much work regarding issues of gender and sexism, but there was something deeper about the ways TJ cried out against his experience with gender categories and in a voice I had not heard before. I later came to understand that he felt imprisoned by a binary gender system. This gender system only allowed for two gender identities—male or female—that labeled individuals based on what were perceived as their sex assignments and maintained rigid norms for acceptable behavior based on this sex. TJ's voice caused me to question my assumptions about training and education about lesbian, gay, bisexual, and transgender (LGBT) issues and transgender identities in particular. It was a profoundly powerful conversation—one that has continued to influence the direction of my career. TJ invited me to begin a journey that would lead to a personal and scholarly exploration of genderism, cisgender privilege, and my role as a facilitator in gender-inclusive social justice education.

TOWARD A FRAMEWORK FOR UNDERSTANDING GENDERISM

When I reflect on my early social justice education efforts, gender roles and stereotypes were discussed in the context of addressing sexism, yet these efforts reflected binary notions of gender as biologically based, male or female gender identities. My efforts did not account for any notion that gender identity and expression reflected a fluid framework. In a fluid context, gender is viewed as a spectrum of male and female identities. Related examples include individuals whose male or female gender identity differs from sex assignment at birth, such as transsexuals; those who blend male and female identities, such as androgynous people; and individuals who experience gender completely outside the notions of male and female gender identities, such as genderqueer individuals or third gender identities. For the purposes of this chapter, the words *transgender* or *gender variant* are used as umbrella terms to refer to a wide spectrum of gender identities.

In the early 1990s many social justice educators and allies began to explore the complexity of gender identity as more students were sharing their gender variant identities and experiences. During this time, training efforts on gender identity at Michigan State University (MSU) reflected much of what was happening nationally in higher education. Similar to other institutions, MSU experienced its first "out" transgender people. At the time, these individuals identified as transsexual, male-to-female staff in their 40s and 50s who were undergoing gender transition and desired support and inclusion on campus. As a result of the courageous efforts of these people, MSU examined issues regarding related gender policies and practice for the first time. Suddenly our human resources department, counseling office, and health center were called to address the needs of an emerging transgender population. Staff education was identified as a top priority.

When I reflect on these early efforts, I'm struck by the lack of critical consciousness I had concerning my educational paradigm and training approach. My social conditioning that supported the "rightness" of a binary sex assignment gender system that I believed was based on biology fed a largely unconscious goal of these initial efforts. In this context, the unspoken focus of transgender inclusion and related training was to support transgender individuals in transitioning to the "correct" male or female gender. The training sessions offered focused on a traditional panel discussion model. Campus transsexual staff members disclosed details of their personal histories, family and partner relationships, gender transition processes and related surgery, and ongoing support needs. They spoke of great challenges related to these concerns and shared powerfully positive and horrifically traumatizing experiences. The MSU community greatly benefited from the leadership, courage, and openness of these first educators. Yet, as I reflect on my response to these initial training efforts, I realize there was a perspective they offered that I was unable to understand.

Through my binary gender lens, I heard the pain and hurt in the voices of the transsexual staff as a direct reflection of their failure to conform to one of two sex-assignment-based social standards for gender. "If only they had the freedom to experience gendered life the way I did," I thought. They were individuals born in the wrong body. I felt a sense of pity for them. Today, I'm disturbed by my initial assumptions, yet I also realize that such thinking was and is shared by many well-meaning student affairs professionals (among others). What I completely missed was that transgender people do not necessarily have a problem. I failed to see that the real problem was that a broader system of binary gender was operating powerfully, that I was a product of it, and that this system encouraged me to see a transgender person as a tortured other, made exotic, who desperately needed to be corrected. I did not know what I could not see. Wilchins (2002) commented on this experience of life in the gender binary, saying,

> Gender is like a lens through which we've not yet learned to see. Or more accurately, like glasses worn from childhood, it's like a lens through which we've always seen and can't remember how the world looked before. And this lens is strictly bifocal. It strangely shows us only black and white in a Technicolor world. . . . There may certainly be more than two genders, but two genders is all we've named, all we know, all we'll see. (p. 13)

Wilchins was encouraging me to see "beyond the binary" (p. 11) in the same ways TJ explained in that profound conversation. I was called not just to gain a deep understanding of dual gender systems but to question my conscious and unconscious role in their perpetuation. This journey would ultimately include a reexamination of my role as a facilitator of gender identity education.

My exploration began with a focus on gender identity and transgender people, beginning with literature related to medical, psychiatric, and human development. Many transgender activists, scholars, and allies describe this literature and related practices as dominated by themes of transgender identities being forms of mental illness, deviance, and disorder (Bornstein, 1994; Lev, 2004; Wilchins, 2002). One often-cited example is the American Psychiatric Association's (2000) *Diagnostic and Statistical Manual on Mental Disorders, 4th ed., Text Revision* (*DSM-IV-TR*) and the upcoming revised edition, *DSM-V*. Among these concerns are *DSM-IV-TR*'s classifications related to gender identity disorder (GID) and transvestic fetishism (TF). The GID diagnostic category is viewed by many in transgender communities to be highly pathologizing (Szymanski, 2008). In this context, transgender individuals who seek medical care and gender-related surgery must essentially be documented as having a mental illness.

A growing number of scholars and social justice educators assert that medical and psychiatric models lack attention to a diverse spectrum of gender identities, overly emphasizing transition from one sex to another, to become male or female. These approaches marginalize transgender individuals who identify as genderqueers, androgynous individuals, gender-benders, transsexuals who do not desire surgery, and the expanding gender variant identities embraced by today's youths (Renn & Bilodeau, 2011). Many transgender activists and allies are calling for the removal of the GID and TF categories from the pending revised *DSM-V*, comparing the action to the removal of the category of homosexuality as a mental illness from the 1973 *DSM* manual.

Through my exploration, it became clear that nonstigmatizing literature on transgender college student identity development did not exist. This led me to conduct a study that examined healthy transgender student identity development processes (Bilodeau, 2005). Although this research provided me with a deeper understanding of transgender college student development concerns, I became increasingly aware that I could not provide meaningful gender identity education without understanding the related system of oppression that operated in society and on campus. Exploring the dynamics of gender privilege and oppression became essential to understand the lived experience of transgender college students and their identity development. A second study led to a definition and characteristics of a dual gender oppression system termed *genderism*. I define *genderism* as the belief or assumption that there are only two genders. Genderism links biological male or female sex assignment to an assumed gender identity as a man or a woman and expected masculine or feminine gender expression and heterosexuality. In this definition, all gender identity and expression is essentialized as one of two options. "Genderism is supported socially by a binary gender system characterized by explicit and implicit rules, rewards, and punishments for conforming to either male or female identities. At its core, genderism asserts that biological sex assignment predetermines gender identity destiny" (Bilodeau, 2009a, p. 61).

Genderism is systemic because it permeates all aspects of an individual's life and is institutionalized though implicit and explicit laws, rules, and policies. Genderism's four primary characteristics and related examples are discussed next.

First, a forced social labeling process sorts and categorizes all individuals into male or female identities, often at an institutionalized level. For individuals who express gender identity outside binary norms, often genderqueer or androgynous students, this experience can be particularly pronounced. Students in the study described an almost daily occurrence of having individuals inquire about their gender identities. "Are you a boy or a girl?" was a common question.

Second, there is social accountability for conforming to binary gender norms with related punishments. Individuals who fail to conform are viewed as deviant or having a disorder. This often takes the form of direct harassment or, for those who fail to conform, fear of harassment. For example, a study participant discussed life in a male residential community that was characterized by threats of "implied violence" (Bilodeau, 2009a, p. 80) for failing to conform to male gender norms. Further, study participants universally described interactions with cisgender individuals that became intimidating because of these individuals' perceptions of the participants' lack of gender conformity, often leaving them feeling highly stigmatized and treated as gender deviants (Bilodeau, 2009a, p. 73). One participant, who was returning to college to finish her degree following a male-to-female gender transition reflected on her interaction with advising office personnel:

> I knew that the office staff were looking at me. They all stopped what they were doing. . . . they tried to be unobtrusive, but I could obviously tell that they had handled my records and they wanted to look at the freak and you just gotta roll with it. But it's demeaning. (Bilodeau, 2009a, p. 73)

Regarding the third characteristic, genderism focuses on personal marginalization being enacted through an overt and covert privileging of binary systems. In the college setting, those who express the greatest degree of conformity to dual gender norms are given advantages over those who do not. As an example from the study (Bilodeau, 2009a), a faculty member admitted that his discomfort with a female-to-male student caused him to favor calling on cisgender individuals during class discussions. Transgender-identified study participants also talked about binary privilege being particularly pronounced in LGBT communities. A student described the experience of a supposedly inclusive LGBT student organization as "really more focused on you're either gay (male) or lesbian (female) and they gave up the B and the T" (Bilodeau, 2009a, p. 94).

Finally, the fourth characteristic of genderism occurs when binary systems promote invisibility of gender nonconforming identities and isolation of transgender individuals, making transgender identities inaccessible. Many participants in the study described feeling their personal gender identities were different from their sex assignments at a young age, yet they received no messages from the environment that gender-variant identities even existed. One student said, "Growing up in the suburbs, there wasn't any language for it" (Bilodeau, 2009a, p. 104). Others described the impact of the social obliteration of gender variant as having a significant negative impact on their emotional health. Another participant reflected, "If I didn't have to deal with it [a binary society], I don't think I'd be so depressed all the time" (Bilodeau, 2009a, p. 108).

IMPLICATIONS FOR MY FACILITATION AND DESIGN OF GENDER-INCLUSIVE EDUCATION

The years I spent researching genderist systems were life changing. The work forced me to take a long and, at times, uncomfortable look into my identity as a cisgendered person. The journey gave me a new awareness of my gender privilege, despite my experiences being targeted as a gay man. My identity as male was rarely questioned or scrutinized, particularly when my sexual orientation was not known. The routine socially gendered dimensions of my life went on comfortably and unconsciously. When identifying my sex on life-affecting documents, whether a driver's license, job application, or insurance and passport forms, my cisgendered status assured instant approval. Shopping in the men's department and the daily tasks of using restrooms and locker rooms never caused my presence in those spaces to be questioned or put me at risk for harassment (again, particularly if my sexual orientation was not known). Going to a new doctor never carried a threat of humiliation or being rejected service because of my gender identity. I never received awkward stares and was never pointed at or whispered about. Although some experiences with homophobia may have led to my masculinity being questioned by others, overall I never had to wonder if I was passing well enough as my gender. My cisgender privilege also showed up in ways that surprised me. Swimming is a great joy of my life. The sensations of being suspended in the water—of having the ability to dive, splash, submerge, and float—carry a powerful sense of physical liberation and freedom for me. I remember feeling embarrassed by my ignorance when transgender students shared with me that they had forgone the simple, freeing pleasure of swimming in any environment. The risks of being discovered were too great.

As I reflected on my experience of cisgender privilege, I realized it was imperative that I consider the impact of this privilege on my own identity and role as a facilitator. What did it mean for me to serve as a cisgender facilitator of social justice education sessions? How did my socialization into binary gender systems consciously and unconsciously affect my facilitation?

I became aware that when I look out into a room, my eyes are trained to see binary gender, and my ears hear voices I instantly associate with male or female gender categories. In what ways did I interact with session participants that demonstrated my unconscious support of a gender binary? As I pondered many of these questions for the first time, I realized that gender-inclusive education, with a social justice framework, must engage all participants in a similar self-examination. The following is how I approach facilitation of gender education in light of these questions.

Exploring Socialization

My approach to campus educational efforts changed as my understanding of genderism changed. The first step is to prioritize the exploration of personal gender identity socialization with participants. The self-examination activities I designed were informed by literature regarding human socialization and related binary gender constructions, some of which the following examples serve to illustrate. Much scholarship suggests that from the birth moment (and often beforehand), sex assignment determines socialization practices, such as gender-specific pink blankets (for girls) or blue (for boys), and dolls (for girls) or trucks (for boys) (Bornstein, 1994; Feinberg, 1996). Other authors suggest a cycle of socialization reinforces binary constructions of gender whereby individuals are systematically rewarded and punished for gender-conforming or nonconforming behavior (Griffin, 1997). These socialization activities include birthing, how we are treated in early childhood within parental relationships (e.g., boys reprimanded for crying, girls needing to cross their legs when sitting), the messages from institutions such as schools (e.g., boys encouraged to engage in tough play and violent sports, girls encouraged to be cheerleaders) and religious organizations (e.g., men are the head of the household, women raise the children), adult workplace experiences, community and regional norms, and policy and legislation (Griffin, 1997). Thus, from birth to death, not only are gender binary systems reinforced and institutionalized, there is no place for people who don't identify with a particular gender. Transgender scholar and activist Pat Califia (1997) posed a provocative, related question: "Who would you be if you had never been punished for gender-inappropriate behavior?" (p. 3). The aforementioned scholarship was used to inform the design of activities for exploring gender identity socialization, genderism, and the related dynamics of power and privilege in educational settings. For example, participants in one exercise of a training that TJ and I often facilitate are asked to think about a time in their lives when they felt like they had to act like a man or act like a lady because they felt pressured, were told to, or feared reprimand. They are asked to reflect on the details of the incident, what they felt, and what they learned.

Another activity used to explore personal gender identity involves dividing training participants into groups based on binary gender categories and asking them to draw a collective picture of the "ideal" man or woman. Follow-up processing included a focus on exploring ways the drawings were influenced by messages received from early childhood through experiences growing up and related to the impact of K–12 schools, local community and faith experiences, workplace dynamics, media influences, and the impact of related legislation. These discussions allowed for a deep self-examination of ways participants may consciously or unconsciously be influenced by social systems and institutions that support binary gender (Bilodeau, 2009b; Bilodeau & Jourian, 2010).

A related and powerful exercise is to ask training participants to introduce themselves by stating their names and preferred gender pronouns. Cisgender participants often report awareness of a unique privilege—that their names, gender identities, and expressions have always felt congruent and have never been socially questioned. In privileged binary systems, pronouns never need to be identified. They are implicit. For me as a facilitator, and for other cisgender participants, this self-exploration process lays the foundation for developing a broader, systemic understanding of the experience of transgender students and genderism.

Applying the Genderism Framework

Following workshop participants' exploration of personal gender socialization, I move to introducing the ways this socialization can be harmful to us all, particularly for transgender students. Through the application of the genderism framework, I illustrate each of its four characteristics with personal experiences and voices of transgender college students. Quotes are displayed on slides and read aloud, and training participants are asked to write initial reactions to hearing the voices. The following training slide serves as an example:

> Genderism Characteristic 1:
>   There is a *forced social labeling process* that sorts and categorizes all individuals into binary "male" or "female" identities, often at an institutionalized level.

Related voices of transgender students:

"'Are you a boy or a girl?!' It's like they had to know, like it was really disturbing that I didn't fit the category."—Razi

"And everyone keeps asking me, like every two weeks I have these people asking me, 'How are you identifying? We just want to make sure that we're making you comfortable.' I'm like, 'Just stop asking. Just call me whatever you want.'" —Charlie

Related participant process question:

What are your reactions and feelings to hearing the student voices? (Bilodeau, 2009b; Bilodeau & Jourian, 2010)

Following the presentation, participants are asked to discuss written reflections with a partner. Ultimately, this activity is designed to promote deep reflection and awareness through multiple activities: seeing, hearing, writing, and discussing. Feedback from these sessions indicates that participants appreciate this opportunity, particularly given that it is often their first exposure to the concept of genderism.

Addressing Intersectionality

Because issues of gender identity represent one dimension of the multiple identities students carry, such as race/ethnicity, disability, nationality, and socioeconomic class, it is also important to design training that reflects genderism's intersections with other oppression systems. All our lived experiences are influenced by the various intersections of our identities, making this level of analysis critical. In training sessions, TJ and I address intersectionality by including opportunities for participants to explore the intersections of multiple social identities and genderism, such as experiences of media invisibility of gender variant and transgender people of color, ways transgender visibility is limited to and defined by drag culture, language and the conception of gender identity across multiple cultural groups (e.g., the use of the term *two spirit* in Native American communities, and *stud* in African American queer culture), historical erasure of the contributions of transgender people of color from the Stonewall rebellion (an event that has been cited as the beginning of the gay rights movement), intersections of gender-based violent crimes with age and race, and the intertwining of race, poverty, and gender identity with higher education access (Bilodeau & Jourian, 2010).

The focus of this chapter does not lend itself to an exploration of these topics in more detail, but I provide two examples used in our training model. In the sessions we examine the murders of two gender variant teenagers: a 15-year-old African American named Sakia Gunn and a 17-year-old Latina named Gwen Araujo. In 2003 Sakia and her friends were propositioned by two men at a bus stop, located near a popular socializing spot for gay and lesbian youth. Sakia was stabbed and died after she identified herself as a lesbian and rebuffed the men's advances. Gwen was a transgender teenager who was beaten and strangled in 2002 after her four male acquaintances, two of whom she had been sexually intimate with, discovered she was transgender. These cases have often been compared to the 1998 torture and murder of Matthew Shepard, a White cisgender gay college student, that drew national and international media coverage. The deaths of Sakia and Gwen drew limited media coverage and raised questions about the legal protections for transgender individuals, particularly as victims who did not identify as White. The analysis includes the marginalization of their deaths by mainstream media as trans identified and the ways race and socioeconomic class were contributing factors to the media silence.

In addition to this example of training content, TJ and I believe it is important that we discuss our personal social identities and ways these identities may influence our facilitation. We do this by disclosing our personal points of privilege and oppression throughout the workshop. My experiences being raised a middle-class White and cisgender male in California and TJ's growing up in Cyprus as Lebanese Armenian, working class, and transgender are shared and discussed as illustrations of ways racism, xenophobia, and classism are mutually reinforcing systems (Bilodeau & Jourian, 2009).

IMPLICATIONS OF FLUID IDENTITIES FOR THEORY AND PRACTICE

In addition to focusing on the impact of intersectionality across oppression systems, training models should also address the fluid nature of gender identity and implications for theory and practice. Concepts of fluid gender identities, genderism, and cisgender privilege offer multiple challenges related to providing definitions and terms for gender-inclusive facilitation. Discrete definitions of terms such as *gender variant, transgender, cisgender, genderqueer*, and so forth are important for establishing a common language in training, but they are not enough to explain the related complexities of sex and gender. When facilitating, I introduce a number of models that help individuals explore gender through contexts of identity development, social construction, and systems of power. Such models include the work of scholars Lev (2004) and Griffin (1997). These models reflect a perspective that language and definitions related to gender identity are evolving, just as the social contexts and related norms, culture, and language change and vary across cultures.

Further, gender-inclusive facilitation must also address issues related to overly simplistic explanations of gender and power. What happens to binary gender and its inherent power and oppression systems when transgender identities are involved? Are the experiences of transsexual men and women similar to their cisgender counterparts? For those who are androgynous, genderqueer, have more fluid gender identities, or don't always pass as male or female, what are their experiences of gender privilege and oppression? In the genderism study (Bilodeau, 2009a), student participants Triston and Razi shared conflicting perspectives regarding male privilege and their identities as tranny boys. They used the term *tranny boy* because they felt it best captured their feelings of being preadolescent boys. Both had been assigned the category female at birth and at the time of the study were living full-time as men. They talked about feeling preadolescent because they had not yet begun taking hormones or engaged in any gender-related surgical procedures. Regarding male privilege, Triston believed it was inaccessible to him because he was not able to pass as male, and even post–gender transition, he would likely never have the same experience of privilege as cisgender men. In contrast, Razi thought hormones and surgery would result in his receiving a high degree of male privilege. His desire was to use this privilege to give him the credibility necessary to challenge sexist behavior he saw in cisgender and transgender men.

As I reflect on my experiences as a facilitator of gender-inclusive education, I believe more initiatives should thoughtfully explore the implications of gender fluidity and related dynamics of privilege. Related educational efforts should recognize the complex implications for all our efforts related to exploring sexism, genderism, and other systems of privilege and oppression.

CONCLUDING REFLECTIONS ON
GENDER-INCLUSIVE EDUCATION

As a student affairs administrator, I am often called to facilitate conversations or general social justice workshops that are not specific to genderism. It remains important, however, to strive to incorporate gender-inclusive practices into all my efforts, not just when facilitating sessions on sexism, genderism, or heterosexism. This would include continuing to be aware of how my own socialization of my multiple identities (including gender) influence me as a facilitator. Other examples include using gender-inclusive language, not generalizing experiences to binary gender categories when using examples (e.g., saying "men often do this" or "women often do this"), and using gender-neutral language and pronouns. Effective gender-inclusive facilitation requires that I be sensitive to how and when I ask people to share their salient identities or break into smaller groups based on social identity. Being gender inclusive also has me consider whether to do training in a building that does not house an all-gender or single bathroom.

This chapter reflects much of my journey toward gender-inclusive facilitation. It has required that I begin with an examination of self and my socialization into binary gender systems. This exploration has demanded that I explore ways I may consciously or unconsciously support the perpetuation of binary gender systems. It has included work on understanding genderism, cisgender privilege, and ways these are enacted on college campuses and in educational contexts. It requires recognizing genderism's intersections with multiple forms of systemic oppression. As we embrace a multigendered reality on college campuses, inclusive facilitation is critically important. With a framework for addressing genderism at personal, institutional, and cultural levels in all our educational efforts, we may powerfully aid in the liberation of all gender identities. It really is about freedom for all of us. Ultimately, I think that's what TJ was trying to tell me in 2002. I hope I have finally begun to hear him.

NOTE

1. In honoring my ongoing collaboration with TJ and his contribution to this chapter, I use his name with his permission.

REFERENCES

American Psychiatric Association. (2000). *Diagnostic and statistical manual of mental disorders: Text revision* (4th ed.).Washington, DC: Author.

Bilodeau, B. L. (2005). Beyond the gender binary: A case study of two transgender students at a midwestern university. *Journal of Gay and Lesbian Issues in Education, 3,* 29–46.

Bilodeau, B. L. (2009a). *Genderism: Transgender students, binary systems and higher education.* Saarbrücken, Germany: VDM-Verlag.

Bilodeau, B. L. (2009b, November). *Understanding genderism.* General session presented at the annual conference of Michigan State University Best Practices in Diversity, East Lansing, MI.

Bilodeau, B. L., & Jourian, T. (2009, March). *Genderism: Transgender students, binary systems and higher education.* Preconference and general sessions presented at the annual meting of ACPA–College Student Educators International, Washington, DC.

Bilodeau, B. L., & Jourian, T. (2010, March). *Genderism: Transgender students, binary systems and higher education.* General session presented at the annual meeting of NASPA–Student Affairs Administrators in Higher Education, Chicago, IL.

Bornstein, K. (1994). *Gender outlaw: On men, women, and the rest of us.* New York, NY: Routledge.

Califia, P. (1997). *Sex changes: The politics of transgenderism.* San Francisco, CA: Cleis Press.

Feinberg, L. (1996). *Transgender warriors: Making history from Joan of Arc to Dennis Rodman.* Boston, MA: Beacon Press.

Griffin, P. (1997). Introductory module for the single issue courses. In M. Adams, L. A. Bell, & P. Griffin (Eds.), *Teaching for diversity and social justice.* (pp. 61–79). New York, NY: Routledge.

Lev, A. I. (2004). *Transgender emergence: Therapeutic guidelines for working with gender-variant people and their families.* New York, NY: Haworth Clinical Practice Press.

Renn, K. A., & Bilodeau, B. L. (2011). Lesbian, bisexual, gay and transgender identity development theories. In B. Bank (Ed.), *Gender and higher education* (pp. 55–62). Baltimore, MD: John Hopkins University Press.

Szymanski, Z. (2008, May 29). *DSM* controversy could overshadow opportunities. *Bay Area Reporter, 38*(30), 1.

Wilchins, R. A. (2002). A continuous nonverbal communication. In J. Nestle, C. Howell, & R. Wilchins (Eds.), *Genderqueer: Voices from beyond the sexual binary* (pp. 11–17). Los Angeles, CA: Alyson.

5

Engaging Whiteness in
Higher Education

Rebecca Ropers-Huilman

Whiteness is less of an essence and more of a choice.

(Leonardo, 2009, p. 174)

EXPLORING WHITENESS is an essential part of facilitating and promoting social justice in educational settings. People are taught by their families of origin, their communities, and social media to view race and racism in ways that challenge, reinforce, question, or resist dominant understandings of race. Educators working toward social justice have the opportunity to help White people see that they have choices about how to enact and respond to whiteness. Failing to explore whiteness may perpetuate the oppression that many educators are attempting to dismantle in their facilitation.

To provide a context for the narratives that follow, I first present concepts related to whiteness and some scholarship that can guide facilitation that is meant to disrupt unexamined whiteness. I then turn to discuss some uncomfortable questions that often underlie facilitators' efforts to explicitly consider whiteness and White privilege in their classes, workshops, or staff development programs. I subsequently present three stories that illustrate the complexity and importance of examining whiteness in educational experiences. The chapter concludes with implications for practice and for the role of postsecondary education in society.

EXPLORING WHITENESS

The concept and the influence of race have received much attention in the past several decades from higher education scholars who are interested in ensuring that all faculty, staff, and students in postsecondary education settings have the opportunity to have experiences they find useful and enriching. This interest is grounded in the belief that to serve our communities, prepare a competent workforce, and behave ethically, educators need to consider how practices in postsecondary education are racialized and have implications for and within a racialized society. Research has focused on who comes to college and how they get there (Adelman, 2006; Hossler, Schmit, & Vesper, 1999; Tierney, Corwin, & Colyar, 2005), students' experiences while in college (Kuh, Kinzie, Schuh, Whitt, & Associates, 2005), how students are affected by those experiences (Harper & Quaye, 2009; Pascarella & Terenzini, 2005), and the structures of opportunity associated with college that shape groups in different ways (Bowen, Jurzweil, & Tobin, 2005; McDonough, 1997). Additional research focuses on faculty and staff and includes quantitative and qualitative assessments of their experiences and choices (Bataille & Brown, 2006; Berry & Mizelle, 2006; Neumann & Peterson, 1997; Nidiffer & Bashaw, 2001).

Research related to race in higher education focuses primarily on how racial inequality serves as a barrier to non-White participants. It addresses much less frequently the ways people who identify or are identified as White benefit from those structured inequalities, or how White privilege (McIntosh, 2004) limits the experience of everyone involved. Yet race is employed in nearly all social institutions in contemporary U.S. society in ways that privilege whiteness. For example, about 85% of all Fortune 100 board members, federal judges, and college and university presidents are White (Alliance for Board Diversity, 2008; American Council on Education, 2007; Biographical Directory of Federal Judges, 2009). Nationally, the U.S. population is estimated to be 78.1% White, 16.7% Hispanic, 13.1% African American, 5.0% Asian American, 1.2% Native American, and 2.3% two or more races (U.S. Census Bureau, 2012). Further, in many metropolitan areas, school districts are made up predominantly of children of color (Kewal Ramani, Gilbertson, Fox, & Provasnik, 2007). Yet there are racial differences in the percentages of high school graduates who attend college immediately upon high school graduation (National Center for Education Statistics, 2009). The changing demographic composition of our country creates an urgency that begs response. How can those of us in postsecondary education teach ourselves, our colleagues, and our students to think about whiteness as a culturally constructed category? How can we challenge the idea that to be White is to be normal and foreground understandings of whiteness as a system of meanings that is institutionalized in our society?

White privilege is not easy for White people to see, in large part because it is constructed as normal. It is normal to have a college president who is White; after all, 86% of them have been (American Council on Education, 2007). It is normal for White students at most postsecondary institutions to enter a class and expect to be in the majority; after all, nearly 80% of college students not attending an historically Black college or university or Hispanic-serving institution are White (Li, 2007). And it is normal that White groups will be least affected by the increasing poverty in the United States, thereby increasing their access to social institutions including higher education, since in 2009 the poverty rate for non-Hispanic White people was 9.4%, compared to 25.8% for Black people, 25.3% for people classified as Hispanic, and 12.5% for those classified under the broad category of Asian (DeNavas-Walt, Proctor, & Smith, 2010).

Despite these numbers, McKinney (2005) found that many White college students did not think of their whiteness as significant except when juxtaposed with others' races. In other words, often when people of color articulated their racially conscious understandings and experiences, White college students recognized their own racialized identities and, generally, became unsettled by that recognition. McKinney pointed out, "A primary characteristic of modern racism is the denial that it still exists. . . . This line of reasoning assumes that because Whiteness is not important to Whites, Blackness is not, or *should not* be important to Blacks, Latino-ness to Latinos, and so on" (pp. 13–14). Grillo and Wildman (1997) emphasized this point:

> Whites are privileged in that they do not have to think about race, even though they have one. White supremacy privileges Whiteness as the normative model. Being the norm allows Whites to ignore race, except when they perceive race (usually someone else's) as intruding on their lives. (pp. 48–49)

Despite this sense that current race relations are normal and not affected by ongoing racism, there is just too much historical and contemporary evidence to the contrary. Very little about it is normal.

Many scholars with various racial identifications have studied the concept of whiteness (Anzaldúa, 1990; Bonilla-Silva, 2006; Fine, 1996; Frankenberg, 1993, 2000; Harper & Hurtado, 2007; Kendall, 2007; Leonardo, 2009;

McIntosh, 1988; Roediger, 1998; Thandeka, 1999; Trepagnier, 2006), yet its manifestations in postsecondary education need further attention to denormalize it and work toward the social justice potential of our institutions. While several scholars have attempted to better understand how whiteness frames the identities and actions of faculty, staff, and students (Barajas, 2009; Helms, 1990; McKinney, 2005; Ropers-Huilman, 2008), many complexities and questions continue to trouble those of us who care about achieving that potential. Especially for those who choose to explore whiteness through their facilitation efforts in a variety of education and community settings, existing scholarship does not provide easy answers.

A FEW UNCOMFORTABLE FACILITATOR QUESTIONS

The concept of whiteness is uncomfortable for many White people to approach for multiple reasons. Nevertheless, its continued significance should move those who are interested in facilitating social justice in educational settings to address it. In this section, I highlight some of the more salient questions resulting from interactions with participants and suggest the importance of facilitators' grappling with these questions as they develop and move through their classes and workshops.

(How) Am I Responsible for Racism?

One reason some White people feel uncomfortable thinking about their whiteness relates to their sense of responsibility and guilt associated with the effects of racism (Kendall, 2007). While I believe that as educators we each have a responsibility to be cognizant of whiteness and its effects on our social systems, it is useful to think about the distinctions between individual people and larger social systems. Leonardo's (2009) scholarship is instructive here: " 'Whiteness' is a racial discourse, whereas the category 'White people' represents a socially constructed identity, usually based on skin color" (p. 169). Whiteness and its associated White privilege are racial discourses—ways of thinking, being, and acting in a given context. People who, like me, identify as White, are part of this discourse in that our identities are shaped by what we know—and don't know—about our cultural backgrounds. We are also shaped by how others perceive the color of our skin and make meanings based on their perceptions of what that skin color means in contemporary contexts.

Who I am as a White person is an individual choice made within the parameters of what whiteness means in the contexts I live in. Likewise, staff, students, and faculty make choices about their own self-representation and communities of affiliation. Simultaneously, their identities are interpreted and shaped by others' perceptions of what it means to be members of a particular racial group. Many educators who explicitly center race relations in their teaching and learning have heard from their colleagues and students, "(How) am I responsible for racism?" We are all responsible for racism because it continues to exist. Yet, no one of us created what we have inherited. While each of us has the power to individually interrupt racism, greater potential for change exists in alliances with those who have lived and thoughtfully analyzed its effects.

Am I Only My Race?

A second set of questions that are important to think about come from community members, students, staff, and scholars alike: "Am I only my race? I have other identities that are very important to me. Isn't my identity as a woman/man/trans person, gay/straight/bi person, working-class/middle-class/wealthy person, and so on just as important? If I am oppressed as a woman, for example, doesn't that matter?" Activists and scholars have taken up these questions in multiple ways.

One particular approach that is theoretically and practically useful is the theory of intersectionality. Intersectionality challenges the idea that any one social category, such as race, class, or gender, can be used in isolation as *explanatory* of a particular group's or individual's experience. Instead, it suggests that an investigation of the intersections of social identities as they take shape in particular contexts is useful in facilitating understanding and action (Cole, 2009; Collins, 2000; Crenshaw, 1991/2009; McCall, 2005; Wing, 2003). According to the theory of intersectionality, social categories are not firmly fixed, even though there is importance in acknowledging that race, sex, class, national origin, and sexual orientation are each meaningful in shaping people's experiences (Delgado & Stefancic, 2001; Parker & Lynn, 2009). As educators and students grapple with whiteness and race, then, it is important to think about how whiteness has taken different shapes in different people's lives. It is also important to respect the many potential intersecting identities we each bring to our learning and developing, since how one comes to know is shaped by our interactions with individuals and social institutions.

Some scholars have focused primarily on a particular intersection of identities to better understand that experience. For example, in postsecondary education, an emerging body of research has focused on how race and gender intersect to affect women faculty members' and administrators' experiences in academic settings (Glazer-Raymo, 2008; Montoya, 2000, 2003; Neumann & Peterson, 1997; Patton, 2009; Wallace, Ropers-Huilman, & Abel, 2004). Since women encounter many different experiences when attending postsecondary institutions, and increasingly diverse women bring their full selves to their educational experiences, intersectional approaches help to disrupt overgeneralized assertions about women's experiences or the experiences of any particular racialized group.

This enriched approach to studying experience in social institutions helps to avoid the minimization of certain groups' experience throughout postsecondary scholarship and in programming and policy making related to college students (Alemán, 2003). It also urges those of us interested in facilitating social justice in our institutions, communities, and lives to acknowledge the diverse identities we and our colleagues and students bring with us to our interactions. Yes, each of us is much more than *just* our race. However, in our current United States context, race matters. Choosing to ignore or downplay how it matters in our local and national contexts, and how it is shaped in intersection with other identities, impedes our abilities to dismantle privilege and discrimination in our social institutions.

WHY THINK ABOUT WHITENESS? LET'S FOCUS ON THE PROBLEM

One of the most uncomfortable questions for me about exploring whiteness relates to the risk of refocusing scholarly and practical resources on a group that has already enjoyed much attention. This risk is especially prevalent during this time when higher education administrators have to make difficult choices about where to allocate their energies and financial resources. Shouldn't educators focus on those who are not being well served by our systems? Why would it make sense to think about whiteness as a key part of social justice efforts?

I hope that these questions are in the hearts and minds of educators who seek to explore whiteness. I hope those who intend to facilitate social justice in any sphere constantly question how their efforts might inadvertently recenter whiteness (and understandings of White experience) as well as White people, especially if the facilitator embodies and enacts whiteness. It is fair to ask, Is it possible to disrupt inequities in higher education settings by examining whiteness? But it is also critical to ask, Is it possible to disrupt inequities in higher education settings without examining whiteness?

I believe we need to attempt to privilege non-White perspectives and experiences in our discussions in higher education. At the same time, I think that ignoring the construction of whiteness—and the ways we learn to negotiate our lives around it—ensures that whiteness will always remain in the center, never disrupted or fully understood. It will remain "normal." In order to transform our higher education environments and our society, we must include a critical examination of how we teach and learn with White students about their privilege. For those of us who identify as White, we must also rethink our own privileged positions and those of our institutions. As Leonardo (2009) pointed out, learning about the complexities of whiteness and seeking to identify and disrupt its power is a necessary part of moving toward equity in educational settings. White privilege, currently a part of whiteness, is a problem that needs to be addressed.

FACILITATING AND LEARNING FROM NARRATIVES OF WHITENESS

Stories can powerfully involve theory, practice, and the big ideas that are part of thinking about the educational experience. I am compelled by the data—the evidence—that comes from stories, especially when it comes to issues related to social justice. My definition of *theory*, which is derived from hooks (1984), is simply that theory is a belief about the way the world works. That is not the definition of *theory* I learned in a formal classroom, nor is this the definition used by many people in academic settings. In these settings, theory is assumed to be well-tested, peer-reviewed statements of relationships between social phenomena. This standard definition leaves unquestioned the system that has limited who has access to positive peer review (meaning the favorable assessment by those who have already established their academic credentials). Some people's views will be understood and will resonate in ways that others' will not. Some people have access to the creation of theory—the validation of perspective—that others do not. I believe that theory, practice, and wisdom exist in what we can learn from each other in educational relationships, if only we listen hard enough and make meaning based in community.

I want to acknowledge that my understandings of the narratives in this chapter are influenced by my own perspectives, experiences, and vantage points. I am aware that I am more likely to see and interpret incidents in particular ways given my personal history. I have taught, worked, and learned in several different contexts over the past two decades. After growing up in a nearly all-White rural community in the Midwest, I attended a regional university in the Midwest for my undergraduate work and the University of Wisconsin–Madison for my doctorate. Upon completion of my doctorate, I joined the faculty of Louisiana State University and remained there for 11 years. In 2007 I joined the faculty at the University of Minnesota and remain here. At various points in my life, I have been a resident assistant, hall director, community-based researcher, faculty member, women's center director, Women's and Gender Studies Program director, and chair of a Department of Organizational Leadership, Policy, and Development. In each of these contexts, I was in a position to teach and learn from diverse communities. I participated in many workshops and conversations focused on unlearning racism and attempted to incorporate what I learned into my daily professional and personal practice.

In my time on the faculty, I have developed and taught many different courses focusing primarily on college teaching, college students, and race and gender in higher education. The majority of students with whom I have taught and learned about social justice have been graduate students in higher education leadership programs at Louisiana State University and the University of Minnesota. My teaching is much more oriented toward facilitation of relationships and understandings, rather than a banking model of my "giving" knowledge to student participants. Students have helped me and others in the class on our journeys toward racial understanding through sharing their stories. Some have taught me by sharing their active engagement with and analysis of race and racism throughout their lives, including in their professional positions and personal lives. These have been primarily graduate students of color and a few White students (undergraduate and graduate) who viewed themselves as racial justice allies.

The majority of White graduate students I have worked with in various capacities come to discussions about whiteness and social justice from dramatically different places. I have learned from them how ignorance and a lack of racial understanding are structured into the lives of White people in professional and personal settings. Through our ignorance, those of us who are White can remain comfortably color blind within our "cocoon of Whiteness" (Holland, 2010, p. 119). White students I have worked closely with in various settings have told me the following:

- I have never thought of these topics before.
- I have never talked with anyone about race before.
- I didn't know that my parents made decisions about our family related to race—until I asked them as a result of our class.
- While I am committed to equity, gender (or some other identity) trumps race for me because it played such a salient and hurtful role for me as I was growing up.
- Can't we all just be treated the same?
- Our class is creating problems in my relationship with my family or friends.

In particularly complex moments of class conversations, some White students have gotten up to shut the classroom door so that passers-by would not hear what they were saying. The idea of others outside our class hearing the questions they were compelled to ask or hearing their tentative attempts at making sense of racism and whiteness was too uncomfortable, too risky. In my experience, discussions about race and, specifically, whiteness are threatening and uncomfortable for many White students.

These discussions can be uncomfortable for students of color as well. I have yet to have non-White students, students of color, minoritized students, tell me that they have not thought about race before coming to a class where we focus on it. I have, however, had students of color tell me they rarely feel able to bring themselves and their experiences into a classroom when they are participating in predominantly White institutions. Some students of color have expressed their surprise at the lack of attention many White students have paid to race, while others seem to accept it as the norm.

Often, as part of my classroom teaching, I ask people to think of salient moments related to race in their lives. This approach is an example of facilitation in that I do not have the answer about their lives. Nor do I understand how they, their families, and their communities have experienced race. While I can introduce readings and concepts that might help them clarify their thinking and understand the larger context of race and racism, I simply do not have the knowledge to pass on to them about their own lived experience. We work together to reflect and share stories with each other, and these stories taken together help shape our collective knowledge.

As facilitators interested in fostering understanding of race and whiteness, we need to be cognizant that conversations for some of our participants will be extremely difficult. We should not assume that all our participants will have the language or comfort levels to discuss race, especially as it plays out in their own lives. It is also important to recognize that when we ask students to think about race in their professional and personal lives, we are asking some people to do what they have always done, which is comfortable, and we are asking others to engage in behavior that has been or will be sanctioned. This does not mean we should not foster these types of conversations and stories. On the contrary, I think approaching concepts related to social justice only at the intellectual level will leave educational institutions and society far from our potential. Yet facilitators need to be aware of our responsibility to help people find safe, if uncomfortable, ways to develop understandings about race and whiteness from wherever participants are in their own racial journeys.

One example of my facilitation of this reflection and collective learning is when I ask students in my classes to construct an autobiography of identity. As part of this assignment, I ask that students interview at least one person in their lives who might have insight into how race and other identities might have shaped or influenced them in some way. As I describe this assignment at the beginning of class, it is often met by students with great trepidation. I try to minimize students' emphasis on giving me, as the teacher, what I want by providing full credit if the basic terms of the assignment are met. I also provide sample questions but do not mandate the use of those questions. I emphasize that this is not meant to be a voyeuristic opportunity for me but rather a way for students to think about race in their own lives so that they can better understand how it may have played a part in the lives of those with whom they work and live. I ask that they write only about issues or events they feel comfortable sharing with me and not feel compelled to include issues they do not want to disclose. In a class session near the end of the term, I ask them to share with others in the class either a section of their paper or a reflection on how they experienced doing this assignment and what they learned from those experiences. It is clear to me that crafting one's own story about race is hard and alternatively evokes strong emotion, curiosity, and resistance among students. By the end of the semester, this is also the assignment most students identify as their most meaningful.

Stories about whiteness are far from uniform. To presume that all White people are the same or have the same stories is as false as to assume that all people of color are the same. Instead, we all choose from among the stories—or discourses—we perceive as available to us in constructing meaning from our lives (Gee, 2005; Ropers-Huilman, Winters, & Enke, 2009). The following stories are related to White students' handling of the autobiography of identity assignment previously described. I did not choose them because they are typical or representative in any way. Instead, they illustrate some of the challenges that I and students have experienced as I try to encourage White people to reflect on their racial identity in the context of a college class that focuses on understanding others' identities and race in society generally. I hope the following stories will help facilitators in diverse settings work with the complexities that an examination of whiteness brings forth. For those of us working in education settings, I believe our missions require our careful attention to this topic.

STORY 1: (HOW) CAN WE TALK ABOUT RACE?

When describing the autobiography of identity assignment at the beginning of any class, I inevitably see discomfort among White students. During one semester, though, one student, "Tom," appeared to be more uncomfortable than most. While he didn't approach me immediately, he continued to ask questions about the assignment throughout the first several weeks of the term. When I informally asked the class midway through the semester how that assignment was going, it became clear that Tom was still wrestling with how to begin. As the class period approached when students were to present some aspect of their autobiographies, Tom came to see me.

With his voice shaking, Tom told me he was having trouble determining whom to interview. He didn't feel as though he could interview his parents. Through our conversation, it became clear that race in general, and whiteness in particular, were taboo subjects in his household and there was simply not a way he could open a dialogue about them with his family. I explored with him other ways he could do the assignment, perhaps seeking a childhood or even college friend. I also reminded him that he needed to be responsible for his learning, determining how much discomfort he would find productive at that place on his journey. I encouraged him to take risks, but given that I do not know the dynamics of his family, I was not in a position to mandate a conversation that could harm key relationships. In the end, he interviewed a school friend and minimally met the terms of the assignment. His involvement with the assignment, though, went well beyond what he turned in, as he had wrestled with the power of race perhaps more than anyone else in the class that term. Tom learned from others' stories in the class as students shared sections of their autobiographies with the group. The group also allowed him time to practice discussions related to race, whiteness, and social justice in the relatively safe space of our class-room. I hope this helped him expand the repertoire he might draw on to participate in discussions beyond the classroom, perhaps even eventually with his family.

STORY 2: STRUGGLING TO SEE THE INTERSECTION

Another student's story illustrates the difficulties of understanding the lived intersections of our identities and how they simultaneously shape our lives and the lives of those with whom we work and build community. After hearing about the autobiography of identity assignment, "Ann" questioned if all students had to write about race in their papers. She asked if she could focus on how gender played a part in her life instead, since her perception was that gender was a much more significant factor than race in her life. I explained that while other identities could definitely be explored, I wanted everyone to include a consideration of race in their papers. In making this requirement, I was trying to ensure that White students examined their asso-ciations with whiteness and White privilege, even as they may have experi-enced oppression in other ways.

Throughout the semester, it became clear that Ann was resisting examin-ing how whiteness played a part in her life. She brought in examples to illustrate how significantly gender shaped educational and other social expe-riences, and although she acknowledged race as a significant identity for students, faculty, and staff of color, resisted its meaning in her early life. Eventually, she shared her story that her mother's gender and, relatedly, class severely limited the opportunities that Ann had when she was growing up. She said she was tired of people foregrounding race and forgetting that other people's lives are hard for other reasons.

In this class, I agreed with her that gender and class were absolutely salient identities that shape people's lives. I had conversations with her in and out of class about how all our identities matter and are intertwined to shape the entirety of our experiences. Ann was open to this concept, though it was clear it was difficult for her to reinstate race into her image of herself when she had already thoughtfully constructed a story of her life that omitted her whiteness. Our class readings helped all of us think through this as we read examples from other White people about how whiteness shaped their lived experiences. Eventually, Ann turned in a paper that illustrated her interweaving of race, gender, and class into her experience and challenged other class participants to think hard about how each of our identities informs and shapes the others.

"There is no hierarchy of oppression," Audre Lorde (1983, p. 9) wrote. Yet I have found in facilitating classes and discussions related to social justice that participants' divergent versions of the hierarchy enter into the conversation and, if not addressed, can derail efforts to forge a respectful and productive discussion. I do not think an ordering of oppressions is a useful way to spend our facilitation time. Instead, focusing on the ways different intersections of identities take shape and have power in specific contexts holds the promise for social justice–oriented change. We are all raced and gendered in complicated ways that are simultaneously of our own creation and fashioned for us by others' interpretations of who we are. As facilitators, we can help participants look for and find those intersections in their own lives and the lives of others they work and live with.

STORY 3: UNCOVERING WHITENESS
IN UNUSUAL PLACES

"Sam" was a White student whose commitments to equality were clear. Everyone should be treated the same. If there was discrimination, it should be alleviated. If there was racism, it should be eliminated. In his mind, no individual or group should be treated differently than anyone else. Race and racism did not need to be attended to except when they became problematic in some way. Sam wanted to move quickly to a color-blind society. Race had not affected his life in any significant way, in his mind, and so should not be a significant part of others' lives.

After the assignment was given and explained at the beginning of the term, I did not hear much from Sam. He seemed to be embracing the assignment and did not ask many questions about it. He had set up discussions with his parents over a break and seemed to be looking forward to learning more about his life and their lives as they were informed by race. It is possible that he was happy to use this assignment as a catalyst for a good discussion with his parents. It is also possible that he did not expect to find much that was new.

The process Sam used to construct his autobiography was transforming. I remember his astonishment when he learned that his parents had made the decision to move to another community when he was a small child explicitly because his former community was attracting too many families of color. In an expression of their caring for him, they moved him to an environment that was less diverse. He, of course, had known about the move but not the reasons for it. He was surprised by what he learned and spent a large part of the semester wondering how that move affected his life and how he might be different as an adult had his parents thought about race and diversity differently when he was young. When Sam shared what he had learned with the class, it was transformative for the rest of us as well. It underscored the importance of whiteness and race in individual and collective histories, as well as the invisibility of decisions that were made based on race.

Sam's story is poignant and not atypical among White students who have participated in my classes. More often than not, if they ask the questions, White students find that race played an important part in the decisions that parents, teachers, and others made about their educational opportunities, home communities, and friends. As Tom's story illustrates, in some families, race is not discussed. It is just too hard. Yet its lack of explicit attention does not mean it is not noticed or that it does not sharply influence major decisions such as where to attend school, where to live, and with whom to associate. It is important that facilitators acknowledge that ignorance is structured and enforced in the lives of many White people. Part of learning about and facilitating social justice is exploring what has been ignored. In this case, helping White participants think about the ways whiteness has shaped their lives opens them to thinking about how whiteness shapes others' lives (including White people and people of color) and the social systems in which all of us come together.

INTERROGATING WHITENESS: FACILITATING SOCIAL JUSTICE AS EVERYDAY WORK

Each of the preceding stories describes experiences in postsecondary education settings that could be happening today on campuses across the country.

Students, staff, and faculty are struggling to have meaningful conversations about race and need to carefully think about how to talk about race to include whiteness. Thinking about the intersections of identities among diverse groups of individuals as they take shape in various contexts will help them do that. Purposefully finding ways to acknowledge and dismantle structured ignorance about whiteness is critical as well.

Since race is such a salient part of lived experience in this country, I believe it is the responsibility of those of us in educational institutions to ensure that we and our students have an opportunity to think carefully and in a supportive space about how race influences us and those around us. The everyday work of antiracism and of challenging whiteness is critically important as we transform our institutions and society. Those of us who are involved in facilitation toward social justice need to look inward at ourselves and at our communities to ask the hard questions related to how White privilege limits our social experiences and impedes the relationships that could strengthen every aspect of our institutions. As in the autobiographies of identity in my classes, we need to take an active role in examining the realities of race in our lives so that we can be open to hearing about those realities for others.

Our students need to look inward too to investigate what their own stories might teach them and others about raced lives. As educators who engage in training, supervising, advising, research, teaching, and outreach, we need to help students negotiate what is, while actively envisioning what could be. Part of this includes helping them construct stories of their lives, even as we continue to construct our own.

IMPLICATIONS

A focus on whiteness and White privilege in postsecondary education has many implications for those of us interested in facilitating social justice in our roles as student affairs professionals, faculty members, administrators, student leaders, or other participants on our diverse campuses. First, when higher education facilitators, scholars, and student affairs professionals talk about racial diversity, we so often focus on people of color, leaving whiteness as a normal, unproblematic category of identity. Whiteness, then, is only brought to many White people's minds when they are asked to check a box on official forms or when some have the opportunity to be in a multicultural community and realize they are in the minority. As McKinney (2005) reminded us, whiteness is a *prompted identity*. This means that many White students and colleagues likely will only think of themselves as White when they are juxtaposed with those who are non-White. If we are to see White privilege, we also need to acknowledge that whiteness is not "just normal."

One way to denormalize whiteness is to pay attention to our language. When educators talk about "diverse students," my experience has been they are often referring to all students who are not White. This is problematic for several reasons. White students are likely just as diverse as other groups. If they are seen as standard issue, and not diverse, then they are not prompted to examine their own cultures and the power that has been vested in their racial identification. If they (and we) do not see whiteness as something that is learned and has (contested) meaning, they cannot participate in challenging those meanings and perhaps forging new intersectional identities for themselves.

A second implication of the focus on whiteness that I am advocating relates to the need for multiracial alliances that lead change in social institutions. In the classes where I ask students to complete and then share an aspect of their autobiographies of identities, it is clear that they learn from each other. Their knowledge about race in society is expanded and enriched by hearing others' stories, especially when those stories are different from their own. Their abilities to talk about and take action about race in their lives are expanded by learning from others. As they move forward in thinking about their own work toward social justice, they would benefit from continuing conversations with people with similar and with different identities and experiences. Bringing in and valuing knowledge from multiple peoples and perspectives can facilitate social justice through individual students' and organizations' learning and behavior. In my mind, facilitators seeking to further social justice would benefit from developing and supporting participants' abilities to engage in multiracial alliances.

Telling and listening to stories related to racial privilege is hard. Yet hearing each others' experiences and interpretations helps those of us who see our role as facilitators of social justice better understand the complexities of race. Furthermore, it helps us learn about concepts we have been taught to ignore, including White privilege. We can learn with each other in diverse communities about how to fulfill our potential as members of institutions with great social power and social responsibility.

REFERENCES

Adelman, C. (2006). *The toolbox revisited: Paths to degree completion from high school through college*. Washington, DC: U.S. Department of Education.

Alemán, A. M. (2003). Gender, race, and millennial curiosity. In B. Ropers-Huilman (Ed.), *Gendered futures in higher education: Critical perspectives for change* (pp. 179–198). Albany, NY: SUNY Press.

Alliance for Board Diversity. (2008). *Women and minorities on Fortune 100 boards.* Retrieved from http://www.elcinfo.com/reports.php

American Council on Education. (2007). *The American college president.* Washington, DC: Author.

Anzaldúa, G. (1990). La conciencia de la Mestiza: Towards a new consciousness. In G. Anzaldúa (Ed.), *Making face, making soul: Haciendo caras* (pp. 377–389). San Francisco, CA: Aunt Lute Books.

Barajas, H. (2009, November). *From disequilibrium to multicultural literacy: Diverse students and service-learning.* Paper presented at the annual conference of the Association for the Study of Higher Education, Vancouver, BC.

Bataille, G. M., & Brown, B. E. (2006). *Faculty career paths: Multiple routes to academic success and satisfaction.* Westport, CT: Praeger.

Berry, T. R., & Mizelle, N. D. (2006). *From oppression to grace: Women of color and their dilemmas within the academy.* Sterling, VA: Stylus.

Biographical Directory of Federal Judges. (2009). Retrieved from Federal Judicial Center website: http://www.fjc.gov/public/home.nsf/hisj

Bonilla-Silva, E. (2006). *Racism without racists: Color-blind racism and the persistence of racial inequality in the United States.* Lanham, MD: Rowman & Littlefield.

Bowen, W. G., Kurzweil, M. A., & Tobin, E. M. (2005). *Equity and excellence in American higher education.* Charlottesville: University of Virginia Press.

Cole, E. R. (2009). Intersectionality and research in psychology. *American Psychologist, 64*, 170–180.

Collins, P. H. (2000). Toward a new vision: Race, class, and gender as categories of analysis and connection. In M. Adams, W. J. Blumenfeld, R. Castaneda, H. W. Hackman, M. L. Peters, & X. Zúñiga (Eds.), *Readings for diversity in social justice: An anthology on racism, anti-Semitism, sexism, heterosexism, ableism, and classism* (pp. 457–462). New York, NY: Routledge.

Crenshaw, K. (2009). Mapping the margins: Intersectionality, identity politics, and violence against women of color. In E. Taylor, D. Gillborn, & G. Ladson-Billings (Eds.), *Foundations of critical race theory in education* (pp. 213–246). New York, NY: Routledge. (Reprinted from *Stanford Law Review, 43*[6], pp. 1241–1299, July 1991, Stanford, CA: Stanford University.)

Delgado, R., & Stefancic, J. (2001). *Critical race theory: An introduction.* New York, NY: New York University Press.

DeNavas-Walt, C., Proctor, B. D., & Smith, J. C. (2010). *Current population reports: Consumer income, P60–238. Income, poverty, and health insurance coverage in the United States: 2009*. Washington, DC: U.S. Government Printing Office. Retrieved from http://www.census.gov/prod/2010pubs/p60-238.pdf

Fine, M. (1996). *Off White: Readings on race, power, and society*. New York, NY: Routledge.

Frankenberg, R. (1993). *White women, race matters: The social construction of whiteness*. Minneapolis: University of Minnesota Press.

Frankenberg, R. (2000). White women, race matters: The social construction of whiteness. In L. Back & J. Solomos (Eds.), *Theories of race and racism* (pp. 447–461). London, UK: Routledge.

Gee, J. P. (2005). *An introduction to discourse analysis: Theory and method* (2nd ed.). New York, NY: Routledge.

Glazer-Raymo, J. (2008). *Unfinished agendas: New and continuing gender challenges in higher education*. Baltimore, MD: Johns Hopkins University Press.

Grillo, T., & Wildman, S. (1997). Obscuring the importance of race: The implication of making comparisons between racism and sexism (or other isms). In A. K. Wing (Ed.), *Critical race feminism* (pp. 44–56). New York, NY: New York University Press.

Harper, S. R., & Hurtado, S. (2007). Nine themes in campus racial climates and implications for institutional transformation. *New Directions for Student Services, 2007*(120), 7–24.

Harper, S. R., & Quaye, S. J. (2009). *Student engagement in higher education: Theoretical perspectives and practical approaches for diverse populations*. New York, NY: Routledge.

Helms, J. E. (1990). *Black and White racial identity: Theory, research, and practice*. New York, NY: Greenwood.

Holland, A. (2010). *The place of race in cultural nursing education: The experience of White BSN nursing faculty* (Unpublished doctoral dissertation). University of Minnesota, Minneapolis. Retrieved from http://conservancy.umn.edu/bitstream/101771/1/Holland_umn_0130E_11739.pdf

hooks, b. (1984). *Feminist theory from margin to center*. Boston, MA: South End.

Hossler, D., Schmit, J., & Vesper, N. (1999). *Going to college: How social, economic and educational factors influence the decisions students make*. Baltimore, MD: Johns Hopkins University Press.

Kendall, F. E. (2007). *Understanding White privilege: Creating pathways to authentic relationships across race*. New York, NY: Routledge.

Kewal Ramani, A., Gilbertson, L., Fox, M., & Provasnik, S. (2007). *Status and trends in the education of racial and ethnic minorities* (NCES 2007–039). Washington, DC: Institute of Education Sciences, U.S. Department of Education.

Retrieved from National Center for Education Statistics website: http://nces.ed
.gov/pubs2007/2007039.pdf

Kuh, G. D., Kinzie, J., Schuh, J. H., Whitt, E. J., & Associates (2005). *Student success in college: Creating conditions that matter*. San Francisco, CA: Jossey-Bass.

Leonardo, Z. (2009). *Race, whiteness, and education*. New York, NY: Routledge.

Li, X. (2007). *Characteristics of minority-serving institutions and minority undergraduates enrolled in these institutions* (NCES 2008–156). Washington, DC: Institute of Education Sciences, U.S. Department of Education. Retrieved from National Center for Education Statistics website: http://nces.ed.gov/pubs2008/2008 156.pdf

Lorde, A. (1983). There is no hierarchy of oppressions. *Bulletin: Homophobia and Education, 14*(3/4), 9.

McCall, L. (2005). The complexity of intersectionality. *Signs: Journal of Women in Culture and Society, 30*(3), 1771–1800.

McDonough, P. M. (1997). *Choosing colleges: How social class and schools structure opportunity*. Albany, NY: SUNY Press.

McIntosh, P. (1988). *White privilege and male privilege: A personal account of coming to see correspondences through work in women's studies* (working paper No. 189 of the Wellesley College Center for Research on Women). Weston, MA: Wellesley College.

McKinney, K. (2005). *Being White: Stories of race and racism*. New York, NY: Routledge.

Montoya, M. E. (2000). Silence and silencing: Their centripetal and centrifugal forces in legal communication, pedagogy and discourse. *University of Michigan Journal of Law Reform, 33*(3), 263–327.

Montoya, M. E. (2003). Mascaras, trenza, y grenas: Un/masking the self while un/braiding Latina stories and legal discourse. In A. K. Wing (Ed.), *Critical race feminism* (pp. 70–77). New York, NY: New York University Press.

National Center for Education Statistics. (2009). *Fast facts: Immediate transition to college*. Retrieved December 15, 2012 from http://nces.ed.gov/fastfacts/display .asp?id=51

Neumann, A., & Peterson, P. (1997). *Learning from our lives: Women, research, and autobiography in education*. New York, NY: Teachers College Press.

Nidiffer, J., & Bashaw, C. T. (2001). *Women administrators in higher education: Historical and contemporary perspectives*. Albany, NY: SUNY Press.

Parker, L., & Lynn, M. (2009). What's race got to do with it? Critical race theory's conflicts with and connections to qualitative research methodology and epistemology. In E. Taylor, D. Gillborn, & G. Ladson-Billings (Eds.), *Foundations of critical race theory in education* (pp. 148–162). New York, NY: Routledge.

Pascarella, E. T., & Terenzini, P. T. (2005). *How college affects students: A third decade of research* (Vol. 2). San Francisco, CA: Jossey-Bass.

Patton, L. (2009). My sister's keeper: A qualitative examination of mentoring experiences among African American women in graduate and professional schools. *Journal of Higher Education, 80*(5), 510–537.

Roediger, D. R. (1998). *Black on White: Black writers on what it means to be White.* New York, NY: Schocken Books.

Ropers-Huilman, B. (2008). Women faculty and the dance of identities: Constructing self and privilege within community. In J. Glazer-Raymo (Ed.), *Unfinished business: Women, gender, and the new challenges of higher education* (pp. 35–51). Baltimore, MD: Johns Hopkins University Press.

Ropers-Huilman, R., Winters, K. T., & Enke, K. A. E. (2009, November). *The invisibility of whiteness: White college women (dis)engaging race.* Presentation at the annual conference of National Women's Studies Association, Atlanta, GA.

Thandeka. (1999). *Learning to be White: Money, race, and God in America.* New York, NY: Continuum.

Tierney, W. G., Corwin, Z. B., & Colyar, J. E. (2005). *Preparing for college: Nine elements of effective outreach.* Albany, NY: SUNY Press.

Trepagnier, B. (2006). *Silent racism: How well-meaning White people perpetuate the racial divide.* Boulder, CO: Paradigm.

U.S. Census Bureau. (2012). *USA Quickfacts.* Retrieved from http://quickfacts.census.gov/qfd/states/00000.html

Wallace, D. D., Ropers-Huilman, B., & Abel, R. (2004). Working in the margins: A study of university professionals serving marginalized student populations. *NASPA Journal, 41*(4), 569–587.

Wing, A. K. (2003). *Critical race feminism: A reader* (2nd ed.). New York, NY: New York University Press.

6

Developing and Sustaining Effective Cofacilitation Across Identities

Tanya Williams and Elaine Brigham

S OCIAL JUSTICE FACILITATORS' work centers around translating the
sometimes dense topics of oppression, power, and privilege for participants as they explore their own identities and the impact of oppression
on themselves and other members of society. As this book's contributors
discuss in previous chapters, this translation requires facilitators to reflect
upon their own social identities and exhibit competencies that promote dialogue and socially just practice. When cofacilitation occurs, however, much
more is required. Even with the most thoughtful design and skilled facilitators, the quality of the cofacilitation relationship can be foundational to
participants' learning. As many social justice education experiences are cofacilitated, cofacilitation, then, is an important competency that requires
attention from social justice educators.

At the heart of social justice cofacilitation is the opportunity to model an
authentic, intergroup relationship—that is, a relationship that successfully
honors each facilitator's multiple social identities and navigates the challenges across differences. A strong relationship between cofacilitators rests on
each facilitator's willingness to take risks, to give and receive honest feedback, and to commit to learning together. Through witnessing cofacilitators'
authentic relationships with one another, participants are provided a vision
of what is possible. Seeing and experiencing what is possible, especially across
cultural differences, gives students permission and encouragement to reach
out to each other and build their own relationships and alliances.

COFACILITATION IN A SOCIAL
JUSTICE CONTEXT

What follows is a dialogue between us, the authors, regarding our experience as social justice cofacilitators. In this dialogue we discuss the nature, significance, and skills needed for effective cofacilitation that *facilitates* social justice work (particularly as it relates to understanding our identities) and is *socially just* facilitation.

In a germinal article on cofacilitation, Pfeiffer and Jones (1975) stated, "We believe that co-facilitating a group is superior to working alone" (p. 1). As social justice facilitators and cofacilitators, we support their assertion and hope this chapter provides insight into the effectiveness and intricacies of a social justice cofacilitation experience and relationship. We believe there is power in using one's self as instrument and are using our relationship as long-time social justice cofacilitators to communicate the power of cofacilitation in social justice education (SJE). In this chapter we offer an exploration into the intentionality of our identity development processes, relationship building, and cofacilitation practice to shed light on the strength and possibilities of effective cofacilitation. Though we have grown to become close friends and colleagues, close friendship is not a requirement for effective cofacilitation. Commitment, self-awareness, content knowledge, skill development, and open communication are what is needed.

We began our cofacilitation relationship 10 years ago when we entered the SJE program at the University of Massachusetts Amherst, Tanya as a doctoral student and Elaine as a master's student. Prior to entering the SJE program, Tanya worked in student affairs in higher education and Elaine worked as a teacher in K–12 education. We share a similar urban/metropolitan, working-class upbringing and we both identify as queer women. While we share some core social identities, not all our identities are the same. In our shared multiple, social identities we acknowledge the many ways our identities and experiences differ based on relative power and privilege and advantage and disadvantage within societal systems of oppression. For example, as a White woman, Elaine experiences race privilege and focuses on how her White privilege and advantage manifests for her as a working-class, queer woman. As an African American woman, Tanya experiences race oppression and focuses on how oppression and internalized oppression manifest for her and ways her more privileged identities, such as religion and ability, intersect. Social justice–focused cofacilitation exists within a system of oppression, power, and privilege. It is only effective when it acknowledges this power, privilege, oppression and our varied social locations and positions (Kirk & Okazawa-Rey, 2004) and works with them overtly with or in the group and the cofacilation team.

We recognize that we bring all our social identities with us to our cofacilitation relationship in open, transparent ways and to our work with participants. Since 2002 we have worked together through the intergroup dialogue model. As mentioned in this book's preface and Chapter 1, *intergroup dialogue* is

> a distinct approach to dialogue across differences in higher education. It can be broadly defined as a face-to-face facilitated learning experience that brings together students from different social identity groups over a sustained period of time to understand their commonalities and differences, examine the nature and impact of societal inequalities, and explore ways of working together toward greater equality and justice. (Zúñiga, Nagda, Chesler, & Cytron-Walker, 2007, p. 2)

We were trained in the theory and practice of intergroup dialogue through graduate course work and practicum experiences and subsequently served as facilitative consultants to fellow graduate student intergroup dialogue facilitators, meeting weekly to support their development as cofacilitators across different social identities, observing their dialogues, and providing feedback on their cofacilitation.

For the past nine years we have cofacilitated multiple semester-long dialogues on race, ethnicity, and socioeconomic class, codeveloped and facilitated a semester-long intergroup dialogue for staff and administrators, and codirected a peer-facilitated intergroup dialogue program at Mount Holyoke College. In this capacity, we work together to train and support facilitators in their development across varying social identities. We continue to develop as a cofacilitation team and are deeply inspired and grateful to continue to engage in intergroup dialogue and other SJE work together. We also draw on numerous experiences cofacilitating shorter-term or one-time dialogues and workshops.

As a team who has facilitated together for nine years in different variations, we have tried our best to make our conversation as transparent and vulnerable as possible, and at times the dialogue will feel like you, the reader, have entered a conversation already in progress—because you essentially have. We are in constant dialogue in our relationship as social justice cofacilitators, working to understand the ways our multiple and intersecting identities respond and react to each other, to the participants in the room, and to the experience we are cofacilitating. We provide themed questions to guide you through the conversation. These questions offer insight to some of the questions that have shaped our work together. In this chapter we attempt to go beyond the how-to for cofacilitation but instead share the inner workings of our relationship as two social justice cofacilitators who are attempting to model social justice in their cofacilitation.

THE DIALOGUE

What Is the Process of Developing Your Social Identities as a Facilitator?

Elaine: It's been a lengthy and complex process that continues today. And much of it has been in relationship with you, Tanya, so that's noteworthy. I've cofacilitated with you more than I have with anyone else, and that's significant. A lot of our cofacilitation has been about race and thinking about how to facilitate across difference in terms of our different racial identities. A lot of my academic and personal work has been focused on race and what I have needed to do to work through my own internalized dominance. I've had to notice what that means, how it manifests itself, when it comes up, how it comes up—to notice the places where in the past I didn't have as much confidence or held back, not wanting to mess up or not knowing what to do or doing the wrong thing as a White person.

And that has changed drastically. Part of my internalized dominance showed up when I thought about race and racism. A dominant way of looking at it is to focus on people of color and not look at the privilege White people have. It is sometimes easier to avoid looking at the fact that there's advantage on the other side of the disadvantage. So a lot of my work has been embodying myself more as a White facilitator doing this work, remembering that I'm not an assistant to the person of color. I'm not trying to figure out the right thing to do for the people of color. I'm an equal cofacilitator who needs to act accordingly, who needs to do whatever I need to do to show up, meaning be fully present, in the room and with the group.

So during earlier moments of our facilitation, I deferred to you in moments when it may not have been helpful or necessary, thinking "Am I gonna do this right?" and looked to you. But developing in my identity, I realized I'm just as capable to step in, and differently capable—because we come from different identities—to step in to say something.

Tanya: I laugh somewhat because, regarding race, if you were looking at me for confirmation of anything nine years ago . . . I was looking at you and thinking, "You have all the information," because I was really deeply in my internalized racism around intelligence or the lack of intelligence of people of color and believing that White people had more answers. And so it's fascinating to me that you were looking at me, as your cofacilitator and a Black woman, worried specifically about whether you were being OK as a White person. And so I think that's one of those really important things to name—the ways that internalized racism or internalized oppression about race, dominant and subordinate identities—if they don't get examined when in a cofacilitation pair, who knows what's happening?

Elaine: Exactly.

Tanya: It makes me laugh. I never knew that you were looking at me for any kind of confirmation.

Elaine: Well, for me, it wasn't an either/or in any way. There were plenty of times when I didn't look at you for that, and there were times that I did. There were plenty of times when I knew the thing to say, or *a* thing to say, and I went with my gut and said it because I was really passionate on issues of race and had a good grounding in the topic. So it is in no way an all or nothing. For me, it was more subtle and nuanced. It's more something about doing all the necessary work—it's work and awareness on internalized dominance in terms of whiteness and also work on internalized oppression on sexism and ableism, specifically for me, and the ways that those intersections manifest and don't work very well together.

So I had to do a lot of work on those things, internalized classism included, all simultaneously. But doing that work enabled me to not be so afraid of saying or doing the "wrong" thing or messing up so that I would be less open to feedback. I think, ironically, we end up having more confidence because we're less interested in having all the answers and are OK with messing up. So I've seen that in myself a lot—having more willingness and ability to be open to the places I need to keep working on, specifically in regard to my subordinate and dominant identities.

All our continued conversations about all this have been really significant and influential, from ways that our multiple identities are intersecting to really diving in and focusing on race to then talking about how class or ability or gender intersect, giving each other feedback, doing lots of debriefing, and reflecting all the time before we facilitate and after we facilitate. When I think about the time we've put into reflecting individually and reflecting in each other's company, as a collaborative process, I know it has drastically affected my work as a facilitator, our relationship as cofacilitators, and my ability to cofacilitate.

Tanya: And doing that reflecting work made it not just about the mechanics of cofacilitation because we knew how to take people through activities. Doing the reflection on identity—having conversations and thinking together about how the dynamics of race work, the dynamics of sexual orientation and class and all of those identities, inside our cofacilitation and in the larger world—made us a stronger team and gave us an understanding of how race may have an impact on even the way that we're seen.

When I think about that question, "What is the process of developing your social identities as a facilitator?" much of my developing awareness has come through cofacilitation. You're my most consistent cofacilitator, but even with the other facilitations I've done with other organizations it is rare that I get to cofacilitate with a person of color. When I think about my developing awareness of my identities, I realize I had my original facilitation experiences and learned my ideas about facilitation from my mentor, a White woman. So all of that is in my mind when I think about developing awareness of identities.

In regard to race specifically, I didn't see myself as a Black facilitator until I started teaching a social justice course in graduate school, and the predominantly White class responded to me in a condescending manner. And so now when I facilitate with you, I realize I'm the person of color in this team. And if we're doing facilitation about race and racism, and particularly in an intergroup dialogue, because of my own development of my racial identity and understanding of my race, I can show up differently or I do show up differently or I can tell that I now show up differently. And that's not only in our cofacilitation, but I think it's with all people I get to facilitate with.

I think I would say that I shrank from the challenge of being questioned by White students or participants in general a lot before and was not fully myself in my facilitation because I was less developed in my Black identity. I understand now that as I developed in my racial identity, my sexual orientation identity—whatever identity I worked on—the development showed up differently as a result of the work I had done. It helps to have a cofacilitator who understands how identity development works.

Elaine: Yes. It makes all the difference in the world. As you were speaking, I was thinking one of the countless, literally countless, things I'm grateful for and appreciative of in our cofacilitation relationship is that race is always explicit. Right away, we named it, we talked about it, and we never acted like any of our identities were neutral. Not that I always handled things perfectly or knew how to do things best—certainly I've learned a ton. We were always in the conversation. There was never a depoliticized, neutralized, nonracialized cofacilitation relationship ever with us.

Tanya: That's true.

Elaine: So right from the beginning it was, "So I'm White, you're Black, I'm Black, you're White, here we are cofacilitating about race." And right away, there was the awareness that we were modeling that relationship for the students and any other facilitators we trained. I appreciate our integrity in taking that seriously and having fun with it too—fun in a this-is-wonderful-work way. We have held and continue to hold ourselves up to a bar in that we don't ask participants to do what we don't do ourselves. So when we train other facilitators and say, "You need to team build and need to give each other feedback when something comes up" we mean it, because we're doing it.

Tanya: Right.

Elaine: And I see how our cofacilitation relationship very directly has an impact on my many other cofacilitation experiences. I think we have that in common, that you're also my most consistent cofacilitator. I also have had many other cofacilitation relationships, and it's interesting too because I'm thinking often mine are with people of color. You get paired with White people, often I get paired with people of color. We've both done a lot of work on race. And for slightly different reasons, I think that dynamic happens often.

When you bring that consciousness on identity to a cofacilitation relationship, it either doesn't work or it works, and your relationship is about to get to a whole new level. And I think about our cofacilitation relationship and how much I learned from experience, that we did that right away; we brought that consciousness about identity to our cofacilitation relationship. We were also willing to work on the issues and dynamics that came up within our cofacilitation relationship in addition to what came up with participants. That work is not always easy; it is messy and complex and nuanced, and we continue to hang in there with each other. Being committed to do our work is critical to staying in the process with each other. If I am not willing to do the necessary self-reflection as a White person and to work on and change my behavior accordingly, that does not serve you or me or our cofacilitation, and it certainly doesn't serve our participants. And our cofacilitation has deepened for me over the years about race and also other social identities. We've continued to each individually do our work on all our other identities and be in a relationship and communicate about that.

Tanya: I'm sitting here thinking you're right, yeah. And I think we started our facilitation relationship by facilitating a race intergroup dialogue, and so our acknowledging our racial identities and development had to happen.

How Do You Work With One Another's Triggers About Social Identities?

Tanya: I think back to those first moments of doing that first intergroup dialogue; I think I was still deepening my understanding about race myself.

Elaine: Me too.

Tanya: I was really at the beginning stages of understanding the dynamics of race and just beginning to see how the power dynamics had been working in my life the whole time. Being transparent about my learning with you as my White cofacilitator felt new. It was weird. I remember thinking, "We're gonna talk about that?" And I'm supposed to allow space for other people [the participants] to talk about race and racism while I'm making painful realizations about it at the same time? It's a tricky thing to be an SJE facilitator.

Elaine: No kidding, well said.

Tanya: I think one of the things that works well for us is that we know each other's *stuff,* and by stuff I mean those triggers and hot buttons or whatever you want to call it.

Elaine: Yes.

Tanya: But in the midst of that cofacilitation—because I know your stuff, because you know my stuff—I know there have been moments where I've been very thankful for your sometimes stepping in during a tricky moment or a time when I am triggered and saying, "OK, I'm going to respond to this."

I don't know how you do it, but you figure out which one I need when, or you're willing to ask me. Either you read my face, or you read, "OK, either she's shut down by that one, and I'm coming in as a White person," or "OK, you got this, Tanya." It's tricky to do social justice facilitation because of triggers and even trickier to do it as a cofacilitator when your cofacilitator doesn't know your triggers.

Elaine: Yes.

Tanya: And I think dangerous.

Elaine: Yes, I couldn't agree more. And then it just points to the importance of each person in a cofacilitation team continuing to work on self-awareness, to be willing to work and ask the questions, "What are my triggers? What are my areas of growth? What still gets under my skin? What used to get under my skin, and what has shifted now?" You know, all of that.

Tanya: Yes.

Elaine: And for each of us to be maintaining our own development too. So, for example, if you kept progressing in your process, and I was kind of stuck in general or as a White person, our facilitation wouldn't be as successful. So we have to be ready—you've helped me think about this—it's not just me knowing your triggers as a memorized list. You've helped me understand them; it's a collaborative process.

What work do I need to do in general, not just with facilitation skills, but also work that would prepare me for that moment, in terms of internalized dominance as a White person and in terms of places where I might have internalized subordination, that might then be affecting my ability to speak out because I don't have confidence because of some other reason, such as ableism or classism or sexism? How can I do all that work to help me show up in a way that is going to be helpful—for you, for the whole group, for particular individuals, for myself?

I can think of a situation recently when a White student said something that was really racially triggering to me. And that was one of those moments when I remember looking at you and thinking, "OK, I'm gonna respond to this." I wanted to support you as a cofacilitator and knew you well enough to be able to read your face in that moment. The moment was also about confidence on my part; more specifically, I was able in that moment to really be direct about what was said that was steeped in whiteness and really hard to hear and also move toward that White person, to be direct, really say what needed to be said, which was hard and uncomfortable. I remember there was awkwardness. I also needed to be open to that White person and to be compassionate. And that's where I've seen my own necessary growth and development.

I've learned a lot in the years that I've been facilitating, and one thing is that it is not helpful to people of color for me to push White people away. I ask the question, "Who could I be working with on these issues?" It might make me feel good at the moment, it might make me look like a bad-ass White social justice educator, to come down hard on a White person. It's not about what I look like, it's not about ego; it's about really staying in and doing the work, which means I have to work as a White person on my connections with White people all the time. That White person who's pushing everyone's buttons, and who everybody wants to give up on, and who just isn't getting it—I've got to figure out how to stay with that person in this role—that's part of it. It might not be the popular get-a-pat-on-the-back part, but that's really important. I can't distance myself in subtle or overt ways.

How Important Is It for Both Facilitators to Continue Their Own Self-Development Outside the Facilitation Team?

Tanya: A couple of things came up in my mind. So what happens if one facilitator stops in her process? For example, in a cofacilitation team it's not like one of those one-time cofacilitation moments. If one of us stops in our attempt to continue educating ourselves, or is limited in our own self-awareness, what does that look like?

Specifically, what would it mean if social justice educators stopped doing work on their identities? I already have feelings about us needing an ethics policy in social justice education. One of those ethics should be if you're going to facilitate and be in a cofacilitation relationship with someone else who has differing identities, you have to keep learning, you've got to keep working. There is no end point of development to any identity you have, because you are in cofacilitation with someone and trying to translate social justice to a larger population. And we don't get to stop. So when you said that, I want to acknowledge that continual learning is so important. And we're not gonna be perfect at it.

Elaine: No. A lot of it is about the commitment one brings to it.

Tanya: Yes, right.

How Do You Work With the Intersection of Your Multiple Identities?

Elaine: I've been thinking how consciously and intentionally we've each worked on race, and at the same time, it's interesting because we have several identities in common—our class identities, our sexual orientation identities, being women, being female. And another really important thing is the ways we've worked with those identities, individually and collectively, staying in conversation and modeling that for participants and students who we're working with. And there have also been moments when that's been interesting because there can be the assumption that we're so different. This is racism because people only see us as a White woman and a Black woman. It's interesting that other people only see that.

If my whiteness got in the way of seeing the ways that obviously our experiences about our sexual orientation are pretty darn different, would I be an effective cofacilitator—or even an effective friend but also an effective cofacilitator? So it's important to not only reflect on just race, it's how does race play out connected to sexual orientation, how does race play out connected to class, how does race play out connected to gender, you know—your experience as a woman and my experience as a woman? We have all those conversations, so I just wanted to point that out as well; that's been a significant part of our work, I think.

Tanya: I think for me, what I hear you saying is a great example of the nuance of teaching about something you are. And I just used this quote in the introduction of my dissertation; the point was that it's tricky to be able to be inside a topic, that topic being you, and that's what I think social justice facilitation is. It's like you're trying to educate people about identities and the power and stuff that's working itself out on a daily basis, while you live those dynamics in the midst of not only the cofacilitation team but the experience with the audience you're facilitating. So all of those issues are a triangular starlike dynamic where all of these things are working out at the same time. And for me, having a stable cofacilitation experience, cofacilitator relationship, provides some grounding for the power that works out in the midst of social justice education.

So again, I get back to the point of needing and having to do the work, because I want to focus on the facilitation that we're doing and not on the dynamics that are working out between us in that moment.

Elaine: Right.

Tanya: As facilitators, we need to be on the same page.

Elaine: Yes, we do.

Tanya: So that we can send out some really well-grounded knowledge and facilitation, and be present about social justice, in order to do the best work.

Elaine: Yes, well said. Something in what you said reminds me of needing to continue to work on our internalized oppression, which is so key to cofacilitation going well. And I was thinking in that example, I've needed to really do work on my internalized classism as a low-income person and working-class White person for a lot of reasons. For one, it's helped me do better work on race and racism and antiracism and whiteness, because I need to be able to work with White people of all classes, I need to be able to work with all people on whiteness and White privilege and racism.

If I am single-issue focused, if I'm only race, race, race, I'm missing a lot. Since a lot of the students we work with have a lot of class privilege as well as racism, I need to have done a lot of work so that I know my stuff.

Tanya: Well, and most important for me, I want to connect to your comment about being single-issue focused . . . going back to your earlier point that if you're in a cofacilitation team and you have not begun your process of exploring the ways your privileged identities intersect with your cofacilitator's target identities, that's gonna be a problem in the facilitation team. It makes me think about what kind of space is being made in facilitation teams, not only to have conversations, but just in general. And I'm thinking that when we ask our dialogue facilitators to fill out the cultural identity sheet, we should add the question, "How do they [social identities] affect your way of being?"

Elaine: Yeah, good one.

Tanya: Or, "What is your awareness of how they affect your way of being?" Because I may be able to say that I'm Black, but that doesn't give my cofacilitator a lot of information about how that may have me show up in that facilitation team. If you perhaps were to ask, "So your race is Black. How does that affect your way of being?" I could talk forever about how being Black in a predominantly White area affects my lived experience. But that question takes the facilitator team up a notch and may allow more space in the cofacilitation pair.

So in Our Cofacilitation Relationship, What Have We Learned From This Relationship to Expand Into Other Relationships in Our Lives?

Tanya: I think—and this is funny, I don't know that I've ever thought about this, but this is what comes to mind—I think I try stuff out on you that I think, "Elaine was able to handle it. Other White people can too." And I know that's pretty dangerous.

Elaine: Dangerous, how? Say more.

Tanya: In the sense that you have awareness and consciousness of your White identity that I don't think some White people do. But I may say something to you or about my own identity about race and realize that you didn't crumble into ash upon my saying this, upon my being empowered. And so, therefore, I can go and be empowered with other White people. And I think I reasoned earlier in our cofacilitation relationship that if my White cofacilitator didn't freak out on me, I could try this empowered thing on others too. Oh, they didn't freak out either. And I tried it out more and more.

Elaine: Kind of like your testing ground in a way.

Tanya: Testing ground, at least about race. I know you were totally my testing ground on race. I'm sure I had some conversations with you about race that allowed me to have deeper, more risk-taking, learning-edge stuff with other White people, because I'd done it in this cofacilitation team.

Elaine: Well, the same is true for me. *Practicing* sounds like I'm practicing on you, and it doesn't feel like that at all, because it felt like it's friendship and it's collaborative. Yeah, I mean if we think of practice as repetition, we've had a lot of practice.

Tanya: Practice with a lot of things.

Elaine: And practice having those conversations. And I think the more we talk, the more I realize we really have worked on intersections quite a lot. We've practiced having those conversations and learning how to articulate holding one identity or form of oppression and not erasing another—how to talk about that. We've experienced firsthand how to have that actually work out in our cofacilitation, where multiple identities are being acknowledged, all being worked with, and it's all being honored. I feel as if my muscles have practiced and are toned, I have more strength in that area. And even when I don't know exactly what to do or what to say, I don't shy away. I can really lean into it: "OK, if I'm in a new cofacilitation relationship, there will be lots of multiple identities, places where I'm dominant, places where I'm not." I know I need to have those conversations. I know if my cofacilitator didn't bring it up, I'm going to do it, or that we're going to do it together. It's going to be imperfect, and it's going to be real, but I'm committed to it, and I'm going to do it. And I have some practice, thanks to my relationship with Tanya, with having just about any kind of conversation you could possibly imagine, so I'm going to do it.

Tanya: Right.

Elaine: And things always go better, always.

Tanya: Particularly with social justice. Anything you do will go better if you're able to have these conversations and be legitimately transparent about how your identities are working out in the moment. And so as social justice facilitators, if you're not able to do that, what the heck are you doing? You're not doing SJE or social justice period. You're not moving the world or the participants to a place to see that it can be done. Folks look at us on many levels, I think, and say, "Oh my gosh, you can have a relationship with someone across groups that looks like that?"

Elaine: I think that if it looks like that, it is real and authentic. We've had hard things that we've had to work on and talk through. If the goal is authenticity and realness then, you know, you get to see all of me; I get to see all of you. I don't need to waste energy trying to paint this picture for you that I'm a White person that gets it all. Because guess what: I don't, so it's a waste of time.

Tanya: At least name the places where you don't know, and don't give up. I think that's another thing when I think about translating our cofacilitation relationship. I think we got along pretty well early, and so it was easy to be your friend. But as a cofacilitator, it's a relationship I'm not giving up on because I'm committed to you as a cofacilitator. I'm not giving up on you. So I'm going to sit and either watch or stay with the process. And that, I think, transfers to other across-group relationships I have with other people—that I'm not giving up on other White people, or I'm not giving up on other straight people. That's a big deal. I take that very seriously.

Elaine: Other cofacilitation relationships come and go. Yeah, others come and go, and I feel like this is the ground. It's a total foundation from which I've been able to work and build with you; it makes me braver, like my relationship with you helps sustain my commitment, my integrity, my courage with other cofacilitation relationships. I think about entering into, let's say, a cofacilitation relationship with another person of color, and not knowing the person as well, and thinking I want to do a good job. And just thinking, "I can do this"—to not shy away, to have courage to do whatever I need to do to have that go well, on my end to do whatever I need to do, whatever I need to say. Just having everything be transparent, conscious, intentional, up for conversation, up for feedback, no rock left unturned, nothing is left unnoticed. And if it is, then turning over the rock, checking in, knowing that we model all the time, that's never turned off.

Tanya: It's fascinating to me—and I'm going to close with this—that we haven't talked about design.

Elaine: I've thought about it 10 million times in my head when we were talking, but no, we haven't actually specifically mentioned it.

Tanya: It's as if the design is the vehicle for the facilitation relationship. Design is clearly important to social justice facilitation, but our conversation here at least points to how the cofacilitation relationship brings life to the design. And so the design could be wonderful, it could be crap, but if this relationship is not purposeful and thought out and the conversations had, the design could be wonderful, and it will flop.

Elaine: Yep. And the design does need to be wonderful. So we don't skimp on design. And you're right, you must be able to trust that I have your back or have done work on whiteness and on class, for example.

Tanya: A great design is not going to save a poor facilitation relationship.

Elaine: No, it's really not. And you really have to have both.

COFACILITATION CAN BE A CONTRIBUTION TO PERSONAL AND SOCIAL CHANGE

This ends the conversational portion of this chapter, but the dialogue between us about how to grow in our relationship and facilitate toward social change continues. "Even when intergroup dialogue may not lead directly to change, it can help create the conditions to catalyze greater community collaboration among previously estranged groups" (Nagda & Maxwell, 2011, p. 2). This possibility exists in all social justice–focused cofacilitation. Through embodying an effective cofacilitation relationship, we model the conditions needed to catalyze greater community collaboration among previously estranged groups. This lies at the heart of intergroup dialogue and similar SJE approaches. This also creates the conditions for more effectively understanding and experiencing conflict as an intrinsic part of social justice work. When we, as an African American and White cofacilitation team, show up in the room in authentic ways and directly acknowledge the estrangement of these two racial and social identity groups—and work with conflict in a normalizing way—we create the potential to address and even contribute to the healing needed as the result of the mistrust, pain, disconnection, and inequity caused by oppression.

The need for relationship- and coalition-building across and within difference in the context of oppression is glaring. An effectively cofacilitated social justice dialogue/workshop experience holds out what is possible in the world. It is our experience and hope that cofacilitation relationships built with consciousness, intention, awareness, commitment, and authenticity can contribute to the vision of more just communities, institutions, and a world, and to making that vision a reality. Our experiences with and reflections on our cofacilitation relationship illustrate how powerful a model this can be. Whether cofacilitating a one-time training or engaging in a year-long cofacilitation relationship, we hope we have made the case that taking the time to build an authentic cofacilitation relationship is as important as innovative design. This includes talking openly about our multiple and intersecting identities; our lived experiences with power, privilege, and oppression; and our vision for what is possible. We continue to find in our cofacilitation with each other and all those we cofacilitate with that it is well worth the time.

REFERENCES

Kirk, G., & Okazawa-Rey, M. (2004). Identities and social locations: Who am I? Who are my people? In *Women's lives: Multicultural perspectives* (3rd ed., pp. 59–69). Boston, MA: McGraw-Hill.

Nagda, B. A., & Maxwell, K. E. (2011). Deepening the layers of understanding and connection: A critical-dialogic approach to facilitating intergroup dialogues. In K. E. Maxwell, B. A. Nagda, & M. C. Thompson (Eds.), *Facilitating intergroup dialogues: Bridging differences, catalyzing change* (pp. 1–22). Sterling, VA: Stylus.

Pfeiffer, J. W., & Jones, J. E. (1975). *Annual handbook for group facilitators*. San Francisco: CA: Jossey-Bass.

Zúñiga, X., Nagda, B. A., Chesler, M., & Cytron-Walker, A. (2007). Intergroup dialogue in higher education: Meaningful learning about social justice. *ASHE Higher Education Report, 32*(4).

7

Understanding and Supporting Multiracial Students

Adam J. Ortiz

NUMEROUS COMPANIES and institutions of higher education bring together employees and students of shared racial identity to form what are called *racial affinity groups* (Forsythe, 2004; Nealy, 2009). The specific goals of these groups vary. Many companies encourage employees of the same race to gather in the hope they will find solidarity with others with similar experiences to develop strategies for success (Forsythe, 2004). In colleges and universities, student affairs professionals use racial affinity groups for similar reasons, believing they will result in the attainment of social justice goals.

When used in the context of racism education sessions, many facilitators ask students to form groups based on race as a powerful educational tool. Separating people by race in workshops can provide members of the racially dominant group in the United States (i.e., White people) the space to discuss experiences with privilege, feelings of guilt, and recommended strategies for becoming an ally, while people in subordinated groups (e.g., people of color) find solidarity, provide one another support, and develop ways to challenge racism (Everyday Democracy, 2008). For many, the feelings racial affinity groups elicit are positive; for others, they arouse feelings of guilt and unease. The ideal outcome is that participation in a racial affinity group will inspire participants to learn more about themselves and others in the context of race and that by doing so they will seek to take tangible steps in confronting subtle and overt acts of racism. This praxis, however, is not always present, and individuals can exit the racial affinity group setting with their needs unmet or, worse, feeling further marginalized.

Consistent with the growing body of literature on the experiences of multiracial students, multiracial people are particularly susceptible to well-intentioned but ineffective support in social justice education efforts aimed at addressing racism (Lou, 2011). Assumptions about how multiracial people identify, internal conflict and confusion about who we are, lifelong anxiety about choosing a racial identity, and other experiences that appear in multiracial development theories (Poston, 1990; Renn, 2000; Renn & Shang, 2008; Root, 1990) create difficulties for multiracial individuals when asked to participate in racial affinity groups. In this chapter I share my reflections of my experience with racial affinity groups as a multiracial person, which led to a transformation of these groups into a powerful tool that better supports multiracial students. I conclude with suggestions for successful facilitation of multiracial affinity groups for social justice educators to consider.

THE HISTORY AND FUNCTIONS OF AFFINITY GROUPS

Despite the number of student affairs professionals who use racial affinity groups in social justice education efforts, there is a dearth of scholarly literature on the practice, particularly in higher education. Much of the information on affinity groups has come from activist websites, each with subtle nuances that indicate affinity groups can be formed for a number of different causes ranging from political activism to networking (Forsythe, 2004; Starhawk, n.d.). In some colleges and universities, the culture and practice of affinity groups—particularly racial affinity groups—is widespread and commonplace. Racial affinity groups have tremendous potential for making progress toward the goals of social justice education.

The history of affinity groups originates with Spanish anarchists in the late nineteenth and early twentieth centuries. Groups of workers congregated in nonhierarchical circles and planned mobilization tactics to fight Fascism (Blanchard, Pullin, & Rolley, 2007). In the United States, affinity groups were introduced again on a wide scale in the 1970s when antinuclear activists began to congregate in small groups and develop strategies for nonviolent demonstrations. These decentralized actions led to effective roadblocks, the occupation of nuclear-related spaces, and the general disruption of the nuclear business. Affinity groups have also been used in Black liberation and women's empowerment movements, as well as in union organizing (Blanchard et al., 2007).

The strength of affinity groups lies in their autonomy and lack of hierarchy. Instead of having a consistent leader who makes ultimate decisions, affinity groups offer all participants equal voice and participation, even when led by a facilitator. Although affinity groups can contain any number of individuals, according to Blanchard et al. (2007), the ideal affinity group size should be between 3 and 17 people, all of whom sharing some unified purpose of congregation. Affinity groups can consist of coworkers, students, friends, activists, or community members and can be created for any action-related purpose participants choose. As long as participants are devoted to the goals of the group, historical use has demonstrated that affinity group organizing is a valuable tool in accomplishing difficult feats of social change.

In higher education, particularly in the realm of social justice education, affinity groups have the capacity to help members of dominant and subordinated social groups gather with their own group members to explore their identities in the context of contemporary culture. This exploration can lead to personal insight about one's life, a greater passion for social justice issues, and the development of new and effective ways of supporting peers and other individuals with similar identities. Student organizations that are formed according to shared race, socioeconomic class, gender, sexual orientation, or other social identities are common affinity groups seen on campuses. Although many campus administrators have demonstrated a commitment to supporting affinity groups, consistent evaluation of practices in these groups is vital for the sake of maximum efficacy.

MULTIRACIAL STUDENTS
IN HIGHER EDUCATION

Multiracial college students in the United States face a significant number of struggles in their lives. Inherent in the multiracial identity are complexities and conflicts that are frequently misunderstood or taken for granted by monoracial individuals. Confusion about how to racially identify oneself, internal guilt and anger, and feelings of isolation are a few examples of experiences that are determined largely by a multiracial person's appearance, cultural knowledge, and peer culture (Renn, 2008). The interplay of these three factors combined with the wide array of combinations of racial backgrounds indicates that multiracial students will likely face some level of distress and isolation in their racial identity development.

In 2003 multiracial identity become recognized nationally as a distinct category. This recognition occurred when the U.S. Department of Education complied with Statistical Directive 15 of the Office of U.S. Management and Budget, that allowed people to select more than one race on legal forms (Garbarini-Philippe, 2010). The option to do so gave multiracial students and their experiences some legitimacy they had not been granted previously. It also allowed for the collection of tangible data that could be used to assess their needs. Still, despite best efforts by institutions to collect data and engage in needs assessment of multiracial students, classes about multiracial topics are uncommon, multiracial student groups are rare, and inclusive college environments are often difficult to find (Garbarini-Philippe, 2010).

Fortunately, the literature on multiracial experiences is growing as attention is being given to the needs of these students. At the moment, both student affairs professional associations, ACPA–College Student Educators International and NASPA–Student Affairs Administrators in Higher Education, have designated communities of student affairs professionals to engage in education and outreach. In 2010 alone, numerous works focused on multiracial experiences and identity development have been published (Johnson & Nadal, 2010; Korgen, 2010; Literte, 2010; Spencer, 2010). While the community of scholars and student affairs professionals dedicated to multiracial student issues is encouraging, a need continues for greater research and scholarship on multiracial students' experiences, particularly in educational institutions. As a population that has been "largely ignored in educational institutions" (Garbarini-Philippe, 2010, p. 1), multiracial students deserve diligence in the development of support methods.

MY STORY AS A MULTIRACIAL PERSON

For the better part of my youth, people would ask me about my racial background, and I would answer, "I am half Mexican and half White." The next question was, typically, "Do you speak Spanish?" My response was an embarrassed no. This confession served as a reminder that I never quite fit the racial expectations of those around me. Growing up biracial (Latino and White) in a racially diverse neighborhood in Las Vegas, these questions arose frequently. The ambiguity about my racial identity is further exasperated by my last name, Ortiz. Despite my surname, I have not had much connection with my extended Latino family and have significantly greater familiarity with White culture.

I continued to experience racial uncertainty into adulthood as I moved to New England to attend a predominantly White undergraduate college and then take a postgraduate job in Vermont. During this time I was only asked about my racial identity if my last name was known. If White people had not learned my last name, I passed as a White person. Having never met anybody with whom I was able to process my experiences, I remained confused about my racial identity. White people did not understand my internal conflict because most of them never had to think about race. Monoracial people of color did not understand my confusion because their racial identity is often a core aspect of their lives. I found myself feeling somewhere between two cultures.

Poston (1990) claimed that many models of racial identity development for people of color did not accurately take into account the experiences of biracial individuals and proposed a new model for understanding biracial identity development with five levels:

1. Personal identity: Identity is not connected to a racial or ethnic reference group.
2. Choice of group categorization: The individual is pushed to choose a cultural group to identify with; this either includes both parents' heritage groups or a dominant culture from one background. The choice is influenced by factors such as appearance, social support, and status.
3. Enmeshment/denial: The individual experiences confusion and guilt for not being able to identify with all aspects of his or her heritage; this may lead to anger, shame, or self-hatred.
4. Appreciation: Individuals begin to broaden their racial reference groups, learning about all aspects of their backgrounds.
5. Integration: Individuals have a full appreciation of their multicultural existence and all their ethnic identities.

Consistent with Poston (1990), I was stuck in the enmeshment/denial phase of the biracial identity development model. In this stage, "guilt at not being able to identify with all aspects of [one's] heritage may lead to anger, shame, or self-hatred; resolving the guilt and anger is necessary to move beyond this level" (Poston, 1990, p. 153). In my youth I had experienced brief waves of believing I could securely identify as White. By the time I graduated college,

I was well accustomed to the guilt and shame I felt in sometimes wishing I was White, sometimes wishing I was Latino, and other times wishing I was neither. I even considered changing my last name at one point in the hopes of alleviating some of the pressure to choose a race.

STRUGGLES IN RACIAL AFFINITY GROUPS

My first experience with affinity groups was during a training retreat for my graduate assistantship. I was told we were going to begin with a racial affinity group session, but I did not know what that meant. The next morning, my colleagues and I were told we were going to split into affinity groups and were instructed to separate by race. Immediately a ripple of fear pulsed through my body. Individuals who identified as White were asked to go to another room, while individuals who identified as people of color were to stay in the room we currently occupied. I felt a pang of confusion and anxiety; a culmination of lasting nervousness that I tried many times to repress or ignore. In the past, when confronted about my race I was able to be "half this" and "half that." This time I had no choice; I had to make a decision.

I recall panicking, my eyes scanning the room back and forth in a frenzied attempt to find someone to speak with about where I should go or if I should participate at all. I believed if I went to the White space, I would be rejected because of my last name; yet, if I stayed in the people of color space, I was worried I would be unwelcome because my mother is White. Thankfully, I locked eyes with a colleague of mine, Jackie [to honor our working relationship, I am using Jackie's real name with her permission], who had told me she had a Black father and a White mother. She looked every bit as anxious as I did. While I take no relief in other peoples' suffering, I was glad for the company.

Upon the start of the meeting Jackie expressed to the facilitators that she was unsure of where to go. When I seconded her uncertainty, we were told that we were welcome to choose where to go, but that other multiracial participants most often went to the people of color group. In fact, one of the facilitators told us that while she herself was biracial, she considers herself to be a person of color. With that, and a few more assurances from other participants, Jackie and I decided to stay with the people of color group.

At the start of the meeting the facilitators told us that the affinity group space was intended to be a safe location where people of color could congregate to share their experiences and offer support throughout the academic year. Our department would be hosting the racial affinity groups a few times throughout the first semester, but we were also encouraged to seek out other people of color for solidarity. Unsure of where my whiteness fit in, I was overwhelmed with nervousness, rehashing experiences I generally tried to avoid thinking about or discussing. I thought long and hard about the time in middle school when I was physically threatened by people of color for having White friends. I thought about all the hurtful racist jokes and commentary I heard from White people who believed I was also White. I thought about my grandparents from the U.S. South, who teased me incessantly for being "a half Mexican." Nearly every negative race-related situation I had ever experienced flooded my mind; once again I was balanced on the border between two races.

The first hour of the affinity group meeting was a presentation on a people of color identity development theory. I do not remember the name of the theorist the presenters used, but the model began by describing a person of color's internalized feelings of worthlessness and ended with the experience of fluent multicultural navigation and acceptance. Throughout the facilitators' presentation, I found myself identifying with few aspects of the model. There was nothing about identifying with multiple racial groups in different contexts (Root, 1990), the guilt inherent in not being able to identify with all aspects of one's racial makeup (Poston, 1990), or the prospective resolutions that pertained to my circumstances. What I also did not see in the model was all the confusion and turmoil I have experienced as a result of being biracial.

As the meeting progressed, people began to feel more relaxed and shared personal experiences they had as a result of their racial identities. Most peoples' stories were about struggles and blatant instances of discrimination I could not identify with, having passed as White in so many settings. Yet I felt my own struggles had no validity in the room—not because I was silenced or discouraged in any way but because of my internal insecurities as a multiracial person. I believed no one else would be able to empathize with the shame inherent in not being able to speak a language or embody a culture commensurate with one's last name or the consistent inability to identify with either parent's racial identity. I certainly did not expect anyone to kindly listen to my stories of having made racist comments about my Latino heritage during my youth in an effort to circumvent hearing them from White people. I could not help but feel that my experiences were different from those of the vast majority around me. Although I was encouraged to share my experiences, I remained silent.

After the meeting, Jackie and I found each other and expressed how out of place and uncomfortable we felt throughout the entire session. Having a White mother, she was equally as upset by the feelings of confusion inherent in the situation. Yet, because we were both new to the graduate program, we sought to trust the process and avoid making our feelings public to anyone who would not understand them. We both felt hurt and disappointed that there was no group we could turn to in solidarity.

Our professional staff had numerous official racial affinity group sessions throughout the semester. Most of them consisted of people telling personal stories about events in their lives that were reflective of being in a racial group that has been historically marginalized and oppressed. Eventually, my colleagues' poignant stories of enduring racial oppression made me aware of the extent to which different forms of racism are rampant and varied. In that regard, the racial affinity groups created for me a feeling of urgency about challenging racism that I was lacking prior to the meetings. I also believe that learning about the experiences of the Latino participants helped me begin moving into Poston's (1990) fourth stage of identity development, appreciation. During this stage, "individuals broaden their racial reference group through learning about all aspects of their backgrounds" (Poston, 1990, p. 153). Learning about whiteness, Latino culture, and racism in the presence of people of color was a new experience for me and pushed me to begin transcending some of the guilt and anger I had felt prior to graduate school. Still, I felt as though I did not have the freedom to relate my own experiences because there was a sense of solidarity in the room I did not feel a part of as a result of my multiracial identity. Although no one intentionally made me feel unwelcome, I felt as though I were a fraud, given the nature of my half-White biracial status.

As my first semester of graduate school ended, I realized I had gained a better understanding of race that was profoundly different from my prior understandings. Although I was thankful for the lessons, I envisioned a better place for me, Jackie, and others like us—a space where multiracial people could share their struggles and increase their understanding of race with others who had similar experiences. Despite having had positive experiences in the racial affinity groups, I relived the same discomfort I endured during the initial racial affinity group meeting in some instances. Jackie and I recognized there had to be a better way for us to structurally exist in affinity group spaces.

THE UNEXPECTED GIFT OF SOLIDARITY

During the start of my second semester in graduate school, I participated in a weekend-long social justice retreat. The climax of the retreat was affinity group time. Despite having learned much about race in my previous affinity group sessions, I did not know the people at this retreat and was afraid I was once again going to find myself in a space where people started making emotionally charged statements without an understanding of my biracial identity. I feared hearing people talk about their discomfort with White people, being judged for being light-skinned, and once again experiencing the feeling of not belonging.

At that moment, the group leaders announced there would be a bi- and multiracial affinity group space. Because there were no multiracial facilitators at the retreat, this affinity group space would be self-regulated and optional. I was elated. I felt like the silence that had kept me quiet about my racial experience for as long as I could remember was suddenly on the verge of dissipating.

By the official start time of the affinity group session, five biracial individuals had walked through the door of the cabin. With no official facilitator, the six of us spent the first few minutes in quiet. The silence was broken by my enthusiastic welcome to the group. After each person delivered a short introduction, I decided to continue leading the conversation. For two hours we discussed positive and negative stereotypes associated with multiracial people, the struggles inherent in the multiracial experience (particularly when one parent is White), and the common loneliness each of us felt in our race-related interactions with other people, including our closest friends and family members. Not surprising for me was the feeling of solidarity in the room that was far stronger than any I had experienced in the general people of color affinity group during the previous semester. Each participant was speaking at length, articulating experiences that were affirmed with knowing head-nods and smiles. It was the first time most of us had been in the exclusive company of multiracial individuals, and each one of us expressed similar sentiments about how much we appreciated the experience.

Through my continued connection with other multiracial people, I was learning about many shared experiences: ambiguity in appearance, passing as a monoracial individual, distance from family members on either parent's side, and a profound sense of loneliness, to name a few. I continued to be encouraged that this opportunity to facilitate a multiracial affinity group was one that I needed to take advantage of with full appreciation and intentionality.

FACILITATING A SUCCESSFUL MULTIRACIAL AFFINITY GROUP

At the start of our second year in graduate school, Jackie and I were asked to facilitate a multiracial affinity group space during resident assistant (RA) training. After a summer of planning, we were excited to work with the 10 people who joined us for the affinity group. Everyone was silent as we instructed the RAs to sit down in the chairs we had arranged into a circle. We broke the silence by introducing ourselves by name, professional position, and racial identity. We disclosed our multiracial identities, helping to set the tone for others to share their experiences as we invited them to do so. We also told them that if at any point any of them felt as though they would like to join a different group, they were more than welcome to exit without judgment. Every person in the room participated and remained seated.

We began the meeting with an open discussion about why affinity groups are used and gave suggestions for participation. Guidelines such as being honest, being mindful of our amount of time to speak, and being intentional about creating a supportive environment were identified as agreements to assist in creating a safe and open setting.

Jackie and I showed slides of famous multiracial individuals. We researched and chose to display multiracial celebrities to highlight the fact that there are numerous well-known multiracial people in Western culture whose racial identities are often misinterpreted. Some of our most prominent examples included Bob Marley, Barack Obama, Lenny Kravitz, Cameron Diaz, and Henry Louis Gates, Jr. We believed that doing this would create a feeling of unity in being racially misunderstood and misrepresented. Sharing these celebrities with the group opened up conversation about numerous topics, ranging from the frequent invisibility of the multiracial experience to the fact that self-identifying individuals are often knowingly mislabeled.

We then provided a brief history of terminology related to multiracial people. From *half-blood* to *hybrid*, we discussed a number of terms—derogatory and technical—that have been used historically when discussing multiracial individuals. Using this context was important to clarify a number of misunderstandings about terminology, as well as provide the participants with information about labels they have likely heard throughout their lives (Downing, Nichols, & Webster, 2005). We were careful to acknowledge that the appropriateness of certain terminology is largely individual and that comfort with words varies from person to person, leading to a general conversation about general people of color in-group language use.

We then moved into the most provocative segment of our meeting: the personal narratives. We began eliciting conversation by using the work of Maria Root (1990, 1993, 1994). We projected an image of Root's (1993–1994) *Bill of Rights for People of Mixed Heritage.* The text is a short treatise on rights that should be granted to all multiracial individuals, such as the right to identify differently than siblings and the right to identify differently in different contexts. All Root's proclamations reflect struggles that multiracial people experience on a consistent basis and serve as an ideal way to initiate conversation about people's race-related stories.

For about an hour the RAs shared their experiences. The anecdotes were humorous, heartfelt, and poignant. One woman spoke about her inability to connect with anyone on one side of her family because she looks whiter than any of them, while a man detailed his frustration with being expected to live up to racial people of color stereotypes, despite the fact that he was raised in a culturally White environment. All the experiences, regardless of their context or intensity, reflected the same sense of frustration, confusion, and loneliness that first drove Jackie and me to facilitate this affinity group.

We also discussed how their multiracial identities were going to affect life in the residence halls, particularly working as RAs. The general consensus was that all participants had a newfound understanding of the importance of talking about race. There was also a feeling of optimism in the room as the group members reassured one another that none of us had to be alone in this identity experience. Our final activity was a note-writing session. Students were instructed to write positive words to one another. For about 10 minutes everybody walked around the room, some folks laughing through residual tears, writing words of encouragement. The moment was an affirmation that this group mattered to students and our efforts were well received. Many of the RAs said this was the first time that they had *ever* felt comfortable discussing race. Others expressed a desire to continue building community with other multiracial individuals. All of them mentioned being thankful for the experience.

Reflecting on the session, I have come to believe that having a space for multiracial people to gather is imperative in social justice education. The limited opportunities we have to participate in multiracial affinity groups leave many of us feeling despondent and lonely, as if our entire existences were invalid because we are missing the affirmation of struggle present in the lives of so many monoracial individuals. I do not intend to suggest that multiracial individuals are more disadvantaged than monoracial individuals of any race—many of us certainly have significant privileges—but rather that our experiences are unique, and that failing to acknowledge this leaves us feeling like we are alone in circles of friends and family who can never understand us. With the proper attention and support, multiracial individuals can thrive in racial affinity groups while walking away affirmed and taking greater steps toward positive racial identity development.

PROFESSIONAL RECOMMENDATIONS

I wrote this reflective chapter for two reasons. The first is to serve as an example of how student affairs professionals can make significant positive changes at any institution of higher education. I know it was difficult to believe I had the power to make positive change. Yet this experience, which was coordinated with some thoughtful reflection, careful planning, and the support of other student affairs professionals, left a lasting affirmation that all student affairs professionals have the power to invest themselves in endeavors that can bring substantial modifications to the way an institution supports its students.

My second reason for writing this reflection was a desire to tell educators how vital multiracial affinity group spaces are to multiracial people. As I stated numerous times throughout this reflection, the experiences of multiracial individuals are unique and complicated. People who identify as multiracial have a seemingly endless spectrum of experiences depending on their racial makeup, but consistently I have had multiracial people share a sense of anxiety and loneliness that was derived from having to choose a racial identity that fit the mold of many monoracial people's concepts of race. I would argue that this is, once again, Poston's (1990) development stage of enmeshment/denial, and I am convinced that many individuals never fully transcend it. Once our existences are acknowledged as mixed (or split, halved, and so forth) and allowed to expound on this experience with others who share this identity, I believe we begin the process of becoming psychologically whole.

I also want to present additional suggestions on how best to support multiracial individuals in the context of racial affinity groups based on my experiences. I include them not with the intention of being an authority on the multiracial experience. Rather, I offer these suggestions as a multiracial student affairs professional who experienced a tremendous amount of solidarity and positive identity development while coordinating a multiracial affinity group setting.

First, when facilitating racial affinity groups, creating a space for multiracial individuals is imperative, even if it is within a larger people of color group. An overwhelming amount of multiracial individuals have spent their whole lives with the anxiety inherent in choosing a race to identify with. Root (1990) referred to the process of going back and forth between identities and suggested a nonlinear approach to multiracial identity development. Regardless of how multiracial people identify themselves, there is social pressure to choose a racial identity in the lives of many multiracial individuals. Making assumptions about a multiracial individual's racial identity, or asking him or her to choose between the two in a physical setting, can elicit significant turmoil. Providing a space for multiracial individuals in the context of racial affinity groups offers them the opportunity to find much-needed solidarity along with the psychological security of identifying however they would like.

Second, highly skilled and sensitive facilitators are vital. In my experience, the most effective facilitators in this context are at a point in their own identity development where they are comfortable navigating volatile race-related conversations from a calm and secure perspective. Certainly, everybody has the capacity to become triggered when discussing race or social justice content, but facilitators of racial affinity group sessions should possess the knowledge and skills to respond to emotional outbursts, topical facilitation, and effective follow-up. Multiracial people with one White parent are particularly susceptible to racial triggers when discussing the people of color/White dichotomy and benefit from a facilitator with a deep understanding of the struggles inherent in the identity.

Third, as part of affinity group facilitation, it is helpful to scaffold the information. First offer the history and function of affinity groups. One need not go into a detailed account of Spanish anarchists and how affinity groups have evolved since then, but at the very least hold a brief discussion about their genesis as well as historical successes and contemporary usage. One of the most significant pitfalls of racial affinity groups is a lack of context. When facilitating these groups, we must remember that most students and young staff members engaging in them have grown up in an era where Jim Crow–style segregation is viewed as definitive and egregious racism. Asking people, then, to separate by race without carefully explaining to them the theoretical and practical reasoning is bound to elicit tumultuous feelings and strong opinions that this practice is counterproductive to eradicating racism.

Fourth, understand the complexities of the multiracial experience. A significant amount of literature has been written about the history and racial identity development of multiracial individuals, and professionals working with a multiracial student population should become familiar with it. Based on a multiracial individual's racial identity, ethnicity, and culture, the multiracial experience for one person may be completely different for another. As I mentioned earlier, a few consistent characteristics seem to recur among multiracial individuals: anxiety over choosing how to racially identify, loneliness inherent in not identifying with monoracial friends or family, and a general sense of unease as a result of being misidentified or mislabeled based on racial cultural norms. All these struggles are discussed in the writings of Root (1990), Poston (1990), and Renn (2004), to name a few. In addition, many multiracial people, depending on circumstances, have different privileges than monoracial people of color. Multiracial people who frequently pass as White, in particular, have an additional level of complexity to untangle.

Fifth, use multiracial development theories while facilitating multiracial affinity groups. Even though some identity development models conflict, many students are relieved to learn the anxiety they may have long experienced in their lives is not solely theirs alone. Given that the multiracial identity is one that is inherently alienating at times, individuals who learn their internal struggles are commonplace will likely experience significant comfort. Learning about multiracial identity development models also gives students a map of potential positive outcomes they may never have realized were an option.

CONCLUSION

Multiracial students hold a unique position in higher education. Though the multiracial experience is not new, exploring the needs of multiracial students is a practice that higher education scholars and professionals have only recently adopted. As student affairs professionals and social justice education facilitators, we must actively seek best practices when working with multiracial students, particularly in areas in which we might perpetuate their experiences of trauma and frustration. Although powerful learning tools, racial affinity groups can be difficult for multiracial students if not facilitated with extreme care and intentionality. If done well, racial affinity groups can hold significant potential to advance positive racial development and provide solidarity for historically oppressed groups. As with any facilitation tool, we must recognize the unique and evolving needs of our students to ensure social justice learning outcomes.

REFERENCES

Blanchard, C., Pullin, E., & Rolley, L. (2007, February). *Beyond the knapsack: Effectively utilizing affinity groups for developing anti-racist behavior.* Conference session presented at the annual conference of Whiteness as a Power of Discourse in Education, South Burlington, VT.

Downing, K., Nichols, D., & Webster, K. (2005). *Multiracial America: A resource guide on the history and literature of interracial issues.* Lanham, MD: Scarecrow Press.

Everyday Democracy. (2008). *Dialogue for affinity groups.* East Hartford, CT: Paul J. Aicher Foundation.

Forsythe, J. (2004). *Winning with diversity: Affinity and networking groups.* Retrieved from http://www.nytimes.com/marketing/jobmarket/diversity/affinity.html

Garbarini-Philippe, R. (2010). Perceptions, representation, and identity development of multiracial students in American higher education. *Journal of Student Affairs at New York University, 20,* 1–6.

Johnson, M. P., & Nadal, K. L. (2010). Multiracial microaggressions: Exposing monoracism in everyday life and clinical practice. In D. W. Sue (Ed.), *Microaggressions and marginality: Manifestation, dynamics, and effects* (pp. 123–144). Hoboken, NJ: Wiley.

Korgen, K. O. (2010). *Multiracial Americans and social class.* New York, NY: Routledge.

Literte, P. E. (2010). Revising race: How biracial students are changing and challenging student services. *Journal of College Student Development, 51*(2), 115–134.

Lou, H. C. (2011). Multiracial student acquiescence to empowerment. *Vermont Connection, 36,* 46–57.

Nealy, M. J. (2009, March 10). *Do affinity groups create more racial tension on campus?* Retrieved from Diverse Issues in Higher Education website: http://diverseeducation.com/article/12376/

Poston, W. S. C. (1990). The biracial identity development model: A needed addition. *Journal of Counseling and Development, 69*(2), 152–155.

Renn, K. A. (2000). Patterns of situational identity among biracial and multiracial college students. *Review of Higher Education, 23*(4), 399–420.

Renn, K. A., & Shang, P. (Eds.). (2008). Biracial and multiracial students. *New Directions for Student Services, 2008*(123).

Root, M. P. P. (1990). Resolving "other" status: Identity development of biracial individuals. *Women and Therapy, 9*, 185–205.

Root, M. P. P. (1993–1994). *Bill of rights for people of mixed heritage.* Retrieved from http://www.drmariaroot.com/doc/BillOfRights.pdf

Spencer, R. (2010). *Reproducing race: The paradox of generation mix.* Boulder, CO: Lynne Rienner.

Starhawk. (n.d.). *Affinity groups.* Retrieved from http://www.starhawk.org/activism/trainer-resources/affinitygroups.html

Part Three

Facilitation Design and Techniques

THIS SECTION EXPLORES in more detail the skills and considerations for creating optimal learning environments for participants of social justice education classes and workshops. As many authors have already discussed, social justice facilitators recommend beginning workshops by explaining guidelines for conversations to establish the trust and openness necessary for full participation. In Chapter 8, authors Brian Arao and Kristi Clemens offer a new way to frame these dialogues, called creating *brave space*. Moving away from the concept of *safe space*, the authors offer an alternative that may more effectively help participants understand and expect the challenges required for growth and learning to take place.

In Chapter 9, Kathy Obear introduces the skill of navigating triggers (i.e., difficult emotional responses that arise for facilitators) during social justice facilitation. She explores how facilitators can develop greater self-awareness, skill, and competency to navigate these triggering events in ways that align with their core values and vision for social justice. Social justice educators have an ethical responsibility to be clear instruments of change in their work. By exploring the intrapersonal issues that fuel triggered reactions, opportunities are created for personal healing and insight for facilitators and participants.

In Chapter 10, authors robbie routenberg, Elizabeth Thompson, and Rhian Waterberg introduce a complex technique that is often used by social justice educators: multipartiality. Facilitators use this skill when they closely consider the role of social identity and differential social power in their facilitation practice. The authors provide the reader with tangible considerations for practice by offering their experiences in incorporating multipartiality in their facilitation and offer their learning process as a model to understand the importance of the method and the challenges and benefits it brings to social justice facilitation.

In Chapter 11, the authors introduce a topic that served as the impetus for this publication: how to effectively facilitate a popular simulation exercise, the Tunnel of Oppression. The authors, Gregory I. Meyer, Karen Connors, Rebecca Heselmeyer, Dusty M. Krikau, Tracy L. Lanier, Matthew R. Lee, Chris D. Orem, and Nancy Trantham Poe, broadened this topic to explore the components of effective facilitation of interactive privilege awareness programs. Their chapter emphasizes the importance of employing intentionality from design through implementation. The authors share their successes and missteps working with this program in the hope that the lessons learned can be generalized for use in facilitating similar social justice educational initiatives.

8

From Safe Spaces to Brave Spaces

A New Way to Frame Dialogue
Around Diversity and Social Justice

Brian Arao and Kristi Clemens

THE PRACTICE OF establishing ground rules or guidelines for conversations and behavior is foundational to diversity and social justice learning activities. As student affairs educators, we expect this process will help create a learning environment that allows students to engage with one another over controversial issues with honesty, sensitivity, and respect. We often describe such environments as *safe spaces*, terminology we hope will be reassuring to participants who feel anxious about sharing their thoughts and feelings regarding these sensitive and controversial issues.

But to what extent can we promise the kind of safety our students might expect from us? We have found with increasing regularity that participants invoke in protest the common ground rules associated with the idea of safe space when the dialogue moves from polite to provocative. When we queried students about their rationales, their responses varied, yet shared a common theme: a conflation of safety with comfort. We began to wonder what accounts for this conflation. It may arise in part from the defensive tendency to discount, deflect, or retreat from a challenge. Upon further reflection, another possibility arose. Were we adequately and honestly preparing students to be challenged in this way? Were we in fact hindering our own efforts by relying on the traditional language of safe space?

As we explored these thorny questions, it became increasingly clear to us that our approach to initiating social justice dialogues should not be to convince participants that we can remove risk from the equation, for this is simply impossible. Rather, we propose revising our language, shifting away from the concept of safety and emphasizing the importance of bravery instead, to help students better understand—and rise to—the challenges of genuine dialogue on diversity and social justice issues.

CASE STUDY

We first began to question and rethink the framework of safe space as colleagues working in the Department of Residential Education at New York University. The critical moment that spurred this rethinking occurred when planning and implementing aspects of our fall resident assistant training program. The department approached the task of training our resident assistants on a wide range of content areas before the start of the academic year by developing a series of 90-minute training modules. As members of our department's diversity committee, we were tasked with developing a training module on diversity and social justice. We were excited for an opportunity to channel our passion for social justice education into an important aspect of student leadership training, yet also challenged by the short session time frame of 90 minutes. Our intended learning outcomes for this module were ambitious even without the challenge of time constraints. How, we wondered, would we introduce the concepts of social and cultural identity, power, and privilege; encourage reflection on how these forces moved through and shaped their lives; and draw connections between the session content and their roles as student leaders?

Given our goals for the session, we decided to incorporate the One Step Forward, One Step Backward activity, which is also called Leveling the Playing Field and Crossing the Line. In this exercise, participants are lined up in the middle of the room. The facilitator then reads a series of statements related to social identity, privilege, and oppression; participants determine whether these statements are reflective of their lived experiences and then either step forward, step backward, or remain in place as directed. After all prompts have been read, the facilitator leads a group discussion about their interpretations of the pattern of the distribution of participants in the room. Students who hold primarily dominant group identities usually end up in the front of the room, those who hold primarily target group identities in the rear, and those with a more even split of dominant and target group identities in between the other two groups. The goal of the exercise is to visually illustrate the phenomenon of social stratification and injustice and how participants' own lives are thereby affected. The exercise intentionally pushes the boundaries of the participants' comfort zones in the hope of spurring them on to powerful learning about social justice issues.

After our module on diversity and social justice, we received mixed feedback about the One Step Forward, One Step Backward activity from the student participants and from our colleagues who had served as facilitators for other groups. Some participants reported they experienced heightened awareness of social justice issues as a positive result. Most, however, were critical of the activity. This critical feedback appeared largely dependent on the social identities of the participant and the degree to which their target or agent group identities held salience for them.

Participants who framed the activity primarily through their agent or dominant group identities stated they felt persecuted, blamed, and negatively judged for ending the exercise at the front of the room. Many expressed feelings of guilt about their position in the exercise (though not necessarily their privilege), as well as helplessness when hearing the emotional reactions of those who were closer to the rear of the room. Common reactions included sayings such as, "I can't help being White" and "These problems aren't my fault."

Conversely, those who framed the activity primarily through their target group identities ended up in the back of the room. Many of these participants stated their physical position at the conclusion of the exercise was a painful reminder of the oppression and marginalization they experience on a daily basis. Whereas their agent group peers expressed surprise at the pattern of distribution, many of the target group participants stated they predicted the result of the activity from the beginning. Like their agent group peers, the target group participants voiced frustration with the activity, though their feelings tended to stem from a sense of being placed in the familiar role of educator for agent group members—a role they felt was inevitably theirs but one that made them feel angry, sorrowful, and in some cases, afraid of the repercussions.

Interestingly, a critique shared by many participants across target and agent group identities was that they experienced the activity as a violation of the safe space ground rules established with each participant group at the outset of the module. The profound feelings of discomfort many of them experienced were, in their view, incongruent with the idea of safety.

It was apparent to us that on the whole our session had missed the mark with respect to our intended outcomes, sparking the first of many long discussions between us. Although it was tempting to simply lump the critiques together as the typical resistance you can expect when talking to folks about power and privilege, we knew this was an oversimplification that would not result in improved pedagogical practice or richer learning for our students. What was the critical flaw in our design? Did we select the wrong activities or place them in the wrong sequence? Did we do a poor job of training our colleagues to facilitate the session? While mining these questions resulted in some useful insights—for example, we no longer use the One Step Forward activity as part of our facilitation practice, primarily because we are troubled by its potential to revictimize target group members—we continually returned to the quandary of safe space. Was it the activity that had made our students feel unsafe, or did this sense of danger originate somewhere else? It was here that we began to more closely examine the conventional wisdom of safety as a prerequisite for effective social justice education and question to what degree the goal of safety was realistic, compatible, or even appropriate for such learning. What is meant by the concept of safety, and how does that change based on the identities in the room?

DEFINING AND DECONSTRUCTING
SAFE SPACE

Many scholars have described visions of safe space as it relates to diversity and social justice learning environments. Among them are Holley and Steiner (2005), who described safe space as an "environment in which students are willing and able to participate and honestly struggle with challenging issues" (p. 49). Staff at the Arizona State University Intergroup Relations Center described the contours of safe space in more detail, with a stated objective of creating "an environment in which everyone feels comfortable expressing themselves and participating fully, without fear of attack, ridicule, or denial of experience" (as cited by National Coalition for Dialogue & Deliberation, n.d., §S). To create such spaces, "participants need some basic discussion guidelines in order to develop trust and safety" (Hardiman, Jackson, & Griffin, 2007, p. 54).

Consistent with the literature, we believe facilitators of social justice education have a responsibility to foster a learning environment that supports participants in the challenging work of authentic engagement with regard to issues of identity, oppression, power, and privilege. Student development theorists assert that to support this kind of learning, educators must take care to balance contradiction to a student's current way of thinking with positive encouragement to explore new ways of thinking (Baxter Magolda, 1992; Kegan, 1982; King & Kitchener, 1994; Sanford, 1966). Further, we share the conviction that violence of any kind—physical, emotional, and psychological—is antithetical to the aims of social justice work; indeed, we see the use of violence to achieve one's goals as a patriarchal norm that should be challenged through such work. As such, we see great value in many of the tenets of safe space as well as the common practice of setting expectations, often called *ground rules*, with the learning group regarding how we will engage with one another on these subjects.

We question, however, the degree to which safety is an appropriate or reasonable expectation for any honest dialogue about social justice. The word *safe* is defined in the Merriam-Webster Online Dictionary as "free from harm or risk . . . affording safety or security from danger, risk, or difficulty . . . unlikely to produce controversy or contradiction" (Safe, 2010). We argue that authentic learning about social justice often requires the very qualities of risk, difficulty, and controversy that are defined as incompatible with safety. These kinds of challenges are particularly unavoidable in participant groups composed of target and agent group members. In such settings, target and agent group members take risks by participating fully and truthfully, though these risks differ substantially by group membership and which identities hold the most salience for a given participant at a given time.

For agent group members, facing evidence of the existence of their unearned privilege, reflecting on how and to what degree they have colluded with or participated in oppressive acts, hearing the stories of pain and struggle from target group members, and fielding direct challenges to their worldview from their peers can elicit a range of negative emotions, such as fear, sorrow, and anger. Such emotions can feed a sense of guilt and hopelessness. Choosing to engage in such activity in the first place, much less stay engaged, is not a low-risk decision and, therefore, is inconsistent with the definition of *safety* as being free of discomfort or difficulty.

Indeed, the unanticipated discomfort and difficulty many agent group members experience as a result of participation in a social justice learning activity can also lead to resistance and denial. Here, the truth of how power and privilege have moved in one's life is rejected, and energy is redirected toward critiquing the activity (rather than the content) as the source of her or his discomfort or explaining away others' experiences as springing not from oppression but from some other more benign source, disconnected from oneself. In this manner, the language of safety may actually encourage entrenchment in privilege, which we may be able to curtail more effectively by building conditions in which agent group members understand and expect from the outset that challenge is forthcoming.

Further, it is our view that the agent group impulse to classify challenges to one's power and privilege as actions that detract from a sense of safety is, in itself, a manifestation of dominance. For example, Wise (2004), in his essay critiquing Whites' insistence on safety as a condition of their participation in a cross-racial dialogue about racism, describes this expectation as "the ultimate expression of White privilege" (¶ 15), whereby Whites attempt to define for others—and especially people of color—how they wish to be confronted about issues of race and racism. People of color are then expected to constrain their participation and interactions to conform to White expectations of safety—itself an act of racism and White resistance and denial. In this manner, we suggest that the language of safety contributes to the replication of dominance and subordination, rather than a dismantling thereof. This assertion does not mean we believe anything goes is a better approach; rather, we suggest we do participants a disservice by reinforcing expectations shaped largely by the very forces of privilege and oppression that we seek to challenge through social justice education.

Members of the target group are even more disserved by well-intentioned efforts to create safety. Target group members may, in fact, react with incredulity to the very notion of safety, for history and experience has demonstrated clearly to them that to name their oppression, and the perpetrators thereof, is a profoundly unsafe activity, particularly if they are impassioned (Leonardo & Porter, 2010). They are aware that an authentic expression of the pain they experience as a result of oppression is likely to result in their dismissal and condemnation as hypersensitive or unduly aggressive (Sparks, 2002). This dilemma looms large for target group members in any social-justice-related learning activity; reflecting on and sharing their direct experiences with oppression, and listening to dominant group members do the same, will likely result in heightened pain, discomfort, and resentment. These feelings alone are inconsistent with the definition of *safety* and exacerbated by ground rules that discourage them from being genuinely voiced lest they clash with agent group members' expectations for the dialogue.

Indeed, the pervasive nature of systemic and institutionalized oppression precludes the creation of safety in a dialogue situated, as it must be, within said system. As Wise (2004) observed with respect to race, "This country is never safe for people of color. Its schools are not safe; its streets are not safe; its places of employment are not safe; its health care system is not safe" (¶ 35).

Though Wise focuses on racism, we argue that his formulation about safety can also be applied to examinations of sexism, homophobia, heterosexism, ableism, religio-spiritual oppression, ageism, U.S.-centrism, and other manifestations of oppression. Viewed through this lens, we see that assurances of safety for target group members are just as misguided as they are for agent group members.

We have come to believe, as argued by Boostrom (1998), that we cannot foster critical dialogue regarding social justice

> by turning the classroom into a "safe space", a place in which teachers rule out conflict. . . . We have to be *brave* [emphasis added] because along the way we are going to be "vulnerable and exposed"; we are going to encounter images that are "alienating and shocking". We are going to be very unsafe. (p. 407)

BRAVE SPACE: AN ALTERNATIVE FORMULATION AND FACILITATION PRACTICE

As we developed alternatives to the safe space paradigm, we were influenced by Boostrom's (1998) critique of the idea of safe space, and in particular his assertion that bravery is needed because "learning necessarily involves not merely risk, but the pain of giving up a former condition in favour of a new way of seeing things" (p. 399). Some scholars have suggested that pedagogies of fear (Leonardo & Porter, 2010) or discomfort (Boler, 1999; Redmond, 2010) are in closer practical and philosophical alignment with this kind of learning. Although these provocative theories were useful to us, our primary inspiration was from the concept of "courageous conversations about race" (Singleton & Hays, 2008; Singleton & Linton, 2006; Sparks, 2002), a strategy developed specifically to encourage taking risks in dialogues focused on the topic of race and racism. These ideas affirmed our decision to make a small but important linguistic shift in our facilitation practice, whereby we seek to cultivate brave spaces rather than safe spaces for group learning about a broad range of diversity and social justice issues. By revising our framework to emphasize the need for courage rather than the illusion of safety, we better position ourselves to accomplish our learning goals and more accurately reflect the nature of genuine dialogue regarding these challenging and controversial topics.

We have found that the simple act of using the term *brave space* at the outset of a program, workshop, or class has a positive impact in and of itself, transforming a conversation that can otherwise be treated merely as setting tone and parameters or an obligation to meet before beginning the group learning process into an integral and important component of the workshop. *Brave space* is usually a novel term for our students or participants, especially those who are familiar with the idea of safe space, and frequently piques their curiosity. In response, we often ask participants why they think we use the term *brave space* instead of *safe space*, with the goal of involving their critical lenses immediately. It is common for participants to respond by unpacking the idea of safety much like we did as we developed the brave space framework. Creating this space for the participants to make their own meaning of brave space, in addition to sharing our own beliefs as facilitators, can lead to rich learning in alignment with our justice-related objectives.

This process of actualizing brave space in a social justice learning activity continues, appropriately, with the establishment of ground rules. There are many different techniques for establishing ground rules. Often, the mode selected is dependent upon the total amount of time allotted for the learning activity. If time is relatively short, the facilitators may choose to advance a predetermined list of ground rules to preserve limited discussion time for other aspects of the activity. Alternatively, when time permits, facilitators may lead a conversation in which the participants generate their own list of ground rules. A hybrid version of both approaches is another possibility, whereby the facilitators suggest some ground rules and invite participants to ask questions about these as well as share additional ground rules of their own. In any case, facilitators will likely seek commitment from the group to adhere to these ground rules throughout the activity, although they may also indicate the rules can be revisited and revised as needed as the activity progresses.

We strongly encourage facilitators who use the brave space framework to strive for protracted dialogue in defining *brave space* and setting ground rules, treating this conversation not as a prelude to learning about social justice but as a valuable part of such learning. We have found that so doing allows us as facilitators to demonstrate openness to learning from participants, thereby disrupting and decentering dominant narratives in which knowledge flows one way from teachers to students. A collectivist approach, wherein all participants have the opportunity to shape the group norms and expectations, is more consistent with the overall goal of social justice education than one in which the facilitators dictate the terms of learning (Freire, 1970; hooks, 1994).

Whatever methodology is used to create ground rules, commonly used ground rules include "agree to disagree," "don't take things personally," "challenge by choice," "respect," and "no attacks." We believe that unexamined, these common ground rules may contribute to the conflation of safety and comfort and restrict participant engagement and learning. In the section that follows, we discuss these common ground rules and characteristics of safe spaces. We also offer some alternatives and examples for processing the complexity of these guidelines that are more consistent with social justice education goals and the establishment of brave spaces. In setting up guidelines for social justice conversations, we aim to encourage participants to be brave in exploring content that pushes them to the edges of their comfort zones to maximize learning. We offer all of these to support facilitators in thinking critically about how ground rules can help or hinder students in full and truthful engagement.

Common Rule 1: Agree to disagree. Implicit in this common ground rule is that disagreements often occur in dialogues about diversity and social justice. We welcome the voicing of disagreement and encourage students to offer contrasting views. However, we believe that agreeing to disagree can be used to retreat from conflict in an attempt to avoid discomfort and the potential for damaged relationships. We often hear students say, "I'm not going to change my mind, and neither are they; what is the point of continuing to talk?" In our view, some of the richest learning springs from ongoing explorations of conflict, whereby participants seek to understand an opposing viewpoint. Such exploration may or may not lead to a change or convergence of opinions or one side winning the debate, but neither of these is among our objectives for our students; we find these outcomes to be reflective of a patriarchal approach to conflict, in which domination and winning over others to one's own point of view is the goal.

Further, we believe that agreeing to disagree in a conversation about social justice not only stymies learning for all participants, it can also serve to reinforce systems of oppression by providing an opportunity for agent group members to exercise their privilege to opt out of a conversation that makes them uncomfortable. Consider, for example, a workshop focused on the topic of sexism. The participants are engaging in a lively and contentious discussion about how sexism has an impact on leadership and employment opportunities for women in the United States. Many of the women, and some of the men, in the room have shared statistics indicating that women are underrepresented in positions of leadership and still paid less than men for the same work. Most of the men in the room contest this view and offer high-profile examples of women who have "made it." Weary of the back-and-forth conflict, the men invoke the rule of agreeing to disagree. The conversation is halted, and the result is that the system of sexism that continues to confer unearned privileges to men and restrict freedom and opportunities for women is left unexamined. This outcome is harmful for all involved, but women carry the largest part of that burden.

An alternative rule is needed, one that inspires courage in the face of conflict and continues rather than stops the dialogue process. Without such a guideline, we are compromised in our ability to facilitate learning that advances social justice for all people. To this end, we suggest that facilitators explore the concept of controversy with civility and how it may prove a stronger fit with the goal of dialogue. *Controversy with civility*, a term drawn from the social change model of leadership development (Astin & Astin, 1996), is "a value whereby different views are expected and honored with a group commitment to understand the sources of disagreement and to work cooperatively toward common solutions" (p. 59). We find this proposed rule to be in much closer alignment with our philosophy of social justice education than agreeing to disagree. It frames conflict not as something to be avoided but as a natural outcome in a diverse group. Moreover, it emphasizes the importance of continued engagement through conflict and indicates that such activity strengthens rather than weakens diverse communities.

As we discuss later, it is important to note that the word *civility*, in our view, allows room for strong emotion and rigorous challenge. It does not require target group members to restrain their participation to prevent agent group members from disengaging. It does, however, require target and agent group members to be attentive to the ways patriarchal societies socialize their members to view aggression and dominance as normative means to approach conflict and to use care to avoid replicating oppressive behaviors while engaged in the pursuit of justice for all people.

Common Rule 2: Don't take things personally. We see this often-used rule as closely related to two other common rules: no judgments and it's okay to make mistakes. Invoking these rules seems to be intended to encourage participants to become involved dispassionately to maintain safety in the learning environment—in other words, safe spaces. Moreover, it also primes participants for the inevitability of missteps while they are exploring social justice issues. These rules may be very reassuring to participants who are concerned that at some point in the activity they will betray ignorance attributable to one of their agent group memberships and do not wish to be labeled or dismissed by their peers as sexist, racist, ableist, and so forth. So reassured, they may participate and engage with less fear and greater honesty.

We share the desire for authenticity and see value in the acknowledgment that human beings are imperfect and should not be expected to behave otherwise. However, we have a number of problems with the use of these rules to ground a social justice dialogue. First, they fail to account for another truth we hold about human beings: although we have some choice in how we respond to and express our emotions, we do not have control over which ones we experience at any given time and to what degree. We suggest that the view we can and should demonstrate such control is reflective of patriarchy, whereby emotional restraint—a normatively masculine behavior—is unjustly overvalued.

Further, we argue that these rules shift responsibility for any emotional impact of what a participant says or shares to the emotionally affected people. Those affected are now expected to hide their feelings and process them internally; the rules may even imply to these participants that their feelings are because of some failing on their part. According to the rules, the affected parties are only permitted to react outwardly in a manner that does not imply negative judgment of the participant who has caused the impact, lest this person be shamed into silence. The affected people are in this way doubly affected—first by the event that triggered their emotions and then again by the responsibility for managing them. These rules also prevent the person who caused the impact from carrying a share of the emotional load and preclude the possibility of meaningful reflection on her or his actions.

In our analysis, these rules do not protect any participants' safety and certainly not that of the target group members, who are more often than not the affected and silenced participants. Rather, they preserve comfort for agent group members, who may allow their power and dominance to show without having it reflected to them and without being held accountable for it. We are careful here to avoid saying that agent group members are served by such a rule; we believe it protects their privilege, but in so doing it also does them a disservice. None of these outcomes is consistent with our view of social justice, so we choose different language—*own your intentions and your impact*—to ground our pedagogy. This language acknowledges that intention and impact matter. It also makes clear that the impact of our actions is not always congruent with our intentions and that positive or neutral intentions do not trump negative impact.

For example, in a conversation about gender expression, gender normative or cisgender people (those whose gender expression aligns with dominant social expectations of their biological sex) may inadvertently cause pain to transgender participants by expressing incredulity about how a biologically male person could be a woman. If the trans participants have been supported in choosing to approach controversy with civility by letting it be known they have been harmed and why, there are now opportunities where silence would have left only closed doors and untouched systems of oppression. The trans participants have not been forced, as is so often the case, into silence but rather have exercised agency by participating truthfully. The gender normative participants are aware they have caused harm and can seek to better understand how and why they did so and what role their privilege as gender normative people has played in creating the gap between intention and impact. All participants, if they so choose, can better explore with one another ways to challenge the social scripts that frame gender as binary and essentially as indistinguishable from biological sex. These results would have been discouraged in an environment in which the trans students were directed to not take things personally.

Common Rule 3: Challenge by choice. This guideline emerged in the field of adventure education and outdoor learning and has since been widely applied in social justice education. Challenge by choice means individuals will determine for themselves if and to what degree they will participate in a given activity, and this choice will be honored by facilitators and other participants (Neill, 2008). The principle of challenge by choice highlights what we view as an important truth in social justice education. Though a given activity or discussion question may provide a challenging opportunity for participant learning, much of that learning may be internal. Students may not externalize evidence of the degree to which they are engaged, but this does not mean they are not wrestling with difficult questions or critically examining how privilege moves in their lives and the lives of others. Further, we recognize this kind of engagement cannot be forced. As facilitators, we might make a pointed observation or pose a provocative question in hopes of spurring such engagement. For example, during a conversation about the controversy over same-sex marriage, we might say, "We notice that only folks who have identified as lesbian or gay have said anything in this conversation; we'd like to invite anyone who identifies normatively with respect to sexual orientation to share their thoughts." However, we understand it is ultimately in the participants' hands to decide whether they respond and to what extent they will push the boundaries of their comfort zones.

Given this reality we believe it is important to do more than simply affirm it by establishing challenge by choice as a ground rule. We believe it is also necessary to actively encourage participants to be aware of what factors influence their decisions about whether to challenge themselves on a given issue. We see this awareness as being particularly important for agent group members. Returning to our example of the same-sex marriage conversation, silence from heterosexual participants could signify any number of things. Some of them might have been thinking deeply about what it means to their being able to enter a civil marriage with their chosen partner, while others could not. Some might have even been formulating a thought to share with the group. Some might have been very uncomfortable with the topic and decided they were unable to rise to the challenge of discussing it.

In the latter case, it is our hope the internal process does not stop at the decision not to accept the challenge. Therefore, when discussing challenge by choice, we also ask participants to think about what keeps them from challenging themselves. Do they hold what they believe is an unpopular viewpoint? Are they fearful of how others will react to their thoughts? Are they simply tired and not able to formulate a thoughtful contribution that day? Whatever the reason, we hope our participants will be attentive to it.

We encourage participants to be especially attentive to the degree to which their agent group memberships inform their decision about whether and how deeply to engage in a challenging activity or dialogue. Specifically, we suggest they consider how their daily lives are affected if they choose not to challenge themselves, and by contrast, how target group members' daily lives are affected by the same decision. If they come to suspect or clearly see their privilege enables them to make the choice not to challenge themselves, and that oppression often invalidates such a choice for target group members, we hope this knowledge factors into their decisions about how and when they choose to challenge themselves.

Common Rule 4: Respect. Of all the common rules, we have experienced this one as the least controversial and the least discussed. When respect is offered as a ground rule, most of our participants agree readily that it should be adopted—they want to be respected, and they want to be respectful to others—and move quickly on to the next point of discussion.

We believe it is important to spend more time discussing respect with the group. We often ask them what respect looks like: How does someone demonstrate respect for you? Delving into this question can reveal various cultural understandings of the term and mitigate assumptions participants bring with them about what kinds of behaviors are respectful. For example, participants will often say that interrupting someone who is speaking is a form of disrespect. As facilitators, we use this as an opportunity to demonstrate multipartiality (see Chapter 10) by affirming this particular understanding but also by acknowledging that in some cultural contexts interruption and talking over one another is welcome; we then invite participants to share any examples they might have from their own experiences. The objective here is not to lead participants to consensus but rather to support them in maintaining increased mindfulness of the different ways they can demonstrate respectfulness to one another.

We also circle back to the idea of controversy with civility when conversing about respect. Specifically, we ask participants to give an example of how they might firmly challenge the views of someone else in a respectful manner. By further discussing the examples, the group can develop more clarity about ways to firmly and respectfully challenge others and how to respond when they themselves are firmly and respectfully challenged. Such discussion is a potentially fruitful investment of time that can prevent students from automatically experiencing and interpreting challenges from others as acts of disrespect.

Common Rule 5: No attacks. The fifth and final of our common rules for creating brave spaces is closely connected to the previous rule of respect. Many of our students have described attacks as a form of extreme disrespect, a view we agree with and connect directly to our rejection of any form of violence as a viable means for advancing social justice. As with respect, we find this rule is usually agreed to speedily and, in the absence of facilitator intervention, without discussion.

Here again, we advocate for clarifying conversation. We typically ask our participants to describe the differences between a personal attack on an individual and a challenge to an individual's idea or belief or statement that simply makes an individual feel uncomfortable. These examples are always very instructive. Most of the examples participants identify clearly as attacks—"You're a jerk," "Your idea is worthless," and so on—have never actually occurred in any session we have facilitated. However, those that are classified during this conversation as challenges—"What you said made me feel angry," "I find that idea to be heterosexist," and so on—are ones that in our experience are regularly named as attacks later on by the recipients of the challenges. At this point, we have found it helpful to remind participants of the group's responses during this portion of the ground rules discussion;

doing so has helped participants remember that pointed challenges are not necessarily attacks, but the uncomfortable experience that may result can sometimes lead to a defensive reaction. The attention can then be turned away from the distraction of the nonattack and toward the roots of the defensive response—more often than not, a sense of threat to the privileges of one's agent group membership.

CONCLUDING THOUGHTS

We have found that reframing ground rules to establish brave space is an asset to us in our work as social justice facilitators. It has helped us to better prepare participants to interact authentically with one another in challenging dialogues. Moreover, as compared to the idea of safe space, brave space is more congruent with our understanding of power, privilege, and oppression, and the challenges inherent in dialogue about these issues in socioculturally diverse groups. The feedback we have received from attendees at presentations (Arao & Clemens, 2006) and participants in workshops we facilitate—including students, staff, and faculty—has been universally positive, and many have requested our assistance in learning and using the brave space framework in their own practice. Still, we recognize that brave space remains a relatively new framework with ample room for growth and refinement. Our evidence of its efficacy is primarily anecdotal. We believe qualitative and quantitative studies would be useful in measuring how brave space is experienced by participants in social justice educational efforts and how it influences their learning and participation in these settings. Further, we welcome your additional philosophical and theoretical analysis of the framework as articulated here, as we know that others will see and understand the strengths and shortfalls of brave space in ways we, as yet, do not. We look forward to continued engagement with you in our shared journey to develop ever more efficacious social justice facilitation practices.

REFERENCES

Arao, B., & Clemens, K. (2006, March). *Confronting the paradox of safety in social justice education.* Educational session presented at the annual meeting of ACPA-College Student Educators International, Indianapolis, IN.

Astin, H. S., & Astin, A. W. (1996). *A social change model of leadership development guidebook, version 3.* Los Angeles, CA: Higher Education Research Institute.

Baxter Magolda, M. B. (1992). *Knowing and reasoning in college: Gender-related patterns in students' intellectual development.* San Francisco, CA: Jossey-Bass.

Boler, M. (1999). *Feeling power: Emotions and education.* New York, NY: Routledge.

Boostrom, R. (1998). "Safe spaces": Reflections on an educational metaphor. *Journal of Curriculum Studies, 30*(4), 397–408.

Freire, P. (1970). *Pedagogy of the oppressed.* New York, NY: Continuum.

Hardiman, R., Jackson, B., & Griffin, P. (2007). Conceptual foundations for social justice education. In M. Adams, L. Bell, & P. Griffin (Eds.), *Teaching for diversity and social justice* (2nd ed., pp. 35–66). New York, NY: Routledge.

Holley, L. C., & Steiner, S. (2005). Safe space: Student perspectives on classroom environment. *Journal of Social Work Education, 41*(1), 49–64. doi: 10.5175/JSWE.2005.200300343

hooks, b. (1994). *Teaching to transgress: Education as the practice of freedom.* New York, NY: Routledge.

Kegan, R. (1982). *The evolving self.* Cambridge, MA: Harvard University Press.

King, P. M., & Kitchener, K. S. (1994). *Developing reflective judgment: Understanding and promoting intellectual growth and critical thinking in adolescents and adults.* San Francisco, CA: Jossey-Bass.

Leonardo, Z., & Porter, R. K. (2010). Pedagogy of fear: Toward a Fanonian theory of "safety" in race dialogue. *Race Ethnicity and Education, 13*(2), 139–157. doi: 10.1080/13613324.2010.482898

National Coalition for Dialogue and Deliberation. (n.d.). *Safe space.* Retrieved from http://ncdd.org/rc/glossary#S

Neill, J. (2008). *Challenge by choice.* Retrieved from http://wilderdom.com/ABC/ChallengeByChoice.html

Redmond, M. (2010). Safe space oddity: Revisiting critical pedagogy. *Journal of Teaching in Social Work, 30*(1), 1–14. doi: 10.1080/08841230903249729

Safe. (2010). In *Merriam-Webster's online dictionary* (11th ed.). Retrieved from http://www.merriam-webster.com/dictionary/safe

Sanford, N. (1966). *Self and society.* New York, NY: Atherton Press.

Singleton, G., & Hays, C. (2008). Beginning courageous conversations about race. In M. Pollock (Ed.), *Everyday antiracism: Getting real about race in school* (pp. 18–23). New York, NY: The New Press.

Singleton, G., & Linton, C. (2006). *Courageous conversations about race: A field guide for achieving equity in schools.* Thousand Oaks, CA: Corwin Press.

Sparks, D. (2002). Conversations about race need to be fearless. *Journal of Staff Development, 23*(4), 60–64.

Wise, T. (2004). *No such place as safe.* Retrieved from http://www.zcommunications.org/no-such-place-as-safe-by-tim-wise

9

Navigating Triggering Events

Critical Competencies for Social Justice Educators

Kathy Obear

AVE YOU EVER FELT so hooked or triggered during a conversation about inclusion and equity that you lost your focus and said something you later regretted? As a social justice educator, I have had innumerable triggering experiences where I have reacted in ways that were counterproductive and left participants feeling angry, hurt, and shut down. Early in my career as a consultant, I cofacilitated a three-hour workshop on homophobia and heterosexism in the workplace for business leaders and managers at a national conference in the Midwest. Looking back, I feel embarrassed and deeply regret how I facilitated that session. A few weeks before the conference, the voters of the city where the conference was held rescinded a law that protected people against discrimination based on sexual orientation. As I started the session I was unaware I was feeling deeply triggered and had assumed the people attending the conference were homophobic and had voted to repeal the city's nondiscrimination law. I have little memory of what I actually said as I welcomed the participants, but I do remember that I entered with an intensely angry and aggressive energy and basically demanded that they shift their homophobic attitudes and change their heterosexist policies. Needless to say, I experienced a significant amount of pointed questions and challenges and had great difficulty moving the group through the activities; over half the participants left at the break. Years later, I talked with my cofacilitator about this session and finally realized how my colleague of color had also been negatively affected by my triggered reactions.

I wish I could say this horrendous experience was the impetus for my personal journey to learn how to navigate triggering events. Unfortunately, I did not become willing to take a serious look at myself and my lack of competence until a mentor, Bailey Jackson, gently confronted me about the ways my behaviors undermined learning goals and negatively affected participants. I am deeply indebted to him for starting me on this transformative journey to take responsibility for my triggered emotions and reactions and to facilitate social justice education from a conscious, intentional mindset.

Facilitating discussions about social justice is extremely challenging, stressful work. It involves exploring issues not often addressed in traditional academic environments, including emotions, stereotypes, biases, and personal examples of oppression. Facilitators and participants bring most, if not all, of who they are to the learning environment, including their multiple dominant and subordinated group memberships, fears, prejudices, unconscious needs, values, and life experiences. Social justice education is not about the objective or impersonal facilitation of participant learning. Whether they are conscious of it or not, facilitators are actively engaged in the learning process at all levels of their being and may tend to feel more triggered in discussions about social justice than in other aspects of their work. To be effective facilitators, I believe we have an ethical responsibility to develop greater competencies to navigate our triggered reactions during dialogues about equity and inclusion. It is my hope the personal stories and reflections in this chapter help facilitators realize they are not alone, that all of us feel deeply triggered and react unproductively at every life stage, and there are effective tools, models, and ways of being to help facilitators navigate triggering events in ways that enhance the learning and development of participants.

The term *trigger* is commonly used in the social justice education literature to describe this phenomenon of being hooked (Bell, Love, Washington, & Weinstein, 2007; Goodman, 1995; Griffin, 1997; Weinstein & Obear, 1992). In this chapter, I define a *triggering event* as any stimulus through which facilitators experience an unexpected, intense emotional reaction that seems disproportionate to the original stimulus. Triggered reactions are like an automatic reflex that occurs in a split second without conscious thought (Hardiman, Jackson, & Griffin, 2007). People can feel so overwhelmed and thrown off balance that they are consumed by their triggered reactions and lose touch with the comments and actions occurring around them. During a triggering event, facilitators may feel disoriented and deskilled and have difficulty making conscious, intentional choices about how to respond effectively in the moment.

A triggering event can be almost anything, including a participant's comment, actions, or facial expression or the silence in the group. It may be an image in a film or photograph or a slogan on a button or T-shirt. Social justice educators can also feel triggered by their own actions or thoughts. I remember triggering myself when I was preparing to work with a group of executive leaders on a corporate diversity council. I kept replaying the thought that I was not competent enough to do the session and I soon felt deeply anxious and fearful. As I began to speak, my voice was tentative and I forgot my train of thought.

It is common to experience a strong wave of negative emotions when triggered, including anger, fear, sadness, anxiety, shame, guilt, and embarrassment. When facilitators feel triggered, the current stimulus has usually reactivated an area of intrapersonal roots, including unresolved conflict, personal issues, or suppressed emotions from their past or current life experiences. Most educators report they were unaware of the relationship between their intrapersonal roots and their triggered reactions. Common phrases like "You pushed my buttons," "It scared me," and "You made me yell at you" imply that the responsibility for triggered reactions lies with someone else or something outside of oneself. In reality, triggered reactions are deeply connected to two key elements: how facilitators make meaning of the situation and what intrapersonal issues and memories are restimulated in the moment.

During dialogues about issues of equity and inclusion, triggered reactions can often undermine the learning outcomes and group guidelines as well as violate a facilitator's core values and vision for social justice. I will never forget the moment I realized my unexamined actions can contradict my core values. I had just responded to the comment of a male participant when he looked me in the eye and said, "You just cut me off at the knees." I felt devastated. At my core I believe our work as social justice educators is to do no harm and to meet people where they are as we form partnerships with them to deepen learning, reflection, and productive change. My behavior violated the stated community norms and my social justice intentions. I hope my actions are never experienced as violent or harmful again.

While they may not be able to control when they feel triggered, educators can develop the self-awareness, tools, and competencies to effectively navigate triggering situations. Triggering events are not inherently problematic.

These emotional experiences can provide significant learning opportunities that may be remembered for years. When fully present in the moment, facilitators can more accurately assess themselves, the current context, and group dynamics and then effectively use the incident as a teachable moment. Unfortunately, most social justice educators more often react in ways that are unproductive and not aligned with their core values (Obear, 2000). In the following sections, I outline a set of tools and skills to help social justice educators prepare for, anticipate, and navigate triggers effectively.

CLARIFY INTENTIONS

When we clearly articulate our vision, values, and intentions as social justice educators, we can design and facilitate educational opportunities that align with our intended outcomes. How do you want people to treat each other? How do you want others to feel during interactions? What type of community do you want all people to experience? What do you want people to do differently after your conversation/session on social justice? Considering these questions can help clarify your intentions as a social justice educator. Facilitators may have many intentions for their work, including the desire to create space for honest, authentic dialogue; treat others with dignity, respect, and care; deepen understanding across differences; create safety for the expression of multiple perspectives; facilitate engaged, respectful disagreement; use teachable moments and triggering events to deepen learning and understanding; and discuss dynamics of oppression and examples of liberation.

It is equally important that social justice educators identify the intentions they choose when they react in ways that violate their core social justice values. The more aware they are of their common negative intentions, the more likely they will recognize them in the moment. Common negative intentions include to win the argument, defend oneself, get revenge, prove one's competency, put others in their place, keep the conversation under control, avoid conflict and confrontation, make the person feel the pain one feels, change the person's views or behaviors, gain everyone's approval, and make everyone feel happy. At the moment when the male participant felt I had "cut him off at the knees," I now recognize that my intentions had been to put him in his place and correct him.

Discussing negative intentions openly and authentically can bring a sense of relief and a feeling of empowerment. Once I recognize these unproductive intentions, I can shift my thinking to more closely align with my core social justice values. When facilitators feel triggered and model the skills and values they espouse, the learning can be far more powerful than the most creative activity or engaging lecture.

THE TRIGGERING EVENT CYCLE

Social justice educators are often unaware they feel deeply triggered until after they have reacted in unproductive ways. The triggering event cycle (Obear, 2000) provides a conceptual framework for understanding the complexity of triggering events (Figure 9.1).

The seven steps outline what occurs, seemingly in a split second, between the time a situation happens and the point at which we unconsciously react. The model is consistent with the discussions about how people make meaning of events in the literature on group dynamics (Miller, Nunnally, & Wackman, 1976; Senge, Kleiner, Roberts, Ross, & Smith, 1994) and rational emotive therapy (Ellis & Ellis, 2011; Vernon, 2011; Wessler & Wessler, 1980).

In Step 1, the stimulus a facilitator experiences (i.e., comment, behavior, image, or personal thought) reactivates some of his or her intrapersonal dynamics (Step 2). These dynamics or *roots* could stem from current life issues, memories of past experiences, fears, unmet needs, judgments, and prejudice. In Step 3, these intrapersonal roots form a lens through which facilitators gather selective data and make meaning of what they believe has occurred. In essence, the facilitator uses this meaning to create a story of the person, motives, or events based on these intrapersonal roots, rather than on more detailed information. At Step 4, the facilitators' interpretations influence their initial cognitive, emotional, and physiological reactions, creating strong feelings or triggers. In Step 5, facilitators may still be unaware they feel triggered as they "choose" their intentions for how they will respond and engage in behaviors in light of these feelings. Their reactions (Step 6) may serve as triggers for some of the participants who then enter the triggering cycle, thereby affecting the triggered individuals and possibly the larger group. Facilitators may then experience additional triggers based on their engagement in their own triggered behavior or from the response from participants (Step 7).

I use the triggering event cycle to increase my consciousness in the moment and to diagnose where I am in the seven-step process. This helps

Figure 9.1 The Triggering Event Cycle

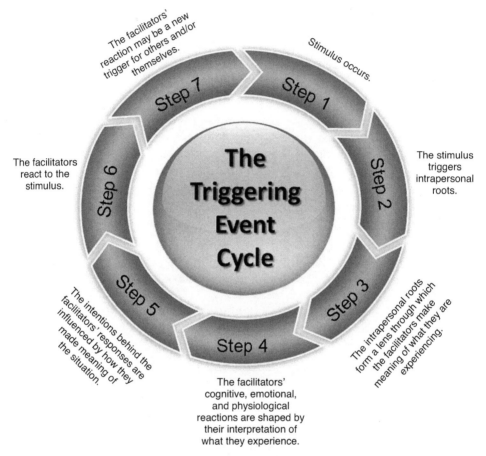

The facilitators may be a new reaction for others and/or trigger for themselves.

Stimulus occurs.

Step 7

Step 1

The facilitators react to the stimulus.

Step 6

The stimulus triggers intrapersonal roots.

Step 2

The Triggering Event Cycle

Step 5

Step 3

Step 4

The intrapersonal roots form a lens through which the facilitators make meaning of what they are experiencing.

The intentions behind the facilitators' responses are influenced by how they made meaning of the situation.

The facilitators' cognitive, emotional, and physiological reactions are shaped by their interpretation of what they experience.

me interrupt my less-productive reactions and intentionally choose more effective ways to navigate the triggering event.

The following story provides an example of the steps of the triggering event cycle. During a workshop on facilitating difficult dialogues, I asked the participants for a personal example we could use to apply concepts and tools we were discussing. I called on the first volunteer, and the example the volunteer provided involved something I had said earlier in the session that made the participant feel deeply triggered (Step 1). I realized I felt triggered when I noticed my chest felt tight and I was having trouble breathing (Step

4). I felt shaky and light-headed, and my heart was pounding in my ears. I felt scared, anxious, and incompetent. I was in shock and afraid that I wouldn't be able to facilitate a productive conversation while also being the source of the participant's trigger. I'd stopped looking at the participant and the group as I tried to figure out what to say next. I noticed my mind chatter and how I had interpreted the situation (Step 3): "I can't believe she did this to me! Is she trying to undermine me, get me back for whatever she felt I'd done?" In addition to judging and blaming the participant, I was also judging and blaming myself: "I can't handle this! I'm going to mess this up and lose all credibility with this group. What will my colleagues think of me? I never should have tried to teach this concept experientially; I just should have given them a lecture!" I knew this moment could be a powerful learning opportunity for the group or a complete disaster. I paused, prayed, took a deep breath, and decided to engage the participant as productively as I knew how (Step 5).

I asked her to say more about the experience and the impact my behaviors had on her (Step 6). As I listened, I also worked to shift my intentions from wanting to embarrass her and put her in her place to more productive ones: I intend to model the tools and skills I'm teaching, I intend to treat this person with dignity and respect, and I intend to stay open to the learning in the moment (Step 5). I paraphrased what I heard, reflecting her triggered feelings and the impact she felt from our initial interaction. As I experienced more empathy for her, I was able to shift my interpretation about the situation from "She's trying to humiliate me" to "She is triggered into a lot of pain and anger; whatever I said or did stirred up a lot for her—maybe as we talk this through she will find some release and peace, and the group can witness ways to respond when someone else is deeply triggered and they feel triggered as well." Eventually, the participant said she felt heard and that her experience had been acknowledged by me. I apologized for the impact of my actions and shared the new insights I was beginning to realize about what I would do differently in the future.

I felt good about how I was able to model in that moment many of the tools and skills to navigate difficult dialogues. After the interaction with the participant had reached an ending point, I asked the group to reflect on what they had observed and discuss effective and less-effective ways to engage in difficult dialogues. It was a powerful learning experience for everyone. In the moment I was not aware of any of the intrapersonal roots that had been restimulated (Step 2), but upon reflection I realize a number of issues contributed to my triggered reactions, including that I was feeling exhausted and depleted, and the situation reminded me of times in my past when I had felt overwhelmed, humiliated, and incompetent after receiving extremely critical feedback from supervisors. I am grateful my response to her did not serve as another triggering stimulus for her, me, or other group members (Step 7).

IDENTIFY WARNING SIGNALS

The triggering event cycle can also be used to identify warning signs so facilitators can recognize they feel triggered before they react automatically (Obear, 2007). They can then consciously choose more productive strategies to navigate triggered reactions and to facilitate the conversation in ways that align with social justice values.

It is difficult to recognize I am triggered at either Step 1 (stimulus) or Step 2 (intrapersonal roots). However, a triggered reaction can be identified at Step 3 (meaning making) if facilitators recognize their interpretations about what they believe is happening in the moment. A useful tool is to suspend the assumptions and judgments that fueled their initial interpretations and refocus their attention on just the facts of what actually occurred. For example, if during a large group discussion I see two male participants talking to each other while a woman is talking about having experienced blatant sexism, I may make up the following narrative in my mind: "Typical sexist men; so disrespectful to women who are claiming their voice and naming the truth of their experiences." As a result of my interpretation, I will most likely start to feel anger, frustration, and resentment toward these men. If I am not able to interrupt the triggering event cycle, I may react in ways that demonstrate disrespect to the male participants and undermine the sense of safety in the room.

Given the same data—two men talking to each other while a woman is sharing a personal example of sexism—I can suspend my initial assumptions and judgments and create a different narrative that opens up greater possibilities for connection: "I wonder if the two men are feeling uncomfortable . . . maybe they're recognizing times they have had similar sexist behaviors . . . or maybe one didn't understand what she is saying and didn't want to interrupt her." This narrative allows me to feel compassion for the two men. I might remember times when I felt uncomfortable as a White person listening to people of color share painful stories of racism. From a more grounded stance, I might respond in a way that invites them into the conversation rather than directly confronting their behavior, such as, "I'm curious how people are feeling as they hear this powerful story. What was the impact on you as you listened?" Even if the men were acting out of sexist attitudes, I increase the chance of furthering their learning and engagement as well as the overall session outcomes by changing my stance from one of judgment and indignation to openness, curiosity, and empathy.

Most facilitators report that if they recognize they are triggered, it often occurs at Step 4 when they notice the disproportionate intensity of their physiological, cognitive, and emotional reactions (Obear, 2000). Common physiological reactions that can serve as early warning signals include a racing pulse, pounding heart, fidgety energy, blushing, an urgent sense to respond, and difficulty breathing. In addition, facilitators may experience a variety of unconscious behaviors that upon reflection were warning signs, including clicking their pens, eye twitches, pointing their fingers, pacing, rolling their eyes, tapping their feet, and making fists.

Social justice educators may experience a wide range of emotions when they feel triggered, such as anger, frustration, defensiveness, fear, anxiety, sadness, embarrassment, guilt, and shame. They might also experience more positive emotions when they feel triggered, such as excitement, joy, compassion, empathy, and enthusiasm. I have felt deeply triggered and distracted in the moment when I was very enthusiastic about a participant's idea and became overly focused on it. At other times, I have felt such deep joy in the moment I lost track of the conversation and the intended outcomes of the activity. By noticing the intensity of our emotional reactions, we increase the chance of choosing responses that further the learning outcomes.

Another category of warning signs is cognitive self-talk. Increasing the ability to recognize inner dialogue helps us shift our thoughts and how we are defining the situation. Common types of self-talk can be organized into five categories: judgments of others, judgments of self, expectations of what self or others should do, thinking in absolutes, and taking the stance of the victim. Examples of judgments of others include "He's so arrogant," "They are so rude and immature," and "They are so resistant!" Judgments of self include "They are so much smarter than me," "This is all my fault," and "I am letting people down." Examples of expectations and "shoulds" include "I should know how to handle this," "I have to maintain control," and "They should treat me with more respect." Absolute thinking includes "They are horrible people" and "I am totally incompetent." Examples of victim stances include "They are humiliating me," "She attacked me," and "They are out to get me."

IDENTIFY COMMON TRIGGERS

A critical competency for facilitators is the ability to recognize the common actions and comments of others that hook them, as well as the self-talk and personal actions that result in triggered reactions. Facilitators can feel triggered from actions or comments of others or themselves. Common triggers from others include belittling comments, disruptive and controlling behaviors, arrogance, offensive comments, challenges to one's credibility, bullying, refusal to self-reflect or engage in dialogue, denial of privileged status, dismissing the conversation as political correctness, portraying themselves as the victim of reverse discrimination, collusion, and the expression of deep pain, grief, or anger. Examples of how facilitators can feel triggered through their own actions and thoughts include making a mistake, thoughts of self-doubt, saying something biased, and not responding effectively in the moment.

Social justice educators report the intensity of their triggered reaction varies based upon the group memberships of the person whose comments and behaviors were the source of the trigger (Obear, 2000). Facilitators more often feel triggered by the actions of those responding from various dominant group memberships, most often White male heterosexuals. A useful activity is to list your common triggers and then reflect on the following: Am I equally triggered by everyone who exhibits this behavior? Or is there a pattern related to the group memberships of the people with whom I am interacting when I feel triggered? For example, as a White person I have often felt angry when other Whites, particularly White men, question the existence of racism or make racist comments. In our dominant group identities we can also feel triggered during interactions with members of the corresponding subordinated group. For instance, if a person of color disagrees with me, I am likely to feel anxious and question my competence and feel fear that I will be confronted on my racial stereotypes and internalized dominance.

I have recognized similar patterns by group membership when I felt triggered out of my subordinated group identities. I have historically felt deep anger when encountering sexist behaviors from men that affect me or other women, as well as by homophobic comments and actions from those I perceive as heterosexual.

The combinations of intersecting group memberships add greater complexity. For example, I tend to feel triggered when other Whites do not recognize their internalized dominance and White privilege, particularly if they have significant life experience as a member of a subordinated group, for example, Whites who identify as lesbian, gay, bisexual, or transgender (LGBT). Similarly, I tend to feel a greater intensity of emotions if these same LGBT White people have privileged status by hierarchical level and class status. In contrast, I feel less triggered if the White LGBT participants are working class or employed in entry-level positions.

It is important for facilitators to recognize the common situations in which they feel triggered and anticipate comments and behaviors that may be triggers for them based upon the multiple, intersecting group memberships of the people involved.

UNDERSTAND COMMON REACTIONS

Another key competency for facilitators is to know how they typically react when triggered. When I am aware of my common triggered reactions, I am more likely to recognize I feel triggered and intentionally choose a response that aligns with my social justice values. I find it helpful to measure the intensity of triggered emotions using a scale of 0 to 10, with 0 being no emotional reaction and 10 being an extremely high level of emotional reaction. When my triggered emotions are around a 3–4 level of intensity, I am usually present enough to use tools to respond more effectively: conduct a systems check of myself, use stress management techniques to get more centered, think through the trigger to realign my self-talk with positive intentions, and then choose an effective response. However, when my emotions are more intense, around a level 6–7, I am far more likely to react without conscious thought. My reaction may be useful in the moment, though more often my behavior runs counter to the learning goals and community guidelines. If I feel triggered to a level 9–10, I rarely have the capacity to respond effectively. When facilitators feel deeply triggered it takes significant self-awareness, focus, and skill to effectively navigate themselves and the situation.

It is important that social justice educators recognize times they have felt deeply triggered and have responded in productive ways that further learning goals. By identifying their effective skills and tools in these situations they may be more likely to use them in future triggering moments. Facilitators have identified numerous responses that were more productive and aligned with their core social justice values (Obear, 2000), including the following:

- Use self-disclosure to share personal thoughts, feelings, and experiences to make a connection with the participant or participants.
- Reflect on their triggered reactions and use them as a gauge for what might be occurring in the group.
- Ask questions to gain time to get more centered, accurately understand the participant's perspective, and intentionally choose a response; it may also help the participant or participants hear themselves and reflect on what they said or did and the impact they had.
- See yourself in the participant and try to relate to the participant or participants whose behavior is the source of the trigger in order to build a connection before offering a differing perspective.
- Ask the participants to walk you through their thought processes so you can better understand how they came to their assumptions and conclusions.
- Invite others to share more about their reactions.
- Ask questions to clarify the other person's intent.
- Acknowledge the triggering moment, and invite others to express their feelings.
- Summarize or paraphrase the central issues or feeling statements you heard mentioned.
- State where you agree as well as where you disagree.
- Describe the behavior that was the source of your trigger.
- Ask others to take the pulse of the situation and reflect on the group process.
- Interrupt the group dynamics to reestablish the group's norms and guidelines.
- Invite participants to explore their triggered reactions.
- Confront the other person with care.
- Invite others to join in the dialogue if only a few people are speaking with each other.
- Pause and meditate or seek reflective insights.
- Use humor to de-escalate the situation before approaching the participant.
- Apologize for unproductive behaviors.
- Take a timeout, or table the discussion for a later time.
- Redirect the conversation to the focus of the discussion.

When I feel centered and present during a triggering event, I am more likely to choose one of these more productive responses.

When facilitators feel deeply triggered they tend to react unproductively in one of three ways: fight, flight, or freeze. Common fight reactions include pushing harder to make their points, shifting into a telling mode, debating and arguing, making sarcastic or patronizing comments, belittling others, and insisting they are right. Flight responses include ignoring the situation, redirecting the conversation away from the topic, downplaying the conflict, minimizing feelings or the impact of behaviors, and judging and blaming themselves. Freeze reactions include withdrawing, having panic attacks, shutting down, and becoming overly focused on a participant.

REGAIN CENTER AND RESPOND EFFECTIVELY

When facilitators feel a sense of urgency, an impulsive energy to fight, flee, or freeze, this is most likely a signal that they are triggered. At whichever step of the triggering event cycle they notice they are triggered, it is critical to immediately stop, assess themselves, and use some of the following tools to regain enough centeredness to intentionally choose an effective response, rather than reacting on automatic pilot.

Conduct a Systems Check

A critical first step is to conduct a systems check, which includes becoming aware of the intensity of your emotional reactions (scale 0–10); your feelings; your physical reactions and sensations; the data you were focusing on before you felt triggered (external or personal comments, behaviors, thoughts, images, etc.); your inner dialogue; the assumptions and interpretations you are creating about the situation; your initial intentions for how to respond; any automatic, unconscious reactions; and any insights on the intrapersonal roots that may be restimulated in the situation.

Once facilitators recognize they feel triggered, it is important to use self-management tools to gain greater clarity and presence. It may be useful to allow time to reflect and slow down their triggered reactions by taking a break, assigning a reflective writing prompt, or having participants pair up to talk about their feelings and reactions (Weinstein & Obear, 1992).

It can be helpful when facilitators use stress-releasing techniques, such as deep breathing, stretching exercises, shifting their attention to the physical surroundings, taking a drink of water, or repeating a mantra ("Everything happens for a reason" or "Trust the process"). They might use visualization techniques to imagine responding effectively. Some facilitators find it useful to quickly talk with a colleague or to write out their feelings, self-talk, and intentions as a way to get more centered.

Recommit to Core Values

A critical tool for responding effectively is to reground oneself in social justice values. Facilitators can breathe deeply as they remember their core intentions for engaging in social justice dialogues. They can bring their attention back to these core values by using them as a mantra. When facilitators shift their intent, they are more likely to respond in ways that align with their integrity and values.

Shift Your Inner Dialogue

We create our own reality by the interpretations and assumptions we make during a triggering situation. Shifting unproductive stories about triggering situations provides a significant opportunity to respond more effectively. Facilitators can ask themselves, "Is what I am thinking a fact or an assumption?" When I clarify the actual facts of the situation I usually experience a decrease in my emotional reactions and a greater capacity to consider alternative narratives. As I change how I interpret the triggering event I usually gain clarity and perspective to help me choose a more productive response. Table 9.1 shows examples of replacing unproductive self-statements with more useful inner dialogue.

When facilitators reframe their thoughts, they can shift their feelings from anger, fear, judgment, and shame to greater openness, curiosity, compassion, faith, and humility. From this stance they are far more likely to choose a response that aligns with core values about social justice education.

EXPLORE INTRAPERSONAL ROOTS

Imagine you are walking in a park and you notice a man and a woman in their late 70s walking hand-in-hand in front of you. What are you feeling as you watch them? And what might be the reasons or roots fueling your feelings? When I have asked this of participants I have been amazed by their

Table 9.1
REPLACING UNPRODUCTIVE SELF-STATEMENTS

If I think	I can shift my thoughts to
I can't handle this!	If I make a mistake, I can use it as a learning moment.
This is going to be disastrous!	What's the worst that can happen? How important is this in the scope of things? I'll do the best I can. . . . This, too, shall pass.
I should know the answer to that!	My role is to help others find their own answers and use their voice. I can say "I don't know" and ask others for input.
They are trying to undermine me!	This isn't about me; it is about them. I wonder what their unmet needs are? What would help the group learn from this moment?
They are such ignorant bigots!	I wonder what threatens or scares them? When have I felt similarly or done something like this before?
Their reaction is so inappropriate!	I wonder what is really going on for them. Did I say or do something that was a trigger for them?
They don't like me.	Some people may not like me. If this is a useful interaction, people may leave feeling confused and full of unsettled questions.
They're not getting it! I'm a failure!	I will do the best I can. People will take away from here what they need.
They are so resistant!	They feel safe enough to be honest about their thoughts and feelings. Now we can get to the heart of this issue.
They are so rude to interrupt me!	I don't appreciate their timing, but at least they are willing to engage in this dialogue.
I made such a stupid comment!	I learned stereotypes just like everyone else. I can model how to explore what I said and apologize for the impact of my behavior.

range of answers. People may feel deeply sad because this couple reminds them of a grandparent who recently died. Another is impatient and afraid to be late because the couple is walking too slowly. Some are joyful and hopeful they might have a close companion in later years. Others feel angry because society allows men and women to show affection but not people of the same gender. Others feel scared because they are in their 50s and do not have anyone close in their lives to take care of them if they get seriously ill. One may feel angry that the example reinforces the gender binary.

People can experience the same stimulus and yet have very different interpretations and feelings. Triggered reactions are rooted in intrapersonal issues, such as fears, judgments, old traumas and wounds, unmet needs and values, and biases and assumptions. Educators are usually unaware a comment or action has restimulated intrapersonal roots (Obear, 2000). These reactivated intrapersonal issues can have an impact on facilitators at every step of the triggering event cycle (Obear, 2007). Those who explore the roots of their triggers and participate in personal healing work experience fewer triggering events as well as greater skill and confidence when navigating triggers they encounter. The following example illustrates how unresolved intrapersonal roots can fuel unproductive triggered reactions.

I remember feeling deeply triggered by the actions of the lead trainer who was an older heterosexual male colleague. As we planned the diversity session I had recommended a number of ideas he did not incorporate into the design. I was feeling frustrated but didn't address the situation. When he didn't use my next suggestion, I felt angry and dismissed, invisible, and very small. My head swirled with questions, including "Is he being homophobic? Is this ageism or sexism? Or are my ideas not that good?" I shut down and had trouble working with him for the rest of the session. I now see how his behaviors had restimulated painful memories and unhealed wounds of when my father and other authority figures had shut me out, ignored me, or dismissed my input. If I had been more centered and self-aware during the planning of the session, I might have honestly discussed my feelings in the moment and explored how my intrapersonal roots were affecting how I was interpreting his behavior. By shutting down, I missed an opportunity to have an honest dialogue with him, deepen our relationship, and possibly cocreate a more effective design.

The following seven categories of roots may help social justice educators explore the intrapersonal issues that influence triggered reactions.

Current Life Issues and Dynamics

When I am feeling centered, joyful, rested, well fed, and healthy, I am far less likely to feel deeply triggered. Daily demands deplete our ability to shield ourselves from the impact of comments and behaviors. Examples of current life issues include illness, relationship problems, financial concerns, challenges at work or school, and stress over national or world issues.

Cumulative Impact of Past Experiences

The emotions and impact from multiple related dynamics may build up over time and overflow in the moment. When the intensity of my triggered reaction is disproportionate to the current stimulus, I may be reacting out of the accumulated impact of similar situations. To untangle this root it can be useful to ask myself, "Does this situation remind me of recent events?"

Unresolved Past Issues, Traumas, and Wounds

Emotional baggage from our past can weigh us down and divert attention from the present moment. Examples of old wounds include past betrayals; violations of boundaries through abuse, bullying, and violence (physical, emotional, sexual, and spiritual); experiences of humiliation; regrets over lost opportunities; experiences of abandonment; witnessing the abuse of others; death of loved ones and cherished pets; and experiences of discrimination. When I think I may have restimulated old wounds it can be useful to ask myself, "Does this situation remind me of any past traumas?" Recognizing when my current reactions are fueled by unresolved old wounds helps me to disentangle myself from the retriggered roots and focus on what is actually occurring in the present moment.

Fears

When I feel significant fear I am more likely to fuel unproductive triggered reactions. Examples of fears include those related to issues of competence ("I can't handle this," "What if I make a mistake?" "They will see how prejudiced I really am"), control ("People will get too emotional"), belonging ("I'll let people down," "People won't like me"), safety ("What if they attack me?" "What if I can't protect others?"), effectiveness ("Things won't change," "I could make this worse"), and worthiness ("Maybe I'm not good enough to do this work," "Maybe I'm a fraud").

Identifying the fears fueling triggered reactions helps facilitators recognize them in the moment and open the possibility to choose courage and faith over fear.

Universal Needs/What I Value

In his book *Nonviolent Communication* (2005), Marshall Rosenberg explored his belief that everything we do is to satisfy our unmet needs. When we feel triggered, the actions of others have most likely challenged some of our core values and universal human needs. Some of the values and needs I believe are related to triggering events include respect, dignity, trust, order, fairness, understanding, honesty, inclusion, competence, harmony, safety, integrity, belonging, consideration, and dependability. I have found Rosenberg's work particularly helpful when I trigger myself into feelings of judgment, guilt, blame, and shame. Instead of unconsciously reacting in a triggering moment, I can focus on the unmet needs that are underneath my feelings and work to get my needs met in ways that further learning goals. For example, if I feel triggered when someone challenges my credibility to be speaking about issues of social justice, instead of reacting by listing my degrees or the group memberships of my best friends, I can stop and consider my unmet needs in the moment. This type of challenge could be related to my values for integrity, effectiveness, and mattering. I can shift my inner dialogue to address these needs by thinking, "I really want to be useful and for my work to matter and make a difference. I intend to work from a place of integrity." If I acknowledge these universal needs, I am less likely to judge others or myself and instead may respond by saying,

> I sometimes have the same question about whether I am competent enough or worthy enough to be facilitating these conversations. I really value integrity and I want to be useful in these dialogues. I am committed to creating greater equity and social justice and to being authentic and fully present with you. I am open to learn what I don't know and am willing to share my knowledge and experience as well. And I hope together we can learn from each other as we continue to figure out how to create greater inclusion and social justice on campus.

Whenever I notice I feel triggered it is helpful to wonder, "What are my unmet needs in the moment?" This question reminds me that everything I feel, do, and say is related to trying to meet some core values and universal human needs and not because I am bad or unworthy. If I can identify the underlying values and needs that were triggered in the moment, I can re-affirm their importance to me and try to meet them in productive ways.

Ego-Centered Desires

Most facilitators relate to struggling with a variety of ego-centered desires when they feel triggered, such as wanting more power and control, trying to change others, wanting to be liked, trying to make everyone happy, and demanding predictability (Obear, 2000). When I feel triggered I can ask myself, "How is my ego involved? Am I more focused on what I want or think should happen and not as grounded in the needs of the participants?"

Biases, Prejudices, Assumptions, Expectations, and Judgments

I am most useful when I am clear, present, and centered. Unfortunately, I often cloud my vision with the biases, judgments, assumptions, and expecta-tions I bring into the conversation. I do not see people in their humanity when I treat them based on prejudice and stereotypes. When I place "shoulds" and expectations on others and myself, I usually trigger myself into frustration, resentment, and disappointment. A more useful way for me to make meaning of an event is to focus on what is more productive or less productive given the context, needs, and intentions of the situation. I am more effective when I focus on the usefulness of behaviors within a given context rather than on my judgment of the goodness or worthiness of other people or myself.

There is a spiritual principle: We are what we judge. I have discovered powerful insights when I have explored what parts of myself I have disowned when I judge these characteristics in others. As I continue to explore and dismantle internalized dominance from my socialization in multiple domi-nant group memberships, I am increasingly able to engage out of compas-sion, connectedness, and clarity when I feel triggered in a situation that I experience from a subordinated group identity.

PATHS TO HEALING

I believe triggering events are a mirror reflecting parts of ourselves that need attention and healing. I have come to view triggers as gifts that indicate our readiness to unpack old baggage and heal from old traumas. I am convinced we can heal ourselves enough to minimize the impact of most of our intrapersonal roots.

Soon after feeling deeply triggered it is helpful for facilitators to create the space to safely release their emotions and explore the roots of the triggering event. They may discover habitual old patterns and survival strategies that no longer serve their higher purpose. It takes courage to honestly explore the past and identify unfinished business and unhealed wounds. Using their current skills and wisdom, facilitators can free themselves from the baggage they have carried for so long. Healing old unfinished business can help them complete this aspect of their past, learn from it, and move on. Unless facilitators examine and heal the underlying roots fueling triggered reactions, they will most likely continue to react unproductively to similar situations in the future.

I believe social justice educators have an ethical responsibility to be a clear instrument of service in this work. By this I mean we do not "work our issues" on the group, we do no harm, and we model the skills and social justice competencies we espouse. I also believe we need to commit ourselves to a lifelong process of personal healing, since the occasional focus rarely yields the necessary results. Facilitators have found it helpful to create a structure for healing work to regularly explore their roots, express emotions, heal old wounds, and practice forgiveness (Obear, 2000), such as therapy; working with a spiritual adviser, mentor, or peer coach; support groups; 12-step recovery programs; and meditation. It has also been critical to continually rebalance my lifestyle to minimize the current life issues depleting my emotional shield and pay more attention to how I work, play, exercise, eat, love, serve, pray, and socialize.

One helpful healing practice for facilitators is to keep a journal about their triggering events using a structure of prompts that align with the triggering event cycle. After writing out the details of the triggering events as if they were experiencing them in the moment, facilitators then describe their feelings, inner judgments, interpretations and accusations, and so on, as if expressing them to a trusted friend. The next step is to identify their unmet needs in that moment and explore how their triggered reactions were unconscious attempts to get their needs met. It is helpful to then identify ways they now wish they had responded that were aligned with their core social justice values. It can be useful to review what they have written and then write in a journal about their insights and lessons learned from the triggering events, how they have grown and changed, and their intentions as they continue to facilitate social justice discussions in the future. Writing about past triggering events in this way is a powerful reminder that triggers are a gift, a valuable teacher, and a window to personal healing.

CONCLUSION

Triggering events are a common phenomenon for social justice educators (Obear, 2000). Facilitators can use the triggering event cycle as a diagnostic tool and use stress management techniques to shift their interpretations and intentions as they choose effective responses that further learning goals and model the behaviors they espouse. The end goal is not to never feel triggered again, but to recognize that triggers signal the opportunity for deeper work. Welcome the wake-up call and commit to a lifelong process of deepening self-awareness and healing. I believe it is our ethical responsibility as social justice educators to respond in ways that model our core values of respect, dignity, equity, and growth. Triggering events challenge me to live my values each and every moment. As I continue to learn and complete deep healing work, I am more self-aware, confident, and skilled as an instrument of change and service in the world.

REFERENCES

Bell, L. A., Love, B., Washington, S., & Weinstein, G. (2007). Knowing ourselves as social justice educators. In M. Adams, L. A. Bell, & P. Griffin (Eds.), *Teaching for diversity and social justice: A sourcebook* (2nd ed., pp. 381–393). New York, NY: Routledge.

Ellis, A., & Ellis, D. J. (2011). *Rational emotive therapy.* Washington, DC: American Psychological Association.

Goodman, D. J. (1995). Difficult dialogues: Enhancing discussions about diversity. *College Teaching, 43*(2), 47–52.

Griffin, P. (1997). Introductory module for the single issue courses. In M. Adams, L. A. Bell, & P. Griffin (Eds.), *Teaching for diversity and social justice: A sourcebook* (pp. 35–66). New York, NY: Routledge.

Hardiman, R., Jackson, B., & Griffin, P. (2007). Conceptual foundations for social justice education. In M. Adams, L. A. Bell, & P. Griffin (Eds.), *Teaching for diversity and social justice: A sourcebook* (2nd ed., pp. 35–66). New York, NY: Routledge.

Miller, S., Nunnally, E. W., & Wackman, D. B. (1976). The awareness wheel. In J. W. Pfeiffer & J. E. Jones (Eds.), *The 1976 handbook for group facilitators* (pp. 120–123). San Diego, CA: University Associates.

Obear, K. (2007). Diversity practitioner tools: Navigating triggering events: Critical skills for facilitating difficult dialogues. *The Diversity Factor, 15*(3), 23–29.

Obear, K. H. (2000). *Exploring the phenomenon of triggering events for social justice educators* (Doctoral dissertation). Available from ProQuest Dissertations and Theses database. (UMI No. 304606453)

Rosenberg, M. (2005). *Nonviolent communication* (2nd ed.). Encinitas, CA: PuddleDancer.

Senge, P., Kleiner, A., Roberts, C., Ross, R. B., & Smith, B. J. (1994). *The fifth discipline fieldbook: Strategies and tools for building a learning organization.* New York, NY: Doubleday.

Vernon, A. (2011). Rational emotive behavior therapy. In D. Cappuzzi & D. R. Gross (Eds.), *Counseling and psychotherapy* (5th ed., pp. 237–261). Alexandria, VA: American Counseling Association.

Weinstein, G., & Obear, K. (1992). Bias issues in the classroom: Encounters with the teaching self. In M. Adams (Ed.), *Promoting diversity in college classrooms: Innovative responses for the curriculum, faculty, and institutions* (pp. 39–51). San Francisco, CA: Jossey-Bass.

Wessler, R. A., & Wessler, R. L. (1980). *The principles and practices of rational-emotive therapy.* San Francisco, CA: Jossey-Bass.

10

When Neutrality Is Not Enough

Wrestling With the Challenges of Multipartiality

robbie routenberg, Elizabeth Thompson, and Rhian Waterberg

ULTIPARTIALITY IS A complex facilitation technique used in education and social justice organizations. The term *multipartiality* comes from the field of conflict resolution (Schrage & Giacomini, 2009; Wing & Rifkin, 2001), where social justice educators closely consider the role of social identity and differential social power in their mediation practice. The scholarship demonstrates how critical this consideration is and provides a set of strategies relevant to conflict resolution. In this chapter, we adapt this conceptual framework to the context of social justice education and provide tangible considerations for practice.

Social justice education is unique because of its equity-based learning goals and process. Hackman (2008) differentiated social justice education by its "deep focus on issues of power and privilege and how they impact everything from the ability of students to learn to the ability for justice and equity to be achieved in our society" (p. 27). A common element of social justice education is the commitment to cofacilitation in which two or more people—often with different social identities—work together to guide the group learning. Each of us has had myriad experiences with cofacilitation and believes it affects the ways we convey multipartial approaches. As stated in Chapter 1, Hackman (2005) offered five goal areas for social justice education: (a) understanding of content, (b) experience of critical analysis,

(c) strategies and tools for social action, (d) strategies for reflection and intro-spection, and (e) a mindfulness of group dynamics and patterns related to identity. We believe that to achieve these goals, social justice educators need to demonstrate congruence by embodying an understanding of identity and justice (which includes an understanding of social power dynamics) while working toward these goals. In this chapter, we offer reflections on our experiences with multipartiality—a technique to level power within interactions—in our facilitation. We hope to illustrate the importance of this method, identify the challenges that accompany it, and demonstrate multi-partiality as an important tool in social justice facilitation.

UNDERSTANDING CONCEPTS

In most classroom instruction, an educator is taught to be neutral (or impar-tial), ensuring that all voices are heard equally and the educator's own bias is kept silent (Bens, 2005; Schwarz, Davidson, Carlson, & McKinney, 2005). Impartiality is often perceived as a technique used to avoid enacting unequal power dynamics between groups. However, impartial facilitation may lead to subconsciously ignoring the existing power dynamics or to conscious deci-sions not to name inequities that are brought up when engaging in dialogue. In social justice education, neutrality is not enough. Drawing from critical race theory and racial identity development theory (Hardiman, 1982; Hardi-man & Jackson, 1992), it is suggested that being completely neutral is not possible; all perspectives are biased toward one philosophy or another whether or not bias is explicitly conveyed. This set of literature challenges student affairs professionals to be conscious of the powerful messages learned from society.

As discussed throughout this book, society provides us with a myriad of assumed truths that privileges some social groups while marginalizing many others. Some examples include the notion that if you work hard enough you will succeed, the closure of shops and restaurants on Sundays to respect the Sabbath, and the belief that having bathrooms for women and men provides an appropriate space for everyone. These kinds of assumptions can be referred to as *dominant narratives* or *master narratives* and can be voiced by any participant, regardless of the person's social identities (Stanley, 2007). Stanley defined *dominant narratives* as "a script that specifies and controls how some social processes are carried out" (p. 14) and assumes that all people's experiences resemble those of the privileged groups.

If educators remain neutral (or impartial) when these dominant narratives are shared, the power of these narratives is maintained. While referring to the political nature of narrative interaction, Wing and Rifkin (2001) stated, "When we do not recognize that there is unequal access to the narrative process and when we do not adjust our interventions accordingly, we then support the maintenance of hegemonic power relationships" (p. 191). Challenging dominant narratives is difficult and involves nuanced practice. It is, however, critical that we create opportunities for these narratives to be unpacked and analyzed to better understand the foundations of our personal viewpoints and how these viewpoints were created. Such thinking creates substantial space for counternarratives—those that illuminate the inaccuracy of the dominant narratives—to enter the conversation. Stanley (2007) defined *counternarratives* as "perspectives that run opposite or counter to the presumed order and control" (p. 14). In addition, Stanley explained that counternarratives deconstruct the significance and meaning of dominant narratives while providing alternatives to current dominant discourse.

Social justice facilitation is an exercise in power as we decide how we want to engage with students and challenge them to push themselves and each other. Multipartiality is a method of leveling power within an interaction; it simultaneously identifies inequities perpetuated during discussion and raises awareness of how these inequities have an impact on the lives of people who experience privilege and oppression (Wing & Rifkin, 2001). Multipartiality is a tool that allows us to execute our commitment to equity without it weakening our facilitation; it strengthens our bonds with students experiencing oppression and guides students unaware of their privilege to increased awareness (McClintock, 2000).

Even when understood in theory, multipartiality can be difficult to integrate into practice. Many social justice educators can confuse multipartiality with partiality—or biased facilitation—drawing clear preference to counternarratives and not providing time for dominant narratives. Privileging counternarratives can actually stifle the depth of critical analysis and can cause participants who believe in the dominant narrative (many of whom will) to withdraw from the conversation. Applying multipartiality in facilitation is a delicate balance between impartiality and partiality; it entails navigating this liminality and validating numerous perspectives rather than showing preference for one over another. It is also crucial to incorporate multipartiality with a mindfulness of the role that identities and justice play in any conversation; naming incidents of racism, classism, homophobia, genderism, and ableism reminds us that working toward social justice is an ongoing process that continues during facilitation.

This chapter offers three examples from our experiences in attempting to implement multipartiality. In the first example, an attempt at multipartiality that falls closer to impartiality is described. The second example demonstrates an attempt that comes closer to multipartiality (in that one of the two facilitators attempts the technique) but does not fully incorporate a multipartial approach. The third example is closest to actual multipartiality. By compartmentalizing the examples in this way, we hope to clarify the intricacies of multipartiality and the spectrum of strategies possible.

Terms used throughout this chapter are a product of the literature and social justice education practice that informs our approach and were discussed in this book's preface and previous chapters (i.e., *target*, *agent*, *privilege*, and *oppression*). As demonstrated in the examples that follow, multipartiality occurs in a variety of ways depending on the context; what remains consistent, however, is that these concepts are fundamental to understanding multipartiality as a facilitation technique.

NARRATIVE 1: AN EXAMPLE OF IMPARTIALITY—ROBBIE ROUTENBERG

Multipartiality, as a skill, can be used during facilitation and made into a life philosophy for people working toward social justice. For example, in assigning who would write each example, we intentionally decided to challenge a dominant narrative that exists: people with more experience in something are more skilled at it. Because I have been a social justice educator the longest, we decided that I would write about an experience where multipartiality was not implemented well. Although a subtle challenge to a dominant narrative that more experienced facilitators would make fewer mistakes, this in and of itself was an act of multipartiality.

As social justice educators, it is important to remember that none of us are invincible to society's messages. Although we can strive to be the most thoughtful, intentional, and articulate facilitators, we still fall victim to our socialization and the pervasiveness of dominant narratives. Instead of feeling guilty or embarrassed, we must recognize and accept that we are affected by socialization and the impact of dominant narratives on our actions and behaviors. With this, I offer a time that I attempted to be multipartial as a facilitator and performed as an impartial facilitator.

In my professional role I was responsible for training and supporting undergraduate and graduate students to be campus social justice educators.

I worked with a program that offers a three-day social justice ally development retreat each semester. As program staff, we worked hard to recruit a diverse group of students to attend this retreat. One particular recruitment goal was to improve our outreach to international students who are often left out of conversations regarding social justice issues. Our efforts seemed fruitful one semester when about one quarter of the retreat participants had significant prior international experience, whether they were born outside the United States or had spent most of their formative years living outside the United States. We were excited about this milestone and about having these voices at the retreat. However, many of the facilitators did not realize the U.S.-centeredness of the curriculum and facilitation, creating the potential for silencing international student participants.

This retreat showed me just how pervasive U.S.-centric social justice education could be. I believed that social justice issues had worldwide realities; I know of several countries where racism, gender issues, and related oppressions exist. Inaccessible buildings and outdoor spaces that marginalize people with physical disabilities are prevalent in societies everywhere. This understanding led me to operate from the dominant narrative that everyone would be able to relate their personal experiences to our conversations on particular social inequities and injustices. This expectation was never voiced but was implicit in my facilitation and the facilitation of my colead facilitators.

By the second day, many of the international students had said very little. We knew language was a hindrance for some and attributed their silence solely to this factor. For others, we assumed speaking in a large group of 40 people was uncomfortable, an assumption we made for many of the people in the group regardless of identity. However, we could not ignore their missing voices and perspectives.

On the second day, some of these students expressed their discomfort to the group about an exercise. One of the other lead facilitators and I were facilitating an activity on key concepts in social justice education and hoped to have participants in the group discuss their understandings of these foundational concepts. We posted five scenarios around the room depicting very different examples of *oppression* and *privilege* that we used to illustrate these key terms. Several students voiced their discomfort, accusing the scenarios of being U.S.-centric; the sentiments were that these situations would not happen in most places outside the United States.

I remember feeling frustrated at that moment, believing strongly that some of these scenarios could happen anywhere. I felt these individuals were not exploring their privileged identities and the ways these identities were blocking them from seeing the worldwide realities of these issues. Although I felt frustrated, I thanked people for their sentiments and continued with the exercise and into the break—not advocating for a particular belief (partiality) or challenging the existing dominant narratives that were operating (multipartiality). The activity had already gone on too long, and we were far behind schedule. I believed we could process their resistance at a later time. It was difficult for me to think of a quick way to challenge what I viewed as their discounting the heterosexism and ableism inherent in some of the scenarios, while encouraging them to share their experiences and perspectives at the retreat.

What made this moment especially difficult was the multiplicity of dominant narratives present: (a) the notion that heterosexism and ableism (as illustrated in the scenarios) are only U.S. issues, (b) social justice issues look the same worldwide, and (c) nationality does not affect the ease with which one can access conversations on social justice. To experience all of these at once complicated the facilitation significantly, making it very difficult to unpack each of them. Under this pressure, my response was to do nothing and to remain impartial.

I now realize that taking those few extra minutes would have helped address some of the dominant narratives that arose. Inviting clarification about how these scenarios were U.S.-centric and challenging everyone to imagine these examples occurring outside a U.S. context would have led to a much deeper understanding of the topics being covered. In the absence of these clarifications, misunderstanding concerning global experiences with oppression prevailed.

On the third day, we divided the group into smaller groups to participate in a role-playing exercise. Each small group prepared a five-minute scene in which an ally could intervene but did not. They enacted their scenes for the larger group, while other participants were invited to join the scene as an ally. This was an excellent activity for encountering and processing the nervousness and pressure that can come with interrupting oppression on an interpersonal level. The scene was performed once without an ally and then a second time where we challenged people to join. These scenes are replayed without much time for premeditation, simulating the required spontaneity of many of these moments in real life. One of the international students in the room expressed discomfort again, saying that he came from a more collectivist culture and this exercise felt very individualistic. He was having trouble relating to the scenario and was uncomfortable trying to intervene.

Another student who was born outside the United States offered a perspective to challenge the exercise as well. She said these scenarios felt trivial to her and seemed to be missing the seriousness of these issues, adding that she comes from a country where social justice issues often were matters of life or death.

When this happened, my cofacilitator, who was born outside the United States and had lived away from the United States for more than half his life, took over the facilitation; he created space for these students to further share their sentiments. It seemed this was an appreciated opportunity for these students, as many of them went into depth about their lived experiences in other countries, detailing nuanced differences between individualistic and collectivistic cultures and how political climates affect the ways individuals related interpersonally in their home countries. Several of the U.S.-born students asked questions and shared their experiences too, which were often in contrast to what was being said. I remember feeling this was a truly illuminating conversation and one that needed to happen; I also remember feeling that I did nothing to spark it and did very little to help facilitate it. It was my cofacilitator who shared in this target identity and who had to unfairly carry this responsibility. I wish that as the dominant group facilitator, I had played a more active role.

Lessons Learned

- ◆ In retreats or workshops participants often provide the counternarratives themselves if they are given a space for them to be shared. Inviting reactions and facilitating a sharing process is a useful strategy to unpacking dominant narratives.
- ◆ Even though time can pose a very real challenge, this cannot become an excuse for not following through with multipartiality. At the very minimum, dominant narratives can be named as such, and conversation can be saved for a later time.
- ◆ If counternarratives are not shared by students, you can explicitly describe what you are noticing. By naming the dominant narratives in the room, the group can become more equipped to discuss directly what is being asked.
- ◆ Dominant narratives can exist within the substance of what we say and in what we do not say as facilitators. It is just as important to be aware of the content of the conversation as it is to notice how each of our identities has an impact on how we participate.

As with all social justice topics, it is crucial to continually educate ourselves. Deepening our understanding of social justice and issues of equity directly informs our lives and our facilitation. As I have lived in the United States my whole life, I carry many ethnocentric messages, and this retreat helped uncover some of them. We are each responsible for educating ourselves, whether by reading books, watching films, engaging in conversations that push our learning, or any other means.

NARRATIVE 2: AN EXAMPLE OF PARTIALITY—ELIZABETH THOMPSON

One of the most significant challenges of my work has been cofacilitating with people unfamiliar with social justice concepts, specifically multipartiality. An example of a time multipartiality was moderately put into practice occurred while I was cofacilitating a training as a residence hall director. My cofacilitator was not familiar with a multipartial technique, and our unexamined differences in facilitation perspectives and in understanding multipartiality led to conflict. Exploration of cofacilitators' different experiences, beliefs, and goals requires energy and commitment. This example elaborates on the conflicts that may occur when cofacilitators have not adequately explored these issues individually or as a team.

My co–residence director and I were asked to facilitate icebreakers and team builders for staff training. In an effort to establish communication norms, I suggested we use an exercise called the Counting Game. This exercise asks participants to count to 50 without talking simultaneously, attempting to create equity in the act of counting. The participants are told that everyone else in the group must speak before they may speak again; participants close their eyes so active listening is required before they decide to speak. Although the rule about speaking once is explicitly shared, it is not always followed, which illustrates the power dynamic that exists when people with privileged identities are not fully mindful of their privilege while playing the game. The primary learning goal is for participants to consider how social identities may affect their interpersonal communication and on their choice to speak. When I was a participant, our facilitators carefully guided us through debriefing questions of increased intensity and depth, addressing issues of power and privilege. For example, during my participant experience, it was significant to note that the men in the room continued counting for the duration of the exercise, while those without gender privilege became more reluctant to participate. Upon noting this norm, I was reminded of a narrow definition of accepted masculinity in the United States: Boys and men are often socialized to compete with one another. Another dominant narrative operating was "whoever gets the farthest the fastest wins." With some coaching from our facilitators, we began to collectively understand the importance of social identity and how our socialization to dominant narratives affected whose voices were heard and whose were made invisible. Our previous experience with social justice concepts supported our ability to reach this understanding.

This first experience with the counting exercise had a lasting impression on me; therefore, I wanted to use it in our staff training. In this experience with my colleague cofacilitator, we were unaware of the students' comfort levels and familiarity with social justice concepts, particularly the links between power, privilege, oppression, and communication. Another difference in this experience was that I was in a community composed almost entirely of people of color. I am a White woman, and my cofacilitator was a Mexican American man. We had not thought through how this might affect our cofacilitation or the assumptions we brought to the experience.

My cofacilitator had never heard of the exercise but was intrigued by the description and agreed it would be a good team builder. We decided that I would serve as the lead facilitator, providing the directions and the debriefing following the exercise. My cofacilitator would interject when he felt comfortable, asking processing questions or sharing observations about the group's behavior. Within minutes of explaining the exercise, the students abandoned the guideline that encouraged everyone to say a number. Instead, a group of men clustered together on one side of the circle and dominated the counting, three of them alternating numbers. I waited patiently to see if any students would challenge this pattern, but it continued until they reached 50. "You got to 50 pretty quickly!" I interjected in a panic, hoping a student would comment on how the rule about equity in sharing numbers had been disregarded. No one said a word. "Where did you notice sound coming from?" I blurted out. I naively assumed that they would be actively listening to their peers as I had instructed, especially because their sense of sight was limited by closing their eyes. Evidently, those who offered numbers aloud without waiting their turn did so without following the instructions. As could be expected, the student staff members were at multiple points of openness and readiness to engage in and discuss the social justice issues revealed from the counting exercise. Several students looked squarely in the direction of the cluster of men in the corner. They could immediately point out who called out numbers but could not come up with any thoughts on what might have contributed to this occurence, especially as it related to social power. "Let's start over! Go!" I exclaimed. They rushed through it one more time to appease me but refused to look deeper at the possibilities of its meaning.

Observing the three male participants counting until they reached their goal prompted a strong feeling of frustration in me—often referred to in social justice literature as being *triggered*.[1] (The concept of triggers is discussed in detail by Kathy Obear in Chapter 9). These feelings interfered with my ability to think through how to best approach their behavior in a constructive way. After being triggered, I did not feel comfortable relying on my cofacilitator, who had been caught up in the exercise's competitive nature, offering observations about the speed and efficiency with which people were reaching their goal—the end point rather than the process. "But that's *not* what it's *about*!" I wanted to scream. I felt defeated, disappointed in myself and disheartened by my cofacilitator's reinforcement of exactly what I wanted our students to avoid and then process: how and why we got to the number 50, who contributed to our getting there, and what it meant.

In choosing this exercise, I hoped to prompt students to think about how their social identities, histories, and lived experiences could affect their subsequent experiences as staff members. I had high expectations for myself as a facilitator and for the exercise. I wanted it to affect my students as it had affected me. What I had forgotten was that it takes time to understand the complexities of power, privilege, and oppression. Grasping the consequences of inequity cannot—and does not—happen in a 20-minute exercise, particularly if the participants do not bring with them prior knowledge of social justice concepts. Because my students and I are different people with vastly different lived experiences, they could not possibly have reactions that were identical to mine.

Despite my experience with social justice education, I still receive privilege based on my race, class, sex, and nation of origin. I mistakenly assumed, with my knowledge of oppressive social structures, that a participant group made up of predominantly students of color would thus be able to engage with me in dialogue about what it *meant*. However, experiencing oppression and understanding its complexities are not synonymous. Because a student experiences oppression does not mean that student understands the ways privilege and oppression function or that the student is ready to articulate what it means. Expecting this readiness is neither fair nor realistic of all individuals experiencing oppression.

This example of facilitation may sound like a disaster. I saw it that way for some time, until I spoke with students one-on-one who told me about their independent reflection. "I thought more about it afterwards," one student remarked, "and that after awhile I stopped counting because it felt like there wasn't any room for me. It was so frustrating." I decided not to push her much harder after that, trusting she would get there on her own. I had pushed too hard during the exercise, asking impulsive questions out of frustration about why students behaved as they had. I now recognize that sometimes being present and allowing for silence is a gift as powerful as mindful facilitation with words.

LESSONS LEARNED

- Having realistic and developmentally appropriate learning goals is important. Facilitators should have an understanding of the participants' knowledge and prior experiences to tailor the facilitation to the needs of their group.
- Remember that the effects of socialization run deep. Students cannot unlearn a lifetime of cultural and social norms in a 20-minute exercise.
- Depending on the duration of our connection with students, we may not see the positive impact of our work. Incorporate opportunities for immediate and ongoing reflection, and be at peace with this and trust that students will continue to reflect on their experience.
- Engage as a *collaborator* in the learning process rather than as someone imparting knowledge to students.
- Take the time to have open and honest conversations with your cofacilitator. Discuss your ideas, goals, and areas of discomfort. Engaging in conversation with cofacilitators about our differences and similarities in style prepares us to support one another as we put multipartiality into practice and experience our students' responses and reactions to it. Examples of important questions to discuss include, What do you need from me as a cofacilitator? What are your triggers? Do you anticipate any triggers in this context, in particular? How can I best support you as a cofacilitator when that happens?

Prior to beginning a graduate internship in social justice education, I believed that effective facilitation would require me to become a blank slate—my own beliefs, values, and priorities erased—to avoid inserting bias into the group. Through facilitation I have learned this is not possible. Furthermore, by being unaware of my own social location and subsequent socialization, I can perpetuate the very oppression I am attempting to dismantle through social justice facilitation. Thus, striving to keep multipartiality in mind allows me to become a partner with students in our learning processes.

NARRATIVE 3: AN EXAMPLE OF MULTIPARTIALITY—RHIAN WATERBERG

While facilitating social justice education, I have found multipartiality to be one of the most rewarding and challenging skills to implement. Facilitating the counternarrative requires a unique balance between self-awareness, patience, and historical knowledge. Inviting the introduction of alternative perspectives and experiences also requires facilitators to ensure that the dialogue space feels safe enough and supportive enough for these stories to be shared by participants (e.g., see Chapter 8). The following story describes a challenging and rewarding experience I had introducing and facilitating multipartiality.

This example stems from my cofacilitating a discussion on the prison industrial complex (PIC), prison-related injustices against African Americans in the United States, and the implications of understanding these systems as students providing community-based service. My cofacilitator and I had specific goals in mind, which included exposing relationships between historical injustices perpetuated against African Americans and the history and current status of the PIC. Additional goals included encouraging participants to understand their own identities in relation to criminalized identities and drawing out reflection between their lived experiences and assumptions about individuals and communities affected by the PIC.

The tools used to draw out reflection were documentary films and statistical information, which proved useful and created a dialogue space that was emotionally charged. Many participants voiced shock at the pervasive injustices of the PIC, with some expressing a sense of helplessness. As time progressed and shock settled, many dominant narratives emerged. Early in our discussion most personal stories were told by White participants and supported dominant ideas concerning "bad neighborhoods," "criminals," and the "necessity" of the prison system. Our room grew quiet as dominant attitudes were displayed in succession, seemingly challenging the questions concerning systemic and historical injustice. It began to feel difficult for my cofacilitator and me to maintain a multipartial space.

Facilitation can be challenging whether you are entering a new group of participants or working with an established group. One factor I have found particularly challenging when implementing multipartiality is knowing, as a facilitator, when to *share out* and when to *stay in*. By "share out" and "stay in," I mean understanding when it is my role as a facilitator to share a counternarrative with the group or when it may be more appropriate to acknowledge that narrative internally without telling it to the group. Presenting the counternarrative can be used to challenge a dominant narrative controlling the dialogue, to open the space to the possibility that alternative viewpoints exist, and to create safety for those participants whose lived experiences (or thought processes) are more closely aligned with counternarratives than dominant ones.

In this example, I decided to provide a counternarrative after a student said he was unsure what to do because "bad neighborhoods need to be patrolled in order to keep communities safe." I asked our students, "What makes a community bad?" After a few moments of silence I continued, "When I enter a community, I can find almost anything I'm looking for. . . . I can find crime in my own neighborhood, but I don't see police officers patrolling the streets. I can also enter 'bad' communities and see people in the streets doing things I consider 'good'; I see folks in the streets playing and organizing and helping each other. The difference for me is that when I enter these bad communities, I see police officers looking for bad things happening in them." Providing this counternarrative felt appropriate at that time for a few reasons. Our dialogue space had become increasingly quiet; I identified with a number of agent identities also held by the dominant viewpoints, and nonverbal communication in our space indicated that participants were becoming withdrawn and hesitant about speaking.

After I spoke, and with a few affirming nods from participants, another student spoke. She told the group that she grew up in a family that drew distinct lines between her neighborhood (the good neighborhood) and bad neighborhoods. The student said this led to subconscious assumptions about "bad people" who must reside in these neighborhoods and that her assumptions had gone unchallenged until she became involved with community service (the medium bringing us all together). Her story led to more stories from students who spoke of historical injustices, such as redlining in the housing market, subsequent policing in neighborhoods with higher concentrations of people of color, and the push to address disparities in drug prosecution for crack and cocaine possession (Moore, 2009).

Then my cofacilitator brought it all back, asking, "What does this have to do with the service you are involved in, and what does that mean?" Following her well-timed and much needed question, we engaged in a lively discussion on how to challenge our assumptions, how to gain accurate knowledge about historical injustice, and how to infuse knowledge about systemic injustice affecting the communities we work with into our lives. We also discussed how to act as allies in an effort to challenge injustices related to the PIC and how to become involved in community efforts that already exist (such as livable wage campaigns and transformative/restorative justice organizations).

Maintaining multipartiality and providing challenging counternarratives is rarely easy and never perfect. I believe that maintaining multipartiality in this example worked for a number of reasons. First, my cofacilitator and I discussed our individual identities openly and extensively. Next, we practiced patience in allowing for thoughts of dominance—and their counternarratives—to be fully expressed and explained. Finally, we used historical knowledge as a presentation tool and an affirmation tool.

A few compounding factors indicated to me that I should give a counternarrative at that point in our discussion. First, I had an awareness of the differing agent and target identities my cofacilitator and I held related to our topic. I also acknowledged increasing silence and tension in the midst of multiple dominant narratives. Finally, I owned my capacity to act as an ally of my cofacilitator and other participants in the group by sharing a counterviewpoint. For me, owning the privilege that allowed me to speak in that moment meant keeping it short and spending my time wisely. I asked a single question and shared a personal example. A single question and a single story (dominant narrative or counternarrative) changed the air of our group conversation. In this instance, it opened the space for another student to share a personal experience, which ran counter to her socialization and counter to the dominant narratives of the topic.

Every pair of cofacilitators has set goals and expectations for their experience with a particular group. When things begin to deviate from our expectations and seem to stray from our goals, it can be difficult to quell anxiety and fear that may arise in our minds and hearts. In these intense moments, staying engaged while reassessing the dialogue is crucial to addressing the dominant assumptions being shared and for opening space for the experiences that dispute those assumptions. My cofacilitator and I hoped to encourage our group to think more critically about the PIC, the community members they work with, and their capacity to act as allies to end injustices that span race, gender, and socioeconomic status, to name just a few. When dominant narratives arose and began to lead our conversation, we employed a balance of personal discomfort and patience to understand the underlying assumptions of these perspectives. We also sought to pinpoint the most appropriate time to introduce a counternarrative. Reassessing the space and allowing dominant viewpoints to be explained helped my cofacilitator and me respond in a multipartial and appropriate way to the stories and questions being shared. Allowing participants to fully explain their dominant perspectives while providing the counternarrative also solidified our space as one in which all thoughts are respected, respectfully challenged, and genuinely considered and discussed. In presenting the counterperspective without shutting down the dominant narrative, our space became a positive space for all participants while acknowledging the dominant narrative was not the lived experience of many people in the United States.

Providing historical information as a counternarrative as well as a presentation tool affirms the counterexperiences of many participants while engaging all participants in reflection about unchallenged assumptions. My cofacilitator and I pointed out connections between the 13th Amendment, the PIC, criminal prosecution (of adult and young people), and police force in low-income communities and communities of color. Although the true importance placed on fact is debatable (since factual information can be—and is—manipulated), students embedded in an academic environment may absorb and appreciate the presentation of information that challenges them to think in new ways. For our group of participants, providing historical and statistical information formed a solid foundation from which our discussion could grow. For other groups, beginning with activities that situate the discussion in the lived experiences of participants or providing exercises that actively draw out opposing viewpoints may be effective for sparking dialogue and opening space for dominant- and counterperspectives to be shared. If possible, it may be helpful to gain a little information about the participants in your group, as this will help guide the facilitation tools and activities you choose.

Although counternarratives hold the power to reframe discourse, facilitators must have an understanding of the current stability and status of their group before introducing contradictory perspectives. For instance, as a facilitator, I may plan process and content activities assuming that dominant perspectives will be shared before counterperspectives. Alternatively, I will also prepare for group development toward the exploration of counternarratives. Sometimes this means not introducing the counternarrative at the first hint of dominant narratives. Adaptability and willingness to fully explore dominant and counternarratives pushes the dialogue group toward deeper examination and discussion of alternative experiences and viewpoints.

LESSONS LEARNED

+ When possible, use an array of educational tools (in this example, historical and statistical information) to solicit dialogue content and direction from participants.
+ Be mindful of the delicate balance between the dominant narratives and counternarratives. When appropriate, allow space for dominant viewpoints to be explained, while maintaining a facilitation goal focused primarily on the deconstruction of those dominant viewpoints.
+ Understand your power (figurative and real) as a facilitator to affirm the everyday experiences students have with oppression and to empower students to share counterexperiences and dominant experiences with their peers.
+ Discuss both facilitators' identities prior to the dialogue to be better prepared for emotionally challenging facilitation moments, cofacilitator balance, and mutual support throughout the dialogue.

DISCUSSION OF LESSONS LEARNED

By reflecting on our cumulative years of social justice education experience, we outline some key lessons learned regarding multipartiality. We recognize it benefits us all to share our experiences with other social justice educators and colleagues. Shared exploration facilitates continued growth, which we hope will benefit readers who have varied experiences with multipartiality.

Multipartiality Is a Science and an Art

As a science, multipartiality involves a distinct skill set of key questions that can be asked and ways to bring counternarratives more centrally into the conversation. As an art, a simultaneous emotional experience occurs for facilitators and participants as well as an understanding that each situation is different. Knowing this, it can be difficult to cultivate multipartiality, making it especially hard to teach it to other social justice educators.

Some foundational strategies for cultivating multipartiality are (a) ask the individual contributing the dominant narrative to say where he or she learned this perspective, (b) invite reactions/responses from others in the group, (c) challenge the group to think of alternate perspectives even if they do not hold them and imagine why people might believe them, and (d) introduce other experiences including your own as a tool for learning.

Many times the dominant narrative is not what is said but rather what is not said (e.g., having a conversation on race but only talking about monoracial experiences). At moments when dominant narratives are implied and not made explicit, a successful strategy is to draw attention to the dynamics of the group. This can either be framed as a question or an observation. For example, a question could be, "Does anyone notice anything about our conversation: what we've talked about and what we haven't?" In addition, a possible statement could be, "I've noticed we've only talked about monoracial experiences and haven't addressed that this is not everyone's experience. Any ideas about what additional experiences there might be?" Drawing attention to the group dynamic can be enough to stretch participants' awareness and lead them to critically think about their experiences, perspectives, and values.

The challenge with offering strategies and framing the development of multipartiality as a skill is that it is a very emotional experience, requiring empathy, patience, and heart. Conveying empathy and respect as you challenge dominant narratives is an artful act and one that is important in keeping the learning space open and without judgment. Displaying this kind of warmth can be exhausting, especially when the comment to which you are directing this warmth has negatively affected you. Nonetheless, it is important we model this so that we can encourage our participants to treat each other with this openness as well. This emotional input and impact are part of why we think of multipartiality as an art.

Considering Facilitators' Identities When Cofacilitating Multipartiality

When cofacilitating, it is important to consider your and your cofacilitator's identities when deciding who should challenge dominant narratives. Maintaining balance between who speaks when, who tells which stories, and who asks what questions will ensure that you and your cofacilitator maintain a sense of equality concerning the direction and quality of the facilitation.

This balance is a key component to facilitating multipartiality and can offer a crucial opportunity to lead by example. Participants may feel empowered when the counternarrative affirms their lived experiences or their personal beliefs. As facilitators, we have the capacity to be living examples of narratives that are counter to the dominant narrative—giving voice to those often silenced.

In our experiences, creating multipartiality is often better received by agent participants when delivered by a facilitator who holds similar agent identities. This should not be surprising because dominant narratives surrounding agent identity reinforce the false idea that agent-directed narratives are more justified and believable. In those instances when agent-identified participants are (a) responding favorably to counternarratives presented by agent-identified facilitators or (b) dismissing the counternarratives presented by target-identified facilitators, the agent-identified facilitator holds particular power. This can be embraced by the agent facilitator as a moment to act as an ally in favor of counternarratives. This can also be an instance when agent-identified facilitators stay engaged so that their cofacilitators can speak from their own lived experiences. When preparing for facilitation, the cofacilitators can discuss dominant narratives that may be shared, how to frame the counternarrative, and what role each facilitator is comfortable assuming.

Of course, confronting dominant viewpoints becomes increasingly complicated when considering multiple and intersecting identities. It is beneficial for facilitators to understand differences between personal identity (how you identify yourself) and perceived identity (identities others ascribe to you). For instance, what happens when a participant perceives one facilitator as a straight man and begins to share dominant narratives concerning sexual orientation and sexual predetermination? Undoubtedly, that participant looks to that facilitator for affirmation and support. When that facilitator identifies as neither straight nor male, does presenting the counternarrative require that he out himself to this participant or the group? Boundaries concerning personal identity, outing oneself, and safety vary from facilitator to facilitator and are crucial for maintaining safety and support between facilitator teams. Sharing boundaries, social identities, and support needs prior to the dialogue will better prepare facilitator teams to cope with dominant narratives that depend on their personal and perceived identities.

Participants Can Challenge Dominant Narratives

A wonderful moment in facilitation is when a participant challenges a dominant narrative or adds a counternarrative. This can push the dialogue toward a place of multipartiality with less effort from the facilitators and illustrates the ownership that participants can have over their learning environment. Facilitators have key ways to set up a learning space where this is more likely to happen. We often ask groups to generate guidelines and expectations early so they know each other's needs in order to create a safer space. Sharing hopes and fears early, as well as creating several intentional opportunities for risk taking and trust building, are some helpful tools for creating learning environments where participants challenge each other in productive ways.

When participants share counternarratives, we believe the facilitator still holds responsibility for the overall safety of the space. Facilitators must be aware of the impact their reactions can have on participants. More specifically, if facilitators show excitement or affirm one participant more than others, the group may feel that there is a right or wrong answer or that you have a favored perspective. Directing affirmation toward some participants but not all can silence some participants while encouraging others, an impact that facilitators need to consider. The use of multipartiality as a facilitation tool addresses this concern by encouraging students to share and explain the origins of dominant and counternarratives. When students understand that disagreements in dialogue will be facilitated using respect, exploration, and personal experience as the backdrop, they will be willing to take the risks necessary to learn and build or reconstruct knowledge with their peers.

Multipartiality as an Educational Tool

Sometimes participants resist multipartiality as a legitimate educational style. The introduction of counternarratives and the challenge to dominant narratives can cause significant cognitive dissonance in participants. However, learning happens when we experience cognitive dissonance and are challenged to incorporate new meanings into our frameworks. Experiments carried out by Rydell, McConnell, and Mackie (2008) suggested that "as explicit-implicit discrepancies in attitude increased, people were motivated to carefully consider subsequently presented, relevant information" (p. 1526). Rydell et al. also indicated that cognitive dissonance is aroused by attitudinal discrepancies and that this encourages individuals to seek out additional information associated with the subject of such dissonance. This information seeking and processing is done in an effort to reduce cognitive dissonance and reframe one's own perspectives.

Ultimately, we aim to provide a learning environment with enough challenge and support for all participants to learn and grow. Although we strive to ensure psychological safety for all participants, we are particularly attuned to the safety of target-identified participants whose lived experiences do not fit the expectations delivered in dominant narratives. We believe it is important to foster learning environments where students feel safe enough—physically and emotionally—to experience discomfort. Feelings associated with discomfort may generate responses similar to those associated with danger: anxiety, nervousness, silence, and confusion, among many other reactions. What distinguishes discomfort from danger is that discomfort leads to learning, whereas danger can distract, interrupt, or prevent it.

Applying Multipartiality as a Facilitator

The practice of multipartiality supports our understanding of the theoretical foundation of student learning. Understanding the intersections of developmental theory by Perry (Love & Guthrie, 1999a, 1999b), and King and Baxter Magolda (2005), among others, can support the development and learning of our participants by balancing challenge and growth within the cognitive, interpersonal, and intrapersonal domains. For example, King and Shuford (1996) suggested, "Encouraging multiple voices to be heard in the classroom enriches classroom discussion. It also creates a challenge for faculty in trying to manage emotional responses that may ensue" (p. 160). The challenge of being aware of students' reactions goes beyond the faculty role and may be applied to facilitation more generally, as illustrated by the three situations outlined in this chapter. King and Shuford (1996) further highlighted Fried's assertion that "emotional responses are recognized as a legitimate—and desirable—part of the learning process" (p. 160). Accepting unexpected emotional reactions as part of the learning process encourages cognitive development toward reflective thinking and consideration of not only what happens to each student personally but also why a student has particular experiences and why he or she responds to them in myriad ways (King & Kitchener, 1994; King & Shuford, 1996; Love & Guthrie, 1999b). Recognizing emotional responses as legitimate components of learning is a challenge to the dominant narratives that operate in much of academia: "There is no place for emotions in the classroom" and "Learning is only a cognitive process." Making room for emotions in learning is to practice multipartiality.

Facilitators can support learning by acknowledging that exploring issues of social inequity and social justice are not easy and sometimes generate discomfort. This reinforces the importance of setting up guidelines for conversations (or brave space as Arao and Clemens discuss in Chapter 8) where participants experience discomfort in the spirit of growth in an environment where it is everyone's responsibility to maintain this space.

The Impact of Social Identities on the Utility of a Multipartial Approach

As nonneutral facilitators, our priority is focused on the presentation of materials, the creation of space, and the sharing of stories that challenge dominant narratives and inaccurate conceptions of our social, political, and economic landscape. If in single-issue discussions our privileged participants feel uncomfortable because of multipartiality, this cognitive dissonance can be evidence that learning can take place. For example, in a discussion on gender, if a cisgender-man-identified student with dominant viewpoints about gender leaves the conversation unsettled, this can be evidence of learning. Additionally, as soon as this participant leaves our discussion, society affirms his viewpoints positively and with privilege. Not only are his experiences reinforced, but his dominant viewpoints are easily corroborated by friends, academic sources, and the media. Because of this, facilitators need to be very intentional about creating this cognitive dissonance.

As multipartial facilitators, our goal is very different from biased facilitation. We strive for full engagement of all participants and actively work to avoid shutting down any participant, regardless of that participant's identity statuses. Even though discomfort and cognitive dissonance are productive feelings and lead to learning, feeling upset beyond the time parameters of the dialogue is not ideal, and facilitator follow-up in these situations will mollify ultimate withdrawal or resistance by the student. Understanding that the growth process expands beyond the walls of our facilitated discussions can be one of the hardest parts for a facilitator to wrestle with and may be incredibly upsetting for facilitators and participants alike.

Unlike many targeted participants, participants who experience privilege can find solace in the world around them. Resistance to counternarratives is a common path many students with privilege take. The development of critical thinking skills and the capacity to emotionally and intellectually understand privilege takes more time and experience than can be offered in a one-time workshop or course. As facilitators, we operate knowing the potential for the lasting impact of our practice and believe that asking tough questions concerning privilege and oppression is a first step to change.

Understanding that dominant narratives invade the subconscious of target- and agent-identified participants also makes multipartiality a continued challenge/reward balance. As mentioned, it is possible that agent-identified participants give more credence to agent-identified facilitators. It is possible that target-identified participants may also resist the counternarrative. This experience, perhaps more so than other forms of resistance, may feel particularly devastating to facilitators. Just as agent-identified participants have been indoctrinated with dominant narratives, so have target-identified participants—even if their lived experiences actually are a counternarrative.

Recognizing and Introducing Counternarratives

As facilitators, we may fear that dominant narratives hold the potential to derail our facilitation at any moment. However, we have confidence in Stanley's (2007) assertion that counternarratives deconstruct the significance and social power provided by dominant narratives. Counternarratives challenge messages about what is deemed socially acceptable, normal, and natural. They offer possibilities for how we can respond to power, privilege, and oppression, resisting those messages we do not agree with. For example, parents who allow their male child to play with dolls offer a counternarrative to a binary system of gender that suggests that boys must play with trucks or else they will not be sufficiently masculine. As attentive, skillful, multipartial facilitators, we too can offer counternarratives as we prompt students to dig deeper, to think about what it means when men's voices are consistently heard, while the women in the room stay quiet. Depending on the group's proficiency with social justice concepts, our facilitation can become more complex: In a community of color, what does it mean when the people with the lightest skin speak most often? How are native speakers of Spanish marginalized in an English-speaking facilitation? These are questions to explore collaboratively with a trusted cofacilitator because they may upset us and affect our capacity to think on our feet in facilitation.

Finally, counternarratives are engaging and interesting. They challenge our students to imagine a better world where people have equal access to resources and opportunities. We may not see the effects of counternarratives right away, but trusting our students' abilities to eventually experience their impact can be beneficial in students' and facilitators' mutual growth.

CONCLUSION

As these examples suggest, employing multipartiality can be as challenging in practice as it is to understand in theory. Being multipartial facilitators requires us to choose a more complex method of facilitation, one where we voluntarily bring our whole selves: our experiences of privilege and oppression, our commitment to social justice, and our belief in our students' abilities to engage with us on tough issues. Additionally, approaching facilitation with these complexities means we disrupt dominant narratives about what facilitation looks like in the first place; by being mindful of the questions we ask our students, we increase opportunities for them to experience intercultural awareness. Furthermore, when we open ourselves up to constant reflection, rely on people we trust—including colleagues involved in similar work—and check ourselves when we begin to lean heavily on our privilege, we can hold ourselves accountable to the work of supporting students as they move toward greater cross-cultural awareness and increase our capacities as effective facilitators for whom social justice matters.

It is important to acknowledge that multipartiality is the main characteristic that makes social justice education different from many other forms of education. Many approaches to education encourage neutrality and, at best, encourage discussion concerning multiple or oppositional viewpoints. Social justice education embraces dialogue as a major medium for learning and makes a concentrated effort to provide perspectives in conflict with dominant viewpoints. Providing multipartial facilitation lets our participants know we are not simply passive facilitators but active participants in the dialogue. We are willing to invite the unheard voices, we are willing to tell the untold stories, we are willing to challenge the traditionally unchallenged, and, most importantly, we are willing to listen, affirm, think, and discuss. Not only are we willing to do these things, but in multipartial facilitation, they are our priorities.

NOTE

1. With the increase in incidents of gun violence in the United States through school shootings and similar crimes in recent years (Columbine High School and Virginia Tech, for example) some proponents of social justice education find using *trigger* as a verb problematic. Language is powerful and generates a range of responses from readers; we acknowledge that using *trigger* is controversial in our current historical moment that is rife with violence. The word is used here because it has a history in social justice education literature when describing varying reactions elicited when engaged in dialogue about social identities, power, privilege, and oppression.

REFERENCES

Bens, I. (2005) *Advanced facilitation strategies: Tools and techniques to master difficult situations.* San Francisco, CA: Jossey-Bass.

Hackman, H. (2005). Five essential components for social justice education. *Equity & Excellence in Education, 38*(2), 103–109.

Hackman, H. (2008). Broadening the pathway to academic success: The critical intersections of social justice education, critical multicultural education, and universal instructional design. In J. Higbee & E. Goff (Eds.), *Pedagogy and student services for institutional transformation: Implementing universal design in higher education* (pp. 25–48). Minneapolis: University of Minnesota, Center for Research on Developmental Education and Urban Literacy.

Hardiman, R. (1982). *White identity development: A process oriented model for describing the racial consciousness of White Americans* (Doctoral dissertation). Available from ProQuest Dissertations and Theses database. (AAT 8210330)

Hardiman, R., & Jackson, B. (1992). Racial identity development: Understanding racial dynamics in college classrooms and on campus. *New Directions for Teaching and Learning, 1992*(52), 21–37.

King, P. M., & Baxter Magolda, M. B. (2005). A developmental model of intercultural maturity. *Journal of College Student Development, 46*(6), 571–592.

King, P. M., & Kitchener, K. S. (1994). *Developing reflective judgement.* San Fransisco, CA: Jossey Bass.

King, P. M., & Shuford, B. C. (1996). A multicultural view is a more cognitively complex view: Cognitive development and multicultural education. *American Behavioral Scientist, 40*(2), 153–164.

Love, P. G., & Guthrie, V. (1999a). Perry's intellectual scheme. *New Directions for Student Services, 1999*(88), 5–15.

Love, P. G., & Guthrie, V. L. (1999b). Synthesis, assessment and application. *New Directions for Student Services, 1999*(88), 77–93.

McClintock, M. (2000). How to interrupt oppressive behavior. In M. Adams, W. Blumenfeld, R. Castañeda, H. Hackman, M. Peters, & X. Zúñiga (Eds.), *Readings for diversity and social justice* (pp. 483–485). New York, NY: Routledge.

Moore, S. (2009, April 30). Justice dept. seeks equity in sentences for cocaine. *New York Times*, p. A17.

Rydell, R. J., McConnell, A. R., & Mackie, D. M. (2008). Consequences of discrepant explicit and implicit attitudes: Cognitive dissonance and increased information processing. *Journal of Experimental Social Psychology, 44*, 1526–1532.

Schrage, J. M., & Giacomini, N. G. (Eds.). (2009). *Reframing campus conflict: Student conduct practice through a social justice lens.* Sterling, VA: Stylus.

Schwarz, R., Davidson, A., Carlson, M., & McKinney, P. (2005). *The skilled facilitator fieldbook: Tips, tools, and tested methods for consultants, facilitators, managers, trainers, and coaches*. San Francisco, CA: Jossey-Bass.

Stanley, C. A. (2007). When counter narratives meet master narratives in the journal editorial-review process. *Educational Researcher, 36*(1), 14–24.

Wing, L., & Rifkin, J. (2001). Racial identity development and the mediation of conflicts. In C. L. Wijeyesinghe & B. Jackson III (Eds.), *New perspectives on racial identity development: A theoretical and practical anthology* (pp. 182–208). New York, NY: New York University Press.

11

Facilitating Interactive Privilege Awareness Programs

Employing Intentionality From Design Through Implementation

Gregory I. Meyer, Karen Connors, Rebecca Heselmeyer, Dusty M. Krikau, Tracy L. Lanier, Matthew R. Lee, Chris D. Orem, and Nancy Trantham Poe

THROUGHOUT THIS BOOK the contributors have addressed approaches to social justice facilitation in the context of classroom settings, workshops, ongoing dialogue groups, retreats, and staff training. Typically, facilitation is the process of a person or team guiding participants through a variety of activities and reflection opportunities to help them make meaning aimed at a particular learning outcome (McCain & Tobey, 2004). Effective facilitation, however, begins long before participants enter the room. Intentional program design, preparation, and implementation are all integral to the successful facilitation of participants' achievement of stated learning outcomes. In this chapter, we present our process of developing an intentional program design aimed at social justice goals. We hope to show how the process and the individuals involved in all aspects of executing the program serve as essential components of the holistic facilitation. Based on our experience, we suggest best practices for facilitation that can be used to implement this type of program at other institutions.

THEORETICAL APPROACH TO FACILITATION OF EXPERIENTIAL SOCIAL JUSTICE EDUCATION

Kolb (1984) described learning as a process of knowledge creation by way of transforming experiences. When social justice facilitation occurs through interaction, concrete, observable experiences can be transformed into cognitive growth. Our aim in social justice facilitation is to help students transform their awareness of power, privilege, discrimination, and oppression in society into motivation to create a more socially just world. Experiential learning programs are particularly effective to achieve this goal because they provide opportunities for individuals to think about their own perceptions of an experience and decide for themselves how their understanding of that experience will influence their behavior (Kolb, 1984). By showcasing inequity and challenging learners to think critically about their experiences, social justice educators seek to motivate individuals and groups into action against the oppressive societal structures that create and perpetuate unearned social privilege.

Experiential programs are inherently personal in nature. Participants contemplating the nature of social privilege may exhibit a multitude of emotions ranging from fear and disbelief to validation and inspiration. The presence of these emotions requires careful facilitation of the learning environment. The intentionality of the facilitation can have a substantial impact on how the concept of privilege is understood by participants.

HISTORY OF THE HOUSE OF PRIVILEGE

The House of Privilege (hereafter referred to as House) is an experiential social justice educational program that was first created and produced at James Madison University in 2009. The House is based on the Tunnel of Oppression (hereafter referred to as Tunnel), a popular campus program inspired by the Museum of Tolerance (MOT) in Los Angeles. Billing itself as a "human rights laboratory and educational center" (Our History and Vision, 2012, ¶ 1), the MOT uses multimedia technology and interactive exhibits to educate visitors on the impact of prejudice while promoting personal responsibility to dismantle hate and discrimination in society.

Although rotating exhibits highlight many types of oppression, the main exhibit at the museum has always focused on the Holocaust. In one exhibit, for example, visitors walk through a re-creation of a concentration camp after receiving a card that depicts a child with whom they are meant to identify. The visitors are exposed to images, videos, and artifacts depicting actual Holocaust-era events of abuse and degradation in an effort to have them internalize the child's perspective before they find out whether that particular child survived (Holocaust Section, 2012).

A group at Western Illinois University emphasizing civics, ethics, and social justice adapted the concept of the MOT for their campus. The result was the Tunnel, which has since been re-created and adapted on college campuses across the United States since the early 1990s (Barrett-Fox, 2007). According to the Tunnel's founders, "The program is designed to create an awareness of different types of oppression, and its effects, within society and the campus community. . . . The program is supposed to challenge the senses and feeling [sic] of participants in a safe environment" (Western Connection Group, 1994, p. 2). Participants are escorted through the Tunnel by a tour guide and have the opportunity to observe and often interact with live actors, view elaborate sets, and experience written, audio, and visual media. Each room of the Tunnel is designed to increase awareness of a specific type of societal oppression (e.g., racial discrimination, body image pressures, religious stereotyping, marginalization based on sexual orientation, and gender-based violence; Western Connection Group, 1994).

Most, if not all, Tunnel programs include a disclaimer, typically read aloud before the program begins, acknowledging that some of the material is graphic and may be difficult to experience. Participants are invited to leave at any time if they are uncomfortable and to consult with a counselor who will be available throughout the event. In addition, all participants are led to a debriefing room following the program where licensed counselors facilitate conversation about the program and ensure the experience has not caused harm.

The prevalence of these types of qualifying statements begs a moment of reflection. Why would we intentionally put people into a situation we acknowledge may be traumatic? Furthermore, could some of the scenes potentially revictimize participants? Is this a worthwhile risk in order to achieve the program's objectives? Do we believe that the only—or best—way for our participants to develop empathy for an oppressed group of people is to walk in their shoes? Is it naive, presumptuous, or even insulting to think we could recreate realistic oppressive experiences and assume participants will then know what it feels like to be oppressed?

Emotional arousal, such as that created by the Tunnel, is an important part of creating optimal conditions for experiential learning (Kaufman, 1999). It is important, however, to ensure a proper balance of emotional intensity so learning can occur. Too little emotional connection will not provoke the mind to start processing the experience, whereas too much can create so great a level of anxiety and fear that the individual cannot think clearly or rationally (Kaufman, 1999). Our concern that for many the Tunnel experience resulted in the latter led us to create the House, with the goal of providing an optimally challenging and supportive emotional experience.

Although the House retains many elements from its predecessor, including participant observation of and interaction with live actors, sets, and various types of media, the Tunnel focuses on having participants experience oppression, whereas the House invites them to witness various forms of societal privilege in action. In creating the House, we tried to retain the experiential nature of the Tunnel while also maintaining a safe, optimal learning environment for participants.

To balance the presentation of challenging images, experiences, and conversations, while also meeting participants where they are cognitively and emotionally, we adopted a person-centered approach. In person-centered therapy, a therapist lays the groundwork for a nonjudgmental environment filled with unconditional positive regard (Corey, 1996; Kahn, 1997; Rogers, 1951). We committed ourselves to facilitating an experience that is affirming in nature and that allows participants to achieve the healthiest possible outcome. We intend for participants to be challenged, frustrated, and inspired by their encounters with the realities of different kinds of privilege they are exposed to in the House. The metaphor of a house—a physical structure that is the product of the unseen foundation on which it is built—stands in for social privilege and the often invisible societal and institutional structures that support it.

FACILITATION ROLES

Steering Committee

As the House program comes together each year, facilitation occurs using a variety of media, activities, and volunteers. Overseeing the process is a group of faculty, staff, and students called the steering committee. These individuals represent offices and departments from across campus as well as the undergraduate and graduate student populations. With this interdisciplinary background, the steering committee facilitates learning outcomes through intentional program design, volunteer recruitment and training, and conducting the actual production of the program.

Program Design

The first step to creating an intentional experience is the development of measurable learning outcomes that will guide the planning process and provide opportunities for continual review and improvement of the program through assessment (Schuh & Upcraft, 2001; Upcraft & Schuh, 1996). The House steering committee developed the following learning outcomes:

1. Participants will be able to indicate at least one example of how their definitions of *privilege* have evolved since attending the program.
2. Participants will acknowledge that unearned privilege exists in society and in their own lives.
3. Participants will indicate an increased level of awareness of unearned privilege.
4. Participants will identify at least one source of unearned privilege in their lives.
5. Participants will indicate an increased willingness to confront unearned privilege.
6. Participants will be able to identify one resource or organization they can use or join to minimize the effects of unearned privilege.

Following the establishment of learning outcomes, the design of an optimal learning environment for the House continued with script development. The steering committee created the script and revises it each year based on participant feedback and volunteer input. To facilitate the learning outcomes, we agreed on three principles:

1. The program would present examples of social privilege in action to provoke participants to become aware of their own privilege as well as the institutional and societal mechanisms that allow oppression to flourish in our society.

2. The program would avoid placing participants in the role of the oppressed, potentially causing trauma. Instead, participants would witness and have an opportunity to reflect on their own privilege(s).

3. The program would motivate participants to go beyond passive observation and serve as change agents in their communities.

The learning outcomes and guiding principles led us to create spaces that exhibit multiple levels of privilege and could be interpreted in a variety of ways depending on the perspective and background of each participant. The metaphor of a house allowed us to label the rooms based on their purpose in a real home (living room, dining room, bedroom, etc.) rather than on the one type of privilege exhibited (racial, religious, gender, etc.). Therefore, instead of room-by-room scripted privilege language and content, we structured the experience in a way that would most effectively facilitate learning, regardless of content.

When designing programs that involve high-risk topics, it is important to gradually increase the intensity of the experiential element of the program. Beginning with low levels of interaction allows participants to ease into the experience before reaching the most interactive components. By reducing the intensity level toward the program's end, participants have time to internally process the most intense part of the experience and better prepare themselves to fully engage in the reflection room.

The most interactive and challenging scenario in terms of causing participants to reflect on social privilege occurs in two living rooms at the center of the tour. In the spaces before and after, participants engage primarily by observing actors or objects. The living room scenes, however, challenge participants in a different way: Actors facilitate intentional cognitive dissonance through direct interaction with participants.

The living room concept was developed as two parallel spaces. The first represents the dominant culture family norm: two White, heterosexual, Christian parents with two children. The room is filled with religious iconography, magazines, videos, books, and toys that all feature White nuclear families. The contrasting room is identical in form (same family makeup, same type of set dressings) but different in content. This living space shows people of a different ethnicity and religion illustrated by the same forms of media as the previous room.

In the first room, participants experience actors facilitating a sense of familiarity among the participants. The actors assume the participants can easily draw on their knowledge of the Christmas holiday and its traditions to engage in the festivities. The actors invite the participants into their home, wish them a "Merry Christmas," and ask them to help decorate the tree. Statements such as "Don't be shy—you know what to do" attempt to set a warm and welcoming tone. The family asks everyone to join in singing a Christmas carol before thanking them for visiting.

In the second living room, the actors treat the participants in the same welcoming manner, but the holiday language and traditions are replaced with those of Diwali, the Hindu festival of lights. The family invites the group to create *rangoli* patterns on plates and encourages them with language similar to what was used in the previous room: "Don't be shy—you know what to do." The family then announces it is time for *aarti*, providing no instructions for participant involvement (as none were provided in the preceding room for decorating the tree and singing the Christmas carol). The family invites everyone to join in singing an aarti song before thanking guests for visiting.

In this scenario, the actors in both rooms are trained to facilitate a welcoming atmosphere. In actuality, it is the program design that creates the mood. For most participants from the dominant United States culture, the first space puts them at ease, while the second room creates discomfort and dissonance.

It would be natural to call this the *religion room* instead of the *living room.* The argument could be made that the room is entirely about Christian privilege, specifically privilege over people who identify with the Hindu faith. A number of things, however, allow us to consider this a more general example of privilege in action. Despite its original foundation in race, the room has been adapted over time to be cast without regard to race or appearance. This allows participants to focus less on the people and more on the experience. As a result of the different lenses participants bring to the experience, we have also seen participants view this scenario as exploring socioeconomic privilege.

It is also possible for participants to generalize the learning in the space to more broad concepts. Feedback has consistently shown that the living rooms provide the most powerful experience for participants. Participants leave with the realization that people make assumptions that others share a common background and experience and that when someone makes that assumption about them, it gives them a feeling of "otherness" that feels uncomfortable. We believe the intentional planning and thoughtful consideration that went into developing the script is crucial to the overall facilitation of social justice education the program offers and critical for the creation of similar experiential learning activities.

The Realtor

Another important element of the program facilitation is the realtor, a tour guide who is, ostensibly, attempting to help participants find a home where they can picture themselves living. Although most acting roles are relatively small and simply require reading from a brief script, the realtor is a vital program facilitator. This person has to respond to participant questions, adjust if a previous tour is taking longer than expected, and improvise based on nonverbal feedback from participants.

It is important for the realtor to stay in character at all times. For example, participants may ask questions about a scene or aspect of privilege that we, as the program designers, had envisioned they would process internally to discover the answer for themselves. This situation often occurs at the beginning of tours when participants are looking for quick insight into what they are supposed to learn from the experience. "Which organization is running this tour?" "Are we supposed to like the people we see?" "What types of privilege will be addressed?" By staying in character, actors have permission to remain vague in their responses and thus facilitate further internal processing by the participant. Responses might include

> This tour is being provided by Reality Realty [the invented name of the real estate firm in the script]. We hope that you'll be able to determine for yourself which properties you prefer. You'll be able to see a variety of situations and weigh the advantages and disadvantages associated with each during your discussion with the titling agent [the term used in the script for the reflection facilitator].

Alternatively, if questions are less tied into the learning outcomes of the program, the process of staying in character simply requires actors to fake an answer. For instance, questions like "How many people celebrate *that holiday* in this neighborhood?" can be answered differently each time. The actor can also use this opportunity to offer the questioner some additional information. "There are several Hindu families in the area that celebrate Diwali," might be one option, or "I am unsure how many Hindus are in this area, but there is a large population on the east side of town that celebrate Diwali."

Staying in character is also important when tours are delayed because of a previous slower tour. At these times, actors can ask questions to facilitate the transition into the reflection process. An example would be to ask which properties they would like to know more about or in which spaces they felt particularly at home.

Volunteer Recruitment

Execution of the House, like many grassroots social justice programs, hinges entirely on volunteer time and effort. The intentional cultivation and training of volunteers who are committed to the initiative is critical to facilitating the learning outcomes in the final event.

Recruiting volunteers, however, can often be a challenge, especially when a program is new and time-consuming, and the advertised description of the program is purposefully vague. The House presents an added challenge in that volunteers are asked to act in front of a live audience, a task many seem reticent to do initially. Our success in recruiting nearly 150 volunteers to serve over 500 hours resulted from intentional collaboration among faculty, student affairs staff, and students.

Fortunately, faculty nationwide use multicultural activities in their curricula to help students learn relevant information (Sciame-Giesecke, Roden, & Parkison, 2009; Simoni, Sexton-Radek, Yescavage, Richard, & Lundquist, 1999). A program like the House has the potential to serve as a supplemental educational opportunity for faculty to use with their students. We have been intentional about reaching out to faculty councils and professors in specific departments who would be natural allies with the House. As a result, increasing numbers of professors offer extra credit to students who volunteer with the program. Some faculty have even added the House experience to their syllabi.

Given that many volunteers will need to perform roles, we also collaborate with the theater department faculty and student clubs on campus. This has allowed us to tap into a network of talent that can help us further prepare other volunteers and alleviate performance anxiety felt by many potential volunteers. The importance of these collaborations with faculty, especially in areas related to social justice education, cannot be overemphasized.

Ongoing volunteer recruitment is interwoven with volunteer training, volunteer retention, and the overall volunteer experience. Volunteers who have a negative experience because they feel ill prepared will not return, nor will they recruit additional volunteers (Roberts, Young, & Meyer, 2009).

VOLUNTEER TRAINING

The volunteers who serve as actors, tour guides, and reflection leaders all serve as facilitators of the program's learning outcomes. At our institution, these are mostly undergraduate student volunteers. It is vital for them to be adequately prepared to be effective facilitators of social justice education.

The steering committee developed a training session for volunteers that had three objectives:

1. Engage volunteers in an examination of the concept of privilege as a broad concept and as a personal, relatable experience.
2. Model the type of reflective discussions of experiential exercises related to privilege that we hope to facilitate during the actual program.
3. Orient students to the logistics of the House and the various volunteer roles available.

The training was intended to be more than a how-to lesson to provide an experience that deepened volunteers' awareness and interest in understanding privilege and social justice. We assumed that by virtue of their interest in being involved with the House, volunteers brought a beginning-level sensibility to the concepts of privilege and oppression and how they are linked to an individual's or group's social identity. Several small-group trainings were led by steering committee members. To achieve the first objective, we invited volunteers to participate in three activities: a step-in exercise that engaged participants in physical movement without discussion, a written social identity inventory, and a sharing experience that allowed volunteers to discuss their experiences with one of their many social identities.

Aside from creating opportunities for personal sharing and deep reflection, the intimate and interactive format of the training allowed us to discern any volunteers whose understanding or perspectives ran counter to the values of the program. The training design allowed facilitators to follow up with volunteers as needed, providing opportunities for additional training and reflection to hopefully achieve greater awareness.

The small-group atmosphere and training activities fostered sharing of personal experiences of privilege and oppression that allowed relationships to build. Participants and facilitators grew familiar with one another and came to share a common language. By the time training was completed and the House was launched, trained volunteers understood the goals and their roles and, perhaps most important, had established a sense of community.

Reflection

Just as our volunteers were asked to reflect on their own privilege prior to helping facilitate the program, our learning outcomes necessitate an opportunity for participants to do the same. Rather than assume this reflective process is happening on its own, intentional opportunities for personal and group reflection are facilitated throughout the program.

Windows of Opportunity

Many critics of the Tunnel note that participants are mere passive observers, never challenged to see themselves as contributors to a system that allows oppression to occur or to recognize their own responsibility to serve as a change agent in society (Belmonte, 2008). Some Tunnel designers have attempted to engage participants by providing reaction walls that offer a space for individuals to share what the experience has meant to them. In 2008, for example, Santa Clara University had participants exit to the reflection room through a Tunnel of Hope, a room decorated with images of people working to end oppression (Belmonte, 2008).

After creating the metaphor of a house, the committee added a Window of Opportunity to each room. Similar to the Tunnel of Hope, the windows are visual representations of opportunities for engagement surrounding the issues addressed in each room. The windows serve as a call to action, not just at the end of the event but throughout the program. Participants are supported with avenues for intervention at the same time they are being challenged with information about the existence of privilege.

The windows are intentionally vague to allow groups to move through the House quickly without being bogged down by large amounts of information. The realtor reminds participants periodically that the titling agent will provide them with a brochure that includes detailed information about several agencies and organizations that are working to relieve some of the issues raised in the House and how participants can get involved to make a difference in their communities.

Web of Oppression

Toward the end of the activity, participants are led into the basement where they stand facing the Web of Oppression. This is the first active reflection opportunity in the program and is designed to prepare participants to engage more fully in the group process that follows the tour. The realtor explains that as the foundation of the house, the basement contains the structure that supports the house above. It is suggested that a good home inspection will start here to identify elements that need to be improved. The realtor states that previous inspectors have already left some notes on the web and encourages participants to add their own observations. Examples include social phenomena such as racism, homophobia, and prejudice. The group is given time to write down their own ideas on index cards to add to the web.

Titling Office

At the conclusion of the tour, participants are led to a titling office (reflection room) to meet with the titling agent whose role is to facilitate a safe environment for participants to reflect on their experience, mediate the reflection when necessary, and provide resources for further learning and community engagement.

We initially drew from the Tunnel model and staffed our reflection room exclusively with licensed counselors from the campus counseling center. Over time it became clear this was not necessary. While potential remains for crises to occur throughout the House, staff can refer to the counseling center or on-call counselor as necessary. More important, we learned from using counselors in the past that the most effective reflections occur when the facilitator has intimate knowledge of the program. Steering committee members, through the nature of their work as teaching faculty and student affairs professionals, have the knowledge, skills, and experience to effectively facilitate these reflections. Further, we found that student volunteers may also be capable of leading reflections with the proper training, including the opportunity to observe more experienced facilitators first. In fact, some of the most effective reflection groups were student led, perhaps because the participants (mostly students) felt more comfortable sharing with their peers.

Regardless of the background of the facilitator, it is important that each group has a similarly guided experience. The steering committee created a brief, semistructured group interview to aid participants' meaning making. The interview included these questions:

1. What was the most impactful part of the tour for you?
2. What surprised you, challenged you, or made you uncomfortable?
3. How did it feel looking through the Windows of Opportunity located in each room?
4. In what ways are you already involved in agencies or services that address social privilege and injustice?
5. Having been through this experience, what are some ways you plan to engage with the Windows of Opportunity in your everyday life?

These questions are designed to challenge participants to move past descriptions of the scenes in the House and to explore the nature of the privileges they observed or related to. Facilitators are trained to reflect the privileges inherent in the comments made and to encourage personal story-telling to illustrate the reality behind the activity.

Mailbox

One of the desired outcomes for the House is that participants will be more aware of their own privilege. It can be challenging to share privileged identities with a group of strangers, particularly for participants who are learning about privilege for the first time. In anticipation that not everyone would participate during the group process, we created the mailbox as an opportunity for participants to acknowledge their privileged identities privately.

Before leaving the reflection room, each participant is asked to write one source of privilege they are aware of in their own lives on a postcard (index card). They are informed they will not need to share this revelation with anyone and that they can leave this card in the mailbox on their way out. It is important to highlight for participants that the metaphor is not that they are leaving their privilege behind or ridding themselves of it. Just as we need notes to remind us of all the houses we visit when buying a home, this serves as a written reminder to them of the part of the House that illustrated their personal privileges best. We are simply asking them to acknowledge that this privilege is part of them and to commit to being more aware of its impact in their daily lives.

A NOTE ABOUT VOLUNTEERS

After discussing the ways our volunteers take part in the facilitation of this program, we would be remiss if we did not address the inherent concerns this conversation may raise with respect to undergraduate students leading reflections or improvising the script. We believe our student facilitators are no less capable of facilitating an understanding of privilege than we are. The nature of the program tends to attract volunteers who have some prior knowledge or experience—through class work, life experience, or both—of social justice and privilege. Additionally, the volunteer training prepares students and allows the steering committee to determine the relative level of understanding of each volunteer.

Social justice and privilege awareness education is a process and a journey we are all participating in together. Volunteers, participants, faculty, staff, students, and steering committee members are all at varying levels of their own personal understanding. If we truly believe in the work of social justice education, we must respect this diversity of experience and allow it to enter the conversation. Only by allowing individuals the opportunity to take risks and make mistakes will we all have the opportunity to learn and grow.

CONCLUSION

Programs such as the House of Privilege often occur annually on college campuses. The effective facilitation of learning outcomes for these programs requires year-round attention and deliberate, thoughtful adjustments. The passion and hard work of hundreds of students, faculty, and staff are necessary to help create an optimal learning environment.

Whether you are inspired to build your own House event, or you plan to use some of the techniques here with another interactive social justice program, it is critical to keep in mind that facilitation is a multifaceted process. Careful attention must be paid to proper volunteer preparation and ongoing support as well as to intentional opportunities for reflection and future engagement for participants. Social justice is our ultimate goal, but it is also the process we intentionally engage in to achieve this goal (Bell, 2007).

REFERENCES

Barrett-Fox, R. (2007). Tunnel of reification: How the Tunnel of Oppression reaffirms righteousness for members of dominant groups. *Radical Teacher*, 80, 24–29.

Bell, L. A. (2007). Theoretical foundations for social justice education. In Adams, M., Bell, L.A., & Griffin, P. (Eds.), *Teaching for diversity and social justice* (pp. 1–14). New York, NY: Taylor & Francis.

Belmonte, G. (2008, February 21). Eight student groups host first Tunnel of Oppression. *The Santa Clara*. Retrieved from http://www.thesantaclara.com/2.145 35/eight-student-groups-host-first-tunnel-of-oppression-1.1870107#.UOwuo SqF_kF

Corey, G. (1996). *Theory and practice of counseling and psychotherapy* (5th ed.). Pacific Grove, CA: Brooks/Cole.

Holocaust Section. (2012). Museum of Tolerance. Retrieved from http://www.mus
eumoftolerance.com/site/c.tmL6KfNVLtH/b.4865935/k.B 355/Holocaust_Sec
tion.htm

Kahn, M. (1997). *Between therapist and client: The new relationship.* New York, NY:
Henry Holt.

Kaufman, B. E. (1999). Emotional arousal as a source of bounded rationality. *Journal of Economic Behavior & Organization, 38*(2), 135–144.

Kolb, D. A. (1984). *Experiential learning: Experience as the source of learning and
development.* Englewood Cliffs, NJ: Prentice Hall.

McCain, D. V., & Tobey, D. D. (2004). *Facilitation basics.* Alexandria, VA: American Society for Training and Development. Retrieved from http://proquestcom
bo.safaribooksonline.com/book/communications/1562863614

Our History and Vision. (2012). Museum of Tolerance. Retrieved from http://
www.museumoftolerance.com/site/c.tmL6KfNVLtH/b.4866027/k.88E8/Our_
History_and_Vision.htm

Roberts, M. H., Young, W., & Meyer, G. (2009, November). *Building a bridge:
Recruiting, training and retaining faculty and staff volunteers* [PowerPoint slides].
Presentation at the annual Virginia Student Services Conference, Wintergreen,
VA.

Rogers, C. (1951). *Client-centered therapy.* Boston, MA: Houghton Mifflin.

Schuh, J. H., & Upcraft, M. L. (2001). *Assessment practice in student affairs: An
applications manual.* San Francisco, CA: Jossey-Bass.

Sciame-Giesecke, S., Roden, D., & Parkison, K. (2009). Infusing diversity into the
curriculum: What are faculty members actually doing? *Journal of Diversity in
Higher Education, 2*(3), 156–165. doi: 10.1037/a0016042

Simoni, J. M., Sexton-Radek, K., Yescavage, K., Richard, H., & Lundquist, A.
(1999). Teaching diversity: Experiences and recommendations of American Psychological Association Division 2 members. *Teaching of Psychology, 26*(2), 89–95.
doi: 10.1207/s15328023top2602_2

Upcraft, M. L., & Schuh, J. H. (1996). *Assessment in student affairs: A guide for
practitioners.* San Francisco, CA: Jossey-Bass.

Western Connection Group. (1994). *Tunnel of Oppression activity packet.* Unpublished manuscript, Western Illinois University, Macomb.

Part Four

Supporting Student
Social Action

MANY SOCIAL JUSTICE EDUCATORS would contend that one of the key distinctions between multicultural education and social justice education is social justice education's call for action to address oppressive practices wherever they exist. The act of educating (or reeducating) students about power, privilege, and oppression is a form of social justice, yet supporting students to engage in social justice action is a daunting task. The two chapters in this section discuss these challenges.

In Chapter 12, Heather Wilhelm and robbie routenberg ask us to consider the experience of students who engage in peer-led social justice facilitation. Many campuses across the country identify peer-led workshops and courses as critical components to their social justice education efforts, but students continue to face unique challenges in facilitating social justice education with their peers. Informed by student facilitators from across the country, Heather and robbie identify how social justice educators can refine approaches to peer-facilitation training to promote the tenets of social justice in a sustainable and accessible way.

The book ends with Chapter 13 by Andrea D. Domingue and David S. Neely, who explore how we prepare students for social action engagement. In a dialogic format, the authors reflect upon the educational, professional, and personal experiences that have had an impact on their own social action and inaction. They provide a framework for preparing students for action based on theories of ally development and liberatory consciousness, concluding with strategies and insights the authors have found to be instrumental in preparing students for social action. By illuminating the authors' own successes and shortcomings, other student affairs professionals and educators will be inspired to reflect on the ways they can better prepare themselves and their students in becoming social change agents.

12

Training and Supporting Peer Facilitators

Heather Wilhelm and robbie routenberg

IN OUR WORK AS social justice educators who embrace experiential-learning pedagogy, student peer facilitators fulfill a wide range of responsibilities that include leading peer groups on local and international service trips, facilitating weekly student dialogue groups, and affecting macro-organizational decisions. Anecdotally, we have found student program participants are more engaged when their peers are facilitating, because the material seems more relevant and relatable. The success of a peer facilitation model requires that staff invest significant time and resources training and supporting these students in their work. Thorough training and continuous support are key elements to a successful peer facilitation model. When the content of the undergraduate work is related to social justice education, the risk of promoting misinformation is high, and consequently the demand for comprehensive preparation is a must. Well-intentioned efforts can inadvertently do more harm than good. Staff and faculty are responsible for ensuring student facilitators have the knowledge and skills to be successful social

We would like to acknowledge the following peer facilitators who contributed to this project, and we provide their names here with their permission: Maya Barua, Mitch Crispell, Shaunna Foell, Susanne Fortunato, Maddi Gould, Tara Hackel, Kelly Hodgkins, Ben Huelskamp, Samantha Hyland, Rebecca Ingram Rowe, Mara James, Alex Kulick, Emily Loh, Heather Lou, Elizabeth McDonald, Sunethra Muralidhara, Rokimas Putra Soeharyo, Elizabeth Ramus, Emily Schorr Lesnick, Kripa Sreepada, Autumn Wilke, Amber Williams, and Carrie Wooten.

215

justice educators. This chapter identifies strategies and topics to enhance the learning of peer facilitators to lead to improved learning outcomes for student participants in your programs.

STRENGTHS OF THE PEER
FACILITATION MODEL

Peer facilitation models offer many benefits for participants, institutions, and facilitators themselves. Sometimes staff or faculty can be resistant to giving students this responsibility, unsure of how the discussions will unfold if left up to the discretion of student facilitators. In reality, students are the most intimately knowledgeable about the campus climate, and although seen differently from faculty, peer facilitators can be equally credible because of their ability to relate and establish trust with fellow students. An additional advantage for employing this training technique is that it provides alternate modes for students to learn, thus supporting the multiplicity of learning styles and preferences (Bertram, Luu, & Sumpter, 2010; Nolan, Levy, & Constantine, 1996).

Benefits to Participants

Peer facilitators can support participants in a multitude of ways that extend beyond knowledge and skills acquired in the social justice education setting (Haber, 2011). Less-experienced participants are introduced to positive role models (Brack, Millard, & Shah, 2008; Haber, 2011) who embrace the tenets of social justice and create a means for students to do the same. Witnessing role models who assume leadership roles in academic settings can "assist in [the] overall campus life experience and holistic development" (Haber, 2011, p. 71) of these participants. Brack et al. (2008) suggested this relationship is even stronger because of the factor of trust, which is correlated with similarities in personal values and personality/temperament.

Benefits to Institutions

For the institution, peer facilitators provide a valuable human resource. This benefit extends well beyond the cost of minimal financial compensation, although this is not to be ignored as peer educators often receive little to no pay for their contributions (Sloane & Zimmer, 1993). Incorporating students as genuine colleagues into the program can lead to increased student commitment and interest, relevancy of material and delivery, and general sustainability of the program (Haber, 2011).

Benefits to Student Facilitators

As significant as the benefits to participants and institutions are, possibly the greatest effects are on the facilitators themselves. These leadership opportunities have led facilitators to report acquisition or improvement of existing skills in the areas of leadership, facilitation, communication, decision making, and creative problem solving (Bandura, Peluso, Ortman, & Millard, 2000). Psychologically, student facilitators are shown to have increased knowledge, self-esteem, and self-efficacy (Ehrhardt, Krumboltz, & Koopman, 2006; Sawyer, Pinciaro, & Bedwell, 1997). Beyond these benefits, student facilitators learn how to work with others in interdependent ways, experiencing the experience and metareflecting on the different stages of group development (Johnson & Johnson, 2006). All these examples suggest "peer leadership provides a valuable real-time, experiential learning and development experience for peer leaders" (Haber, 2011, pp. 70–71).

"Students who can play a substantive role in linking academic learning with real-world problem solving represent in many ways an ideal" (Zlotkowski, Longo, & Williams, 2006, p. 5). For student facilitators, this provides an opportunity to engage in integrative learning—linking their academic and cocurricular experiences. Additionally, student facilitators engage in democratic participation, therefore understanding the importance of learning civic responsibility and engagement. Through their practice, they serve as a catalyst of a democratic process on campus. Zlotkowski et al. (2006) contended, "Creating safe, respectful, and democratic spaces allows students to develop, use, and own their voices on a host of public issues" (p. 7). These forums become incubators for peer facilitators and participants alike offering a microcosm of civic-engagement platforms that "lead to deeper levels of involvement . . . that allow young people to become engaged and responsible civic actors" (Zlotkowski et al., 2006, p. 7).

INHIBITING IMPLEMENTATION

Zlotkowski et al. (2006) suggested that many colleges and universities have been slow to adopt a student-led approach to curriculum. Some staff and faculty may be fearful of diluting the potency of their curriculum or jeopardizing the metrics for assessing learning objectives. "Rather than posing a threat to faculty, students engaged in research can connect the community, the faculty, and the university in a powerful, productive alliance" (Zlotkowski et al., 2006, p. 10). Although involving peer facilitation is an optimal learning situation, arriving at this place is not so simple. Zlotkowski et al. went on to say, "Carefully selected, well-trained undergraduates can play decisive roles in making academic-community collaborations powerful, successful experiences" (p. 4). A reader might note the inclusion of the descriptors *carefully selected* and *well-trained*. The pressure of these words can intimidate facilitators from implementing such an approach.

REFLECTIONS FROM PEER FACILITATORS

Transforming social justice theory to pedagogy in practice demands the social justice facilitator give voice to the needs and attitudes of those directly involved in the facilitation experience. In conceptualizing a book on social justice facilitation, we believed it was critical to include a chapter on the experience of peer facilitators. Many social justice educators use student facilitators as a core component of their pedagogical approach, and while we recognize the nature of this chapter is not qualitative research, the reflections expressed by student facilitators point to an array of strengths and challenges experienced in the role. This chapter cannot be generalized to all social justice peer facilitators; still we believe it is important to include student voices to enrich and ground a conversation on best practices in social justice education. We solicited reflections from current undergraduate students or recent graduates who facilitated social justice education opportunities as peers. Invitations to participate in the project were disseminated via a recruitment e-mail through the ACPA–College Student Educators International Commission for Social Justice Educators' Listserv. Additionally, existing networks were used to ensure sufficient breadth in responses with careful attention to survey a cross-section of institutions and peer facilitation roles.

Alumni were graduates within the last three years and served as facilitators during their senior years. Contributors provided responses to the following questions:

♦ In your opinion, what were some of the bigger challenges you faced as a facilitator of social justice conversations?

♦ What have you found to be the most helpful aspects of preparation for your role as a peer educator (e.g., some particular readings, specific experiences or exercises, coaching from a supervisor/mentor)?

♦ What additional types of training and support could have better prepared you for your role as a social justice educator (e.g., something you wished your supervisor/mentor would have told you or provided, information or experience that would have been useful to you)?

Twenty-three individuals responded, offering a variety of perspectives and experience with staff/faculty training and support. These student contributors facilitated social justice conversations in a variety of settings, including residence life, intergroup dialogue, social justice education workshops, social justice education theater, service-learning, ally development programming, student conflict resolution, university diversity communities, and sexual assault prevention education. They represented 13 institutions: Appalachian State University; Cornell University; James Madison University; Macalester College; Purdue University; Saint Louis University; San Jose State University; University of California, Berkeley; University of Maryland, College Park; University of Michigan; University of Northern Colorado; University of the South; and University of Wisconsin–Madison.

In this chapter, we integrate these contributions, theoretical foundations, and our experience into a resource for how to support student facilitators in a sustainable and accessible way.

Challenges Experienced by Peer Facilitators

Despite all the positive reasons to consider peer facilitation, this approach is not without challenges. As shown by the students surveyed, and the literature that informs our exploration of student facilitators in the social justice classroom, the associated challenges fall into four categories: group maintenance, individual participant resistance, environment/institution, and facilitator development.

Group Maintenance As Hackman (2005) articulated through an examination of core components required in social justice education, an understanding of group dynamics is essential. This understanding requires facilitators to be keen to the ways participants' identities affect the group. When facilitation is not sustained over a long period of time but entails working with single-session workshops, this presents a common challenge for the student facilitator. Several contributors discussed group dynamics among their most memorable challenges. Out of a total of 23 respondents, 15 reported that participants' understandings of social justice concepts may vary greatly, therefore leaving facilitators unsure of how to lead engaging and inclusive conversations in these settings. One student contributor offered, "Everyone has to start somewhere in their journey. It was my job [as a peer facilitator] to recognize that and cater to everyone's different steps in their journey." Other contributors shared their frustration in working with a participant group that does not display advanced critical thinking skills, suggesting this is especially difficult when facilitators believe themselves to be well versed in this area. "Respecting where each student is at in their development is challenging," reflected one student contributor, "I oscillated between frustration (why don't they get it?), excitement (look, they're just starting to get it!), frustration (why can't *I* do a better job to help them get it?), excitement (they are talking to one another honestly!), on and on."

Six respondents mentioned controversy or conflict being particularly challenging to navigate, and four students offered detailed accounts of how identity dynamics affected the facilitation experience. One student contributor said, "One pervasive theme I found difficult to mediate was negotiating the share-outs of target groups who would often provide descriptive experiences of violence, silencing, self-blame and 'othering' that would in turn educate and enhance the identity development of agent groups."

Supporters of the social justice classroom must consider the potential for tokenizing identity groups and the unintended consequences that may result.

Individual Participant Resistance   While all groups experience challenging dynamics, some individual participants have also proven frustrating to work with for facilitators. Nearly all contributors mentioned this barrier, including making specific references to tokenizing behaviors, demonstration of apathy and active resistance, and not making connections to societal implications of their experiences. Facilitators struggled with determining how much to challenge a single participant and how much to move the group forward without that participant.

Environment/Institution   The identities and behaviors of groups and participants have much to do with their environments. For example, leading a conversation about race at a predominantly White institution is very different from leading the same conversation at a historically Black college or university. Institutional variations including demographic profile, type and size, academic foci, and geographic location, among others, can influence the dialogue experience. One student contributor pointed out, "Facilitating dialogues with college students at a flagship and predominantly White institution can prohibit many students from globalizing their experience." Another consideration is resources applied to these opportunities, financial and otherwise. The amount of funding, space, staff time, and experience dedicated to the program can have an impact on facilitator preparation and the consequent depth and breadth they are prepared to cover. This resource availability in turn affects the skillfulness of facilitators in addressing the dynamics and behaviors that arise.

Facilitator Development   All these challenges external to the facilitators can prompt reflection about one's preparedness and confidence. Facilitators receive a variety of messages about what it means to be qualified or strong in their practice. Identity can play a key role in their confidence and approach to facilitation. One student contributor acknowledged,

> The biggest challenges I faced in becoming a facilitator of social justice conversations as an undergraduate student were largely internal. I experienced a lack of confidence as a result of my own unrealistic interpretations of who I believed was qualified to facilitate. Due to the social privileges I experienced because of my identity, I felt I was unqualified for the role.

It is important to help these students recognize the value and importance of their engagement in social justice dialogue. Students who demonstrate this lack of confidence particularly benefit in cofacilitation contexts. One contributor noted,

> One thing that would have been helpful to be trained more effectively in would be to communicate effectively across different skill levels of facilitation. For example, having been trained and feeling very confident as a facilitator, it is a challenge to work with others who do not feel this same level of confidence.

Just as there is no point at which one masters social justice, developing one's facilitation skill set is a continual process. Some contributors recognized and embraced this fact, as one contributor stated:

> My social justice educator and mentor once noted that social justice is a process, not a linear trajectory, and that we are all in different stages in the process. And as scholar Audre Lorde once said: "we are all works in progress."

Even as a facilitator, I am still in the process of unlearning my internalized oppressions and unpacking my privilege. As a student facilitator, sometimes my peers would assume that I had already "done the work," that I already knew the answers. Although my facilitation experience might be more extensive than members in discussion groups and forums, I too make mistakes and struggle to embody my politics of social justice each day.

One indicator of confidence in facilitation is a willingness to stray from the predetermined plan, to be spontaneous with material in order to allow for an unanticipated group process. Many students found this process challenging, feeling like they knew only a few activities and wanted to stick to what they were prepared to do. In the absence of ongoing meetings and trainings, they said their facilitator development was stifled. Contributors shared a general dissatisfaction with the little opportunity to explore new and innovative experiential pedagogy as well as additional historical context and analysis of content with staff supervisors or mentors. A failure to provide these components to peer facilitators can lead to a reinforcement of dominant ideologies and taking perspectives in the facilitation setting. It is necessary to integrate and welcome information and beliefs from multiple nondominant sources to allow for a balanced, critical analysis of the discussion focus. This facilitator charge is difficult and advanced, yet critical to preventing feelings of alienation and otherness in already marginalized participants (Hackman, 2005). It is necessary that staff expose peer facilitators to these dialogue tactics and provide ongoing support and resources for their development. One student contributor said, "For me, the only way to become a skilled social justice facilitator is through experience and reflection."

As a peer and a figure of authority in a group, this facilitation responsibility can be even more challenging. "During my first term as a facilitator, I struggled with the fact that I had taken on the dual role of being both a peer and a facilitator," admitted one student contributor. The tension inherent in this conflict results from the facilitator's stretch for empathy and ability to relate to participants and yet struggles for a sense of distance and difference because of his or her role. Three contributors expressed struggling with their emotions when faced with this divide. Relatedly, these students were continually seeking a way to demonstrate integrity in their dual role.

This idea resonated with contributors who expressed a desire to carry authenticity to their own experiences and beliefs while simultaneously being accountable to fostering others' development and critical thinking. Although these concepts need not be in direct opposition, respondents reported feeling pulled between these poles. This dissonance emphasizes the lifelong process of developing and redeveloping one's competence as a facilitator. "I experienced a number of challenges that, while difficult in the moment, ultimately helped play a crucial role in my development as a more effective facilitator of social justice conversations," reflected one student contributor. As staff and faculty, it is our role to promote positivity and confidence in our peer leaders as they engage in this very challenging opportunity.

Implications for Peer Facilitators

The opportunities and challenges presented to peer facilitators are vast, yet faculty and staff mentors can support facilitators irrespective of students' skill level or degree of maturity. It requires that one seek out the literature and create opportunities to advance this discussion with students and staff at the interdepartmental and institutional levels. As shown by the reflections gathered from student contributors, staff and faculty already make a positive difference in several ways in preparing and supporting undergraduate facilitators. What is striking from the student contributions is that they illuminate the inconsistencies in peer facilitators. It is clear that even the most effective methods of training and support (as reported in the literature and through the lenses of the student contributors) are far from universally employed. In order to address a range of ways staff and faculty can be helpful, we have used the structure Hackman (2005) provided when conceptualizing the five major components of social justice education. Although written primarily as curricular considerations relevant to participant learning, they also have value in the planning of facilitator training.

Content Mastery   The first of the major components is content mastery, which is the level of knowledge expertise facilitators have. Hackman (2005) specified content as being micro and macro in nature and focusing on dominant and nondominant narratives. In Chapter 10 of this book, routenberg, Thompson, and Waterberg provide a detailed investigation of dominant and nondominant narratives. It is important to help student facilitators develop this understanding and acquire a working knowledge of the different levels of oppression, how power is exerted, and examples of privilege some groups benefit from daily. This depth and breadth of knowledge can prepare peer facilitators to name dominant and nondominant narratives in the dialogue.

The first step in this process requires that staff support students in developing their own knowledge base in preparation for dialogue settings when such narratives arise. Seven out of 23 respondents identified that familiarity with the theoretical underpinnings of social justice education was very helpful in their facilitator roles. Several expressed that having this knowledge legitimized their efforts by affirming the importance of their roles. Although some students struggled with the flexibility required to facilitate effectively, students who were confident in the theoretical framework of the subject matter mentioned how this knowledge allowed them to be increasingly spontaneous in their facilitation. As a result, their ability to stray from the script led to more enriching learning experiences for participants. More than half of the contributors did not mention theoretical context at all, and some mentioned it would have been helpful to know, demonstrating inconsistency across training. One student contributor said,

> For 3½ years in undergrad, I was constantly learning how to become a better peer facilitator. What could have better prepared me for my role as a social justice educator was a better understanding of, statistically, what kind of impact peer-led social justice facilitations had on students/audiences . . . whether or not there was a substantial weight attached to what WE do.

One student contributor put it this way: "I could benefit from a more in-depth discussion of the process people go through when they engage in a social justice learning." Her comments sum up a trend evident in a variety of reflections offered by peer facilitators across institutions, functional areas, and degrees of responsibility.

Critical Thinking and the Analysis of Oppression   As Hackman (2005) asserted, critical thinking and the analysis of oppression are critical tools of the effective social justice educator. For facilitators in training, this axiom translates to developing a skill set for addressing the dominant narratives that arise in the dialogue setting. Although crucial, "possession of information does not necessarily provide students with a pathway for action" (Hackman, 2005, p. 105). Staff and faculty responsible for training and supporting student facilitators must prepare students to prompt critical analysis in dialogues. Several students alluded to this need, and many are resistant to initiate such discussions for fear of participant resistance or a lack of confidence in their facilitation skills or in their comfort with content mastery. Eight contributors mentioned that watching someone else facilitate this process was very helpful in learning the practice. "I want to state clearly and early on that I have learned the most about this role from watching other facilitators and observing which interventions were effective and which were unproductive," offered one student contributor. When developing a training curriculum for student facilitators, it can be advantageous to integrate shadowing (watching someone else facilitate) into the preparation process.

Personal Reflection   Personal reflection is another key component addressed by Hackman (2005), and this concept was given the most attention by student contributors. Through this process, students apply theory to practice, exploring how social justice concepts relate to their daily experience. More specifically, reflection allows students to personalize acquired knowledge and examine the ways they experience and perpetuate privilege and oppression. This type of introspection fosters empathy for participants' experiences, thus encouraging facilitators to tailor workshop sessions to challenge and support participants in an individualized manner. Staff can model the importance of reflection, demonstrating the importance of congruency in thought and action. As a tenet of social justice education, personal reflection is crucial for all involved to embrace, to acknowledge personal growth and challenge, and to illustrate that participants and facilitators alike have opportunities to cultivate critical consciousness within them. One student contributor's honesty demonstrates this point well:

> [Only] once I stepped back and reflected on why I was bullied, or why others were oppressed when I had never thought about my privilege, did I finally understand WHERE my privilege came from and WHY people never want to give it up! As an aspiring lawyer, this is key to one of the reasons why I chose this profession and will help me when trying to write laws, rewrite laws, or fix our legal system that unfortunately is based on a lot of oppressive thinking.

Eight contributors expressed appreciation for staff and faculty who challenged them to reflect on their identities and the ways they had an impact on their approach to facilitation. Student facilitators were making the connection very strongly between reflection and practice.

Personal reflection can extend beyond the realm of one's social identities and their impact on facilitation. Critical reflection and feedback offer another approach to reflection that proves equally vital in the peer facilitation process. Feedback can be offered on dialogue content, management of group dynamics among participants, dynamics between cofacilitators, and ways social identity has affected the facilitation or the dialogue broadly. Students mentioned such reflection varied between an internal process, an informal process with a few other individuals, or a large group (facilitated) format. From the contributions, it is not clear if one method is preferred; however, it is clear that some form of structure is helpful. One student contributor asserted,

> [The] three most important things I can stress for developing as an effective peer facilitator are training, ongoing reflection, and co-facilitation. These factors make us more effective in our roles, help us develop more effective strategies for facilitation, and help to ensure that as facilitators we are doing more good than harm.

Based on the importance that postfacilitation reflection has had, one pedagogical suggestion is to build in an infrastructure for ongoing training and support. Although we know several contributors have had the benefit of ongoing support, 4 of 23 mentioned explicitly this was something they desired.

Awareness of Multicultural Group Dynamics and Tools for Action and Social Change   Awareness of multicultural group dynamics is the fourth component. Interestingly, this awareness came up several times in the discussion of challenges from student contributors, and yet was not mentioned as something staff and faculty have or should assist in developing. *Multicultural group dynamics* refers to the way the group relates to each other relevant to identity, as well as an exploration of which identity groups are represented in the conversation and which are not. A facilitator should be aware of multicultural group dynamics and name them in the workshop setting to be discussed and learned from. The skills required for naming the dynamics and facilitating the subsequent conversation lead to increased awareness, and an environment that fosters social change relates to the fifth component, action and social change.

Tools for Action and Social Change   "Tools for Action and Social Change are critical to help move students from cynicism and despair to hope and possibility" (Hackman, 2005, p. 106). The fact that no student contributor addressed this competency when asked about ways that staff or faculty have been or could be helpful sends a strong message. We believe there are a few possible reasons this was universally omitted: (a) the students did not recognize that what staff and faculty were doing to support these learning components had value or (b) staff and faculty are doing very little to address these learning components relative to others noted by Hackman (2005). Regardless of the reason, it is evident that these components be included in the training of peer facilitators and value of such components made explicit.

SUPPORT

Beyond the confines of Hackman's (2005) five components of social justice education, several students expressed that support was a key factor in their success. Eight contributors highlighted supportive staff as valuable in their preparation for facilitation. Two contributors named an "ally community" as something currently unavailable at their institution but of great interest, describing this community as a group of peers with whom they can process their social activism in and outside their dialogue group. Of the five contributors who indicated that staff/faculty support in developing competence was helpful, eight mentioned they felt that developing competence was a challenge. This information suggests that although staff and faculty are providing some strong support, a great deal more training and support needs to be provided. Such support requires resources from staff and faculty, particularly additional time. "Having adequate time set aside, on-going meetings, and paying attention to both 'intellectual and emotional selves' are cited as critical ingredients" (Zúñiga & Sevig, 2000, p. 492). Working with peer facilitators is not to be viewed as an easy way to extend your reach, though it does also provide this benefit. With the pedagogical decision to include peer facilitators, the challenges and opportunities are great and implicit.

ASSESSING READINESS

For programs that have peer facilitators, a key part of the preparation process is assessing facilitator readiness. Sufficient assessment at the moment of recruitment and after training minimizes the amount of risk involved. A staff or faculty member can be more certain that the dialogue will be productive and that participants are not at risk of harm, emotional or otherwise. Hackman (2005) provided a benchmark for determining readiness: "To be most effective, social justice education requires an examination of systems of power and oppression combined with a prolonged emphasis on social change and student agency in and outside of the classroom" (p. 104). Schoem and Hurtado (2001) provided a rubric for measuring readiness: passion, awareness, knowledge, skills, and support. Passion is important in that it requires a substantial commitment to persist as a facilitator, particularly in challenging moments within the dialogue group. Awareness is important and includes engaging in self-reflection to be in tune with one's own identities, emotions, perspectives, and communication patterns. Knowledge of social systems and social justice issues is crucial for facilitating a group through the discovery process. The skills to assess are those related to critical inquiry and navigating group process (Hackman, 2005). *Support* is defined as the availability of individualized professional and personal support from staff and faculty for the facilitator. By examining these factors, one can determine if the student is ready to take that next step. It is important to recognize that all of these elements are equally important, and the relationship of these elements and how they inform each other make a facilitator a dynamic and transformative presence.

CONCLUSION

Many social justice educators reject a traditional view of leadership and involve undergraduate students as facilitators in an effort to better embody the values and tenets of social justice education. This practice assumes that a "leader-centric perspective is limiting, as it restricts leadership to an individual and is often viewed as an inherent characteristic that is not developable" (Haber, 2011, pp. 65–66). In contrast, experiential learning, as demonstrated in peer-facilitated spaces, positions the facilitator and participants alike as agents of their learning and in turn "come to see the world not as a static reality, but as a reality in process, in transformation" (Freire, 2007, p. 83). Although many campuses identify peer-led workshops as critical to social justice education efforts, peer facilitators continue to face challenges in such settings. When mishandled, these forums can reinforce stereotypes and dominant ideologies, foster isolation and complacency, create an artificial experience, and fail to identify methods for action and social change. Emergent perspective leadership (Haber, 2011) describes leadership as a process all group members share. Morals, ethics, and perspective are relevant to the construction of collaborative leadership, which requires personal awareness and a willingness to continuously engage in self-development. Peer facilitation allows one to integrate an emergent perspective leadership approach, thus leading to numerous learning opportunities for these facilitators in terms of student development and transferrable skills.

The art of social justice facilitation requires a delicate balance of educating oneself about best practices in the field and in skill and intuition. We believe the whole of this book provides a broad spectrum of approaches to consider. A very important approach includes listening to our peer facilitators and creating opportunities to work alongside them as partners in this venture. Their vantage point is crucial to cultivating a transformative learning environment. As detailed in this chapter, employing a structure of peer facilitation benefits the participants and their opportunity for learning, the facilitators and their leadership development, as well as the institution that is hosting this experience. These benefits exist only if the facilitators are well prepared and receive ongoing support from staff and faculty. As educators, it is our responsibility to provide these students with the tools and support needed for them to reach their potential. The immediate educational experience and the future of the field of social justice education rest in their hands.

REFERENCES

Bandura, A., Peluso, E. A., Ortman, N., & Millard, M. (2000). Effects of peer education training on peer educators: Leadership, self-esteem, health knowledge, and health behaviors. *Journal of College Student Development, 41*(5), 471–478.

Bertram, M., Luu, D., & Sumpter, F. (2010). *Evaluating peer health education: Does reciprocal education occur in mentor-mentee relationships?* Unpublished manuscript, School of Education, University of Connecticut, Storrs.

Brack, A. B., Millard, M., & Shah, K. (2008). Are peer educators really peers? *Journal of American College Health, 56*(5), 566–568.

Ehrhardt, B. L., Krumboltz, J. D., & Koopman, C. (2006). Training peer sexual health educators: Changes in knowledge, counseling, self-efficacy, and sexual behavior. *American Journal of Sexuality Education, 2*(1), 39–54.

Freire, P. (2007). *Pedagogy of the oppressed.* (4th ed.) New York, NY: Continuum.

Haber, P. (2011). Peer education in student leadership programs: Responding to co-curricular challenges. *New Directions for Student Services, 2011*(133), 65–76.

Hackman, H. W. (2005). Five essential components for social justice education. *Equity & Excellence in Education, 38*(2), 103–109.

Johnson, D. W., & Johnson, F. P. (2006). *Joining together: Group theory and group skills*. Boston, MA: Pearson.

Nolan, J. M., Levy, E. G., & Constantine, M. G. (1996). Meeting the developmental needs of diverse students: The impact of a peer education program. *Journal of College Student Development, 37*(5), 588–589.

Sawyer, R. G., Pinciaro, P., & Bedwell, D. (1997). How peer education changed peer sexuality educators' self-esteem, personal development and sexual behavior. *Journal of American College Health, 45*(5), 211–217.

Schoem, D., & Hurtado, S. (Eds.). (2001). *Intergroup dialogue: Deliberative democracy in school, college, community, and workplace*. Ann Arbor: University of Michigan Press.

Sloane, B. C., & Zimmer, C. G. (1993). The power of peer health education. *Journal of American College Health, 41*(6), 241–245.

Zlotkowski, E., Longo, N. V., & Williams, J. R. (Eds.). (2006). *Students as colleagues: Expanding the circle of service-learning leadership*. Providence, RI: Campus Compact.

Zúñiga, X., & Sevig, T. (2000). Bridging the "us/them" divide: Intergroup dialogue and peer leadership. In M. Adams, W. Blumenfeld, R. Castaneda, H. Hackman, M. Peters, & X. Zúñiga (Eds.), *Readings for diversity and social justice* (pp. 488–493). New York, NY: Routledge.

13

Why Is It So Hard to Take Action?

A Reflective Dialogue About Preparing Students for
Social Action Engagement

Andrea D. Domingue and David S. Neely

O NE OF THE CENTRAL AIMS of higher education in the United
States is to help students develop the knowledge, skills, and passion
necessary for being engaged and socially responsible citizens
(Schneider, 2000). While historically these intentions focused on encouraging students to be active participants in government and politics, there has
also been a trend to support students in developing a critical consciousness
about social oppression and building skills for creating a more equitable
society (Hurtado, Milem, Clayton-Pederson, & Allen, 1999). Put succinctly,
"The goal of higher education should not be a database of facts, but the
competence to act in the world and the judgment to do so wisely" (Colby,
Ehrlich, Beaumont, Rosner, & Stephens, 2000, p. xxvii). Student affairs
administrators and other educators play a vital role in training and motiva-
ting students for active engagement in their communities—not only while
enrolled as students but throughout their lives.

Social action is also at the core of social justice education. Bell and Griffin
(2007) proposed three primary goals of social justice education: "to increase
personal awareness, expand knowledge, and encourage action" (p. 70). They
explained that "our goal is for participants to see themselves as agents of
change, capable of acting on their convictions and in concert with others

231

against the injustices they see" (p. 72). However, even those educators who are personally committed to social justice are often not well prepared to take action in their own lives, let alone facilitate social action engagement among their students.

Our goal in writing this chapter is to share the challenges we, as social justice educators, have faced in our facilitation where we plan for, encourage, and reflect on students' social action. Similar to the types of reflection we ask our students to engage in, we reflect on how our educational, professional, and personal experiences have affected our own social action and inaction. A guiding question in our ongoing reflection has been, What am I doing to make facilitating social action central to my practice? We begin by discussing different types of *social action*, defining what the term means to us, and providing a framework for preparing students for action based on a theory of ally development (Broido, 2000).

In the second section of this chapter we shift into a written dialogue format in which we explore how the mosaics of our multiple social identities and our experiences as undergraduate students have shaped the choices we make as facilitators in fostering social action engagement. Finally, based on our experiences teaching and facilitating courses and workshops on topics related to diversity and social justice, we share strategies and insights we have found to be instrumental in preparing our students for social action. Our hope is that by illuminating our own successes and shortcomings, other educators will be inspired to reflect on the ways they can better prepare themselves and their students to become social change agents.

WHAT IS SOCIAL ACTION?

A variety of discussions of social action appear in the student affairs and social justice education literature, ranging from those that associate social action with student activism and acts of student dissent (Biddix, Somers, & Polman, 2009; Chambers & Phelps, 1993; Hamrick, 1998) to broader definitions that are inclusive of different forms of action at varying levels of individual risk. As an example of this broader understanding of social action, Bell and Griffin (2007) suggested that antiracism actions for White students could range from "reading about racism, to objecting to racist jokes or comments in their classes or at the family dinner table, to joining a Third World caucus or White ally group on campus" (p. 77). These different forms of action can be placed at different points along the "action continuum," a scale that ranges from "actions against inclusion and social justice" to "actions for diversity and social justice" (Wijeyesinghe, Griffin, & Love, 1997, p. 109). The four types of action for diversity and social justice identified on the action continuum are educating self, educating others, supporting/encouraging, and initiating/preventing (Adams, Bell, & Griffin, 2007). A distinction can be made among these four different types of action. Some are self-directed, and others are directed outward. Zúñiga, Williams, and Berger (2005) found that students who participated in diversity-related courses and interacted with diverse peers became more motivated to take self-directed actions to "actively challenge their own prejudices and take outward actions to promote inclusion and social justice in their communities" (p. 676).

We understand social action to be inclusive of many forms, such as those presented on Adams et al.'s (2007) action continuum. We also suggest that social action should be seen as an ongoing journey, not as one or more isolated events. Educating oneself is a critical point of entry for many of us at the individual level, but ultimately we should also challenge our students and ourselves to reflect critically upon changes needed at interpersonal and institutional levels and engage in appropriate action to actualize these changes. We would like to emphasize that our conceptualization of action includes critical thinking that considers the benefits as well as the risks of possible consequences associated with interrupting various forms of oppression. This includes reflecting on issues of personal safety, the potential impact on interpersonal relationships, and the repercussions of violating policies and laws. There are many examples of social action on college campuses, most falling into one of two categories: proactive and reactive. Too often college students are not prepared to act but to react, only demanding institutional change or intervention when an unjust act has occurred on their campus. An example of reactive action was seen on our campus when students organized protests challenging the university's response to a race-based hate crime and the subsequent arrest of an African American undergraduate student who acted in self-defense when attacked by two White men in his residence hall (Schworm, 2009). Students of color, White students, faculty, student affairs administrators, and members of the community acted in solidarity to voice their anger and frustration with the university's complacency and with the local court system's unjust prosecution of this victimized student.

In addition to those actions initiated in direct response to specific unjust situations, students also engage in proactive action, taking steps to enact positive social change that help to create a more just and diverse climate on their campus. As discussed throughout this book, a proactive social action can be found in intergroup dialogues, where equal numbers of students from two or more social identity groups with a history of conflict or oppression meet for sustained, facilitated dialogue (often as a part of a credit-bearing course). An important part of the intergroup dialogue process is action planning and alliance building (Zúñiga, Nagda, Chesler, & Cytron-Walker, 2007). Writing about the connection between intergroup dialogue and social action, Chesler (2001) reminded intergroup dialogue facilitators that if the "new insights and understandings, about oneself and one's own cultural group as well as about others' are not translated into new personal and collective action, a major opportunity has been lost" (p. 294). Students studying on our campus, and at an increasing number of campuses across the United States, now have the opportunity to enroll in intergroup dialogue courses and programs that challenge them to enhance their personal awareness, educate others, interrupt oppressive behavior, and work toward institutional and systemic social change.

If we were to plot the preceding examples of action on the action continuum, the students who organized and participated in protests and marches on our campus demonstrated action at the initiating/preventing level. Students who choose to participate in intergroup dialogues exemplify the educating self and supporting/encouraging types of action. Later in this chapter, we explore the potential in intergroup dialogue for students to also engage in the other forms of action for diversity and social justice (Adams et al., 2007).

FACILITATING STUDENTS' SOCIAL ACTION ENGAGEMENT

Having defined what we mean by social action, we provide some context about how educators can prepare college students to engage in thoughtfully considered social actions—how we can facilitate this learning. One theoretical framework that informs our practice is Broido's (2000) research on ally development among college students. Conducting a phenomenological study, Broido examined how college students understand their development as social justice allies and how the college environment may influence this development. Her study provided a number of valuable insights about the experiences of college students involved in social justice work.

Participants in Broido's (2000) study first and foremost shared a commonality of entering college with attitudes that aligned with the aims of social justice work. In particular, these students held egalitarian views; they believed discrimination is wrong and that people in society are fundamentally equal. Further, participants shared a common theme of entering social justice work on campus after being recruited by others. They described entering this work as unintentional and not self-directed. Either their peers encouraged them to get involved, or they discovered a cause or change effort through their membership or leadership role in an organization or club (e.g., diversity training as a resident assistant). Participant responses were also categorized into three major thematic components that contributed to the students' ally development: increased information on social justice, engagement with meaning-making processes, and self-confidence. Specifically they described how learning about different perspectives, understanding why diversity is important, and gaining insights on the experiences of target identities played roles in their becoming allies.

Engagement in meaning-making processes was the second theme Broido (2000) discovered. Participants expressed being able to make sense of the new information they gathered by discussing it with others, reflecting, and attempting to take on another's perspective when speaking. This meaning-making process helped participants build confidence and gain clarity about their personal thoughts regarding social justice. Finally, the theme of self-confidence contributed to ally development as participants discussed how they had to build confidence in their identities but also develop the ability to explain their social justice personal beliefs and address injustice when confronted. Although many participants indicated they already had confidence prior to becoming social justice allies, all mentioned how additional or a different kind of confidence was needed to further pursue this work.

Broido's (2000) work highlights some key findings educators should keep in mind when encouraging their students to pursue social action steps. One interesting finding was the connection between students' ally development and the role of student affairs professionals in their processes. The participants made no mention of how student affairs professionals helped them become social justice allies outside resident assistant positions and residence life programming. In addition, although conducting ally development work in the classroom was mentioned, most of the venues in which participants engaged in their work took place outside the classroom through membership or leadership roles in student organizations or in the residence halls.

As a result of these findings, specific recommendations for student affairs professionals include fostering self-confidence, developing skills, interrupting oppressive instances, and increasing efforts to make ally and social action opportunities more widely known to students (Broido, 2000). Although peer interactions are beneficial to students engaging with social justice work, we believe it is important to consider how we as facilitators can better support students in pursuing this work intentionally instead of by happenstance. There is more we can do as facilitators to move beyond building awareness and guiding the analysis process so that our students can pursue social change and thus build a support network to sustain their action.

The foundations for this chapter, defining social action and identifying a pedagogical framework for preparing students to take action, began as a verbal dialogue between the two of us, Andrea Domingue ("Dre") and Dave Neely. The next section of this chapter is formatted in a conversational style inspired by a chapter written by Beverly Daniel Tatum and Andrea Ayvazian (2004), "Women, Race, and Racism: A Dialogue in Black and White." Tatum and Ayvazian wrote this piece as a means to collaboratively answer questions each had received regarding how one goes about developing a meaningful relationship across racial identities. This dialogic format along with the authentic expression of their collaboration as social justice educators resonated with us, as we too have worked together in facilitating social action among students. We have chosen to continue our ongoing dialogue in the written words presented here. Welcome to the conversation.

OUR STORY: ENTERING INTO SOCIAL ACTION

Dre: Before we discuss how we facilitate social action, Dave, how about giving a brief overview about our backgrounds and how we became friends and collaborators?

Dave: We've had a long relationship as friends, classmates, and colleagues, and I think that one important aspect of our friendship is the way our scholarly and professional paths have mirrored one another's since we first met seven years ago in a student affairs master's degree program. After completing our master's degrees together at New York University, our paths continued to align when we were both admitted to doctoral programs at the University of Massachusetts Amherst. From my perspective, our friendship has continued to grow stronger as we have continued to see the ways our passions are closely aligned. I greatly respect your commitment to social justice education and the incredible energy you bring to this work. Dre, is this how you remember our relationship beginning?

Dre: I totally agree with this, Dave, and would just like to build on how our relationship formed. I think it is also important to discuss how we each became drawn to social action in higher education. Our motivation for writing this chapter together was based on a series of dialogues we have had over the past two years about the intersections between social justice and higher education. While there are differences in the ways our unique interests relate to social justice work in higher education, we share a desire not only to raise students' awareness about oppression but also to help students develop an interest and capacity to pursue some type of social action.

Dave: Also, along with all our similarities, there are also significant differences between us in terms of our social identities. These differences have no doubt had a considerable impact on the ways we facilitate and approach social action. Would you mind sharing some of your thoughts about the ways your social identities have shaped your journey with taking and facilitating social action?

Dre: I agree it is critical to reflect on the impact of our social identities. I am an African American lesbian woman who was raised in a middle-class household in Texas. College was a time in my life where I began to develop a consciousness about oppression in general as well as how it related to my sexual orientation, gender, and racial identities. My campus did have a queer students of color organization that concentrated on social action to address racism and sexism. However, at the time I did not believe I had the skills or experience to join such efforts and mostly wanted to build my own social support network. During my sophomore year I took a sociology course called Deviance, where the primary objective was to identify social norms in the United States, analyze conformity to norms, and explore the various ways people react to norm violations.

Dave: The thought of taking a course on social deviance really intrigues me. Can you say more about the structure of the course and how it shaped your thinking about social action?

Dre: While there were readings, lectures, and film clips in this course to help illustrate concepts regarding social deviance, the most significant learning for me came from our interactive homework assignments. These assignments could be as low or high risk as we wanted, and we had to be sure to document others' reactions to our deviant actions as well as our own reactions. I can clearly recall one assignment that has had a lasting impact on me to this day. The setting for the activity was in my role as a resident assistant, and this felt like a slightly higher risk to me. To pursue my assignment about disrupting social norms, I decided to stand up for a portion of a staff meeting where we normally all sat around a table while participating in team-building activities and discussing the week's agenda. Initially, my supervisors and peers were inquisitive about why I was standing and asked me questions, mostly related to my health, regarding why I did not want to sit down. When I assured them that everything was fine, I noticed stares and glances from the staff throughout the experience. My peers reacted by laughing and making jokes and some even tried a variety of tactics to persuade me to sit down. At one point, one of the supervisors became noticeably frustrated and distracted, ultimately expressing that she viewed my act as disruptive and defiant, despite the fact there were no rules or guidelines that required me to sit during a meeting. I later had a conversation with my supervisors and explained to them that my actions were part of an effort to meet a class assignment.

Dave: It sounds as though your experiences related to this course were very meaningful to you. Do you feel they were connected to your development as a social justice facilitator?

Dre: Yes, the events related to this course and my undergraduate experiences with student organizations have had a lasting impact on my life. It took me several years to realize how these moments served as a catalyst to my commitment to social justice work and taking social action and how my instructor's facilitation of experiential activities became the foundation of my social action engagement work. The course assignments provided me with some insights on the wide range of reactions others may have to interruptions of social norms. It also put me in touch with my own individual reactions and emotions to taking such steps. Unfortunately, my instructor did not prepare me for the ways my decision to stand up for the duration of a staff meeting would have an impact on the way others viewed me. I gained a complex reputation as a courageous person, committed to challenging social expectations, and in some instances as an instigator—labels that have continued to follow me through my career as an educator. Had my instructor facilitated an intentional debriefing about the experiences we had when participating in the activities and offered some insights about the ways people might respond to these actions, it would have made the affirmations and critiques of my later action work more informed.

What about you, Dave? How have your social identities affected your commitment to social action?

Dave: As with you, my social identities have connected with my motivation to engage in social change efforts and have shaped the ways I approach action. As a middle-class, able-bodied, heterosexual White man, I arrive at my work as a social justice educator with a knapsack overflowing with unearned privilege (see McIntosh, 2004). My journey toward becoming a social justice ally began as an undergraduate student, where friendships, course work, and campus activities helped me begin to understand the vast social inequalities in our society and the immense privileges my social group memberships give me. These experiences as an undergraduate student not only paved the way for me to engage in critical self-reflection and social action but also led to my passion for working with college students. It has been my hope that I can help in some way facilitate the type of reflection and consciousness-raising I myself experienced as an undergraduate student.

Dre: Do you remember any specific experiences as an undergraduate student that facilitated a shift in your consciousness?

Dave: If I were to single out one critical moment from my time as an undergraduate student that moved me forward the most on my path toward becoming a social justice educator, it would be a project that I completed for a course on multicultural education. The project was supposed to help me become better prepared to teach and support students from a diversity of backgrounds. At that time I planned on becoming a high school music teacher. For the project I chose to survey a group of gay friends who sang with me in the men's glee club about their experiences in their high school choir classrooms. I asked them if their choir classes and activities were safe and supportive spaces for queer or questioning students. I was interested in learning for myself and educating other teachers about ways to make their music classrooms safer environments for queer students.

Dre: Can you say more about how this experience affected your commitment to social justice?

Dave: While completing this project, I began to truly recognize my heterosexual privilege for the first time. This was also the first time I identified as an ally to a socially disadvantaged group, and I made this commitment known to my classmates, friends, and family. After taking a stand to confront homophobia in myself and in others, I also became more passionate about understanding the struggles of other oppressed groups and peeling back the layers of my own multiple privileged identities. This class project provided me with one of my first opportunities to engage in social action by inspiring me to continue educating myself.

Dre: What were some of the reactions you faced as a result of your taking on an ally role?

Dave: Some of my friends and family members were confused over why I had become so passionate about supporting disadvantaged groups. My commitment to social justice seemed to make some of my friends feel uncomfortable or guilty about their own privileges. I began to recognize who I could go to for support as an ally and who I could not. There were also positive outcomes for me, including an increased sense of integrity and being able to build more authentic and trusting relationships with friends from other races, ethnicities, religions, and sexual orientations.

Dre: My call to action was slightly different from yours, Dave. I was involved with my campus's Safe Space program and held a number of general workshops to educate others on terminology and how to support lesbian, gay, bisexual, and transgender (LGBT) individuals. My motivations for this work stemmed from my own struggles with gaining support from family and peers, and it was my hope to make the campus, if not society as a whole, less difficult than what I had experienced. Within a year of being involved with this program, I had a desire to increase my sphere of influence and make a deeper impact. My next step was to advocate for the establishment of an LGBT resource center.

Dave: It sounds like you were really breaking new ground on your campus. How did you sustain this momentum?

Dre: Through conversations, my peers and I decided that student organizations were insufficient and that the campus administration should better support our needs. While we had a women's center and multicultural center on campus, the LGBT students did not have a centralized location, funding, or staff liaison. We decided the way to get support was through the student government. We tried to create a greater awareness and support for LGBT issues by running for leadership positions and joining with a party of ally candidates that supported our platform. While the party did not win the election that year, we did have an impact. The student government formed an LGBT agency position that I cochaired, and we were given funds for a cubicle space.

I was eager to be in this position and had high aspirations of next steps to have a staffed center with a definitive space. However, the stress of the position and perceived pressure from the whole campus community was too much to bear. Ultimately I made the very difficult decision to step down from the position. This has been a regret I have carried with me for many years and one that I rarely speak about with others. I chose to share my personal struggle with stepping down from a social action opportunity to highlight first how burnout and pressure can affect students who are committed to social justice work, especially if they do not have a support network to sustain them. I also wanted to express the necessity of practicing self-care as social justice allies. While I do regret my decision somewhat, I also feel it was a necessary decision for my mental and academic well-being. Making that decision to take time to step back from the work helped me to rejuvenate myself and gain clarity on how much of myself I give to this work. This balance is something I struggle with to this day, but this decision was foundational in my future to become a facilitator and to model self-care to my students.

Dave: I agree that finding balance is essential to sustaining efforts for social action. Can you say more about this?

Dre: The primary way I instill self-care in my work as a facilitator is to help students develop personal boundaries for themselves and to encourage them to have the agency to speak up when they need a break. One technique I use often is to have students develop lists of all the projects they are currently or hope to be involved with. Once the students have completed these lists, I have them prioritize their lists and develop an action plan to complete these current and intended activities. Through a series of guided questions I first ask students to consider if their goal is realistic given a specific time constraint. I also encourage them to consider how their initial action plan will coincide with their academic responsibilities, personal relationships, and health. While at times I am transparent and honest with students regarding my opinions about the feasibility of their work, it is my first choice to have them critically reflect and make decisions about their social action work and self-care on their own.

Dave: Thank you, Dre, for sharing this personal experience related to your own social action engagement. Similarly there have been times when I have joined efforts to make positive social change, but there have also been occasions where I have held back from engaging in action because of my fear of potential consequences. I participated in direct action for the first time as an undergraduate student when I participated in a rally and march organized by fellow students who were outraged with the United States' invasion of Iraq. It was thrilling for me to raise my voice in solidarity with others as we made our collective frustration and calls for change known to the broader public. However, less than two years later when I was a graduate student in New York City, I found myself holding back from engaging in any of the numerous antiwar actions that were taking place in Manhattan during the 2004 Republican National Convention. Only a year into my first student affairs assistantship position, I was concerned that I could jeopardize relationships and opportunities that were important to my academic and financial success if I was detained or arrested while involved in a protest. Though difficult for me to admit, the potential costs to my own personal success held me back from engaging in action. This kind of fear poses a challenge for me when facilitating social action with students. I find myself encouraging students to take risks and engage in social action but to be prepared for the potential repercussions of their actions. I think it is important to encourage students to find ways to take actions that align with their comfort levels in terms of risk. I have found the action continuum mentioned previously to be a helpful tool in helping students decide the ways in which they are prepared to act.

Dre: Are there other forms of social action that you have taken?

Dave: On a more personal level, I continually attempt to confront my own oppressive attitudes and behavior and strive to educate others about social inequalities. Over the past decade, I have become more confident sharing my passion for social change and concerns about racism, sexism, and homophobia in academic circles with my classmates and at home with my partner. However, until recently, I have largely remained silent outside these more comfortable settings. In fact, only in the past few years have I felt prepared and confident enough to directly confront my friends, colleagues, and family members when I observe them embracing negative stereotypes or attitudes or making comments about disadvantaged groups. Today, I am continuing to work through the fears I associate with confronting others.

Dre: Clearly we both have a passion for engaging in social change efforts to create a more socially just society, but we have also encountered personal challenges including overcommitment and the fear of repercussions. In the same way, taking action is challenging for our students.

Dave: Yes, taking action can be challenging for students despite a long legacy of campus activism. Turning to facilitating social actions, what challenges have you encountered?

Dre: One of the first significant challenges when facilitating social action is that individuals have very different understandings of what it means to take action. Just as there are varying theoretical meanings of social action, there are also various practical interpretations of what taking action means. These differences were particularly poignant when I cofacilitated a discussion with students in an intergroup dialogue course. When I asked the group participants what they envisioned when I said the word *activism,* responses ranged from interrupting a joke to participating in rallies or a demonstration. These differences became even clearer when I asked the students to explain the difference between being an ally and being an activist. Some students viewed being an ally as supporting social justice in name only, while others viewed being an ally as vital to interrupting oppression. Few students wanted to claim the term *activist* to describe themselves, and they said they often associated this term with someone who had significant organizing skills and the ability to recruit others and motivate them to take action on a specific issue.

Emotional barriers can also prevent individuals from taking social action. Considering how deeply ingrained oppression is in our society, taking steps to stop or change these systems may frighten individuals. For those students who are committed to social justice, they may find their values differ from those of their peers or family. They may experience judgment or ridicule from other students, friends, or family. In addition, individuals may encounter repercussions from the campus administration or law enforcement if action efforts knowingly or unknowingly break policies or laws. In some cases, the ramifications of such violations may follow individuals well through their college and professional careers.

Dave: Has your reflection on your experience as an intergroup dialogue cofacilitator had an impact on how you facilitate now?

Dre: Since leading this intergroup dialogue, I have learned to take a different approach in facilitating social action and unpacking the various forms it can take. Through my teaching of another social justice course, Social Diversity in Education, I have altered my facilitation of exploring social action in two main ways. First, discussions about defining and understanding social action take place multiple times throughout a semester. Having regular conversations about social action provides students with a space to continually question and shape the actual action projects they will ultimately implement before the conclusion of the course. The second strategy I now use is to supplement these conversations by incorporating multiple video clips of college student activism. Students have appreciated seeing these videos, as they can more tangibly grasp what social action looks like on campus, and they also describe feeling more empowered and hopeful of its possibility as they see individuals with comparable college experiences taking these steps toward change.

Dave: I have to admit that, like many students, I also have fears about the potential repercussions of encouraging my current and future students to take social action in terms of my job security and career advancement. Even though higher education is often perceived to be more socially progressive than other institutions, colleges and universities can be hostile environments for employees who question the status quo or encourage their students to challenge unjust policies or practices. Going back to the action continuum, some forms of action are more public and controversial than others. I have few fears about encouraging students to educate themselves and others about forms of oppression and injustice. However, I still fear that participating in or preparing students for the types of action that fall within the initiating/ preventing category, such as working to change institutional actions and policies, could lead to my gaining a reputation as a troublemaker or whistle-blower. While I aspire to grow in my career as a socially engaged educator, the headlines of higher education periodicals remind me of the costs student affairs administrators and faculty pay when they challenge campus policies or call for progressive change that runs counter to an institution's financial bottom line. Courage, collaboration, dialogue, and patience are often necessary for successfully navigating the political waters in higher education.

Dre: I agree with you, Dave. It is important for us to remain in continual dialogue with ourselves about the factors that motivate us and hold us back from acting in different situations. I also want to share some of the specific lessons that I have learned from my students regarding the unique challenges they face in taking social action. One example comes from my experience as an adviser of an LGBT peer education program. As the adviser, it was my responsibility to design and facilitate trainings for students to help prepare them for the educational programs they were to lead on campus. This intensive one-week training took place during the beginning of the academic year, just before new and returning students arrived on campus. As we discussed earlier, integrating the intersections of our multiple social identities has been a driving force in my student affairs practice, so it was important to me that I included this ideology in my work with the program. While a few sessions focused primarily on teaching content about race, religion, and social class, the training included little room for action beyond students' practicing facilitating workshops, and it lacked collaboration with other diversity-focused peer education programs on the campus.

Dave: Were you able to build on what you learned from this experience?

Dre: Yes, recognizing this shortcoming, the facilitators of the multicultural office and I had a series of conversations about ways to have our peer educators interact and work together to better address social justice and diversity issues on campus. We felt that having a few joint training sessions would help foster a more collaborative relationship that would hopefully generate some innovative programmatic efforts addressing multiple identities. While we developed a few content-based sessions throughout this training, we also implemented an action project called the New York City Borough Tour, an effort led by one of the graduate assistants of the multicultural office. The goal of this project was provide students with an opportunity not only to expand their knowledge base of LGBT and multicultural resources beyond the local area (mostly lower Manhattan neighborhoods close to campus) but also to have the students from two peer education groups explore new places together and work across differences. Students were assigned to groups by the facilitation team and given the following guidelines: travel to the assigned borough, visit and collect information from a variety of landmarks in those areas that relate to multicultural and LGBT topics, and finally, create a presentation to share with their peers about their experiences.

Dave: How did that turn out?

Dre: The reactions from each group included a mixture of excitement, nervousness, and resistance. Some students struggled with the action project as it moved them out of their comfort zones, particularly as it relates to social identities. While the students represented varying socioeconomic backgrounds, this project asked them to move outside the privileges they experienced while studying at a large private institution. Language was also a concern as some neighborhoods in the other boroughs had concentrated areas where English was not the primary spoken language. Considering intergroup relations, some White students, who were predominantly in the

LGBT peer education group, showed discomfort in traveling to racially diverse locations. Similarly, students of color, who were mostly in the multicultural peer education group, showed discomfort in visiting LGBT landmarks.

Despite their initial resistance, the students ended up enjoying the project and had some important takeaways from the experience. They planned new programmatic initiatives on multiple identities that were implemented throughout the academic year. Perhaps the most significant benefit was observing the gradual ways that the relationship between the two peer education programs grew stronger. However, I do think there were some missteps in this effort to foster collaboration and mindfulness of the intersectionality among target identity groups. I think the advising team could have done a better job setting up this project by allowing more time for team building in the small groups. Students were informed of their group assignments the day of the project and had no time to get to know each other and strategize about how to complete the project beforehand. In addition, because the project was so heavily directed by the facilitators, students had little opportunity to develop ownership of the initiative, which may have influenced some initial resistance from the students. Rather than giving students an exhaustive landmark list or borough locations, facilitators could have had student groups brainstorm to find these places themselves. Finally, the reflection component of the project could have been improved. Other reflection components such as pre- and postproject journal entries could have been useful, particularly if these entries connected to the training's content sessions.

Dave: It is very exciting for me to learn about the successes you have had creating action partnerships between students from different social identity groups. Hearing about some of the limitations of this project reminds me of other limitations I have encountered in my own facilitation. One of the greatest challenges of preparing students for action in my current role as a teaching assistant has been working in a very limited amount of time. A course in which I facilitated class discussions held to a more traditional format with all the students attending a large lecture once a week and then meeting in their smaller discussion sections once a week for slightly over an hour.

While the faculty instructor of the course gave me substantial autonomy over teaching my section, a portion of 75 minutes I spent with students each week needed to be set aside for reviewing the assigned readings and material presented in the lectures as well as for answering questions about the syllabus and class assignments. In my efforts to create a class community where students felt comfortable sharing personal stories with one another and engaging in dialogue, I also devoted a considerable amount of class time to icebreakers and to sharing personal experiences in small groups and pairs. Often I found myself trying to find ways to squeeze in preparation for and reflection about action around the edges of my lesson plans, instead of as a central theme.

Dre: This has been a struggle for me as well. What have been some strategies you have used to work around this?

Dave: One strategy I have found effective for working with limited time is incorporating action planning into small-group activities at the beginning of class meetings. In the classes before Thanksgiving weekend and spring break, I dedicated the beginning of the class to a group planning activity where students helped one another think of the types of opportunities that exist for engaging in action during these holiday breaks. I encouraged the students to think specifically about the different people they would be spending time with, such as members of their immediate or extended families and groups of friends from high school or college. In these small-group dialogues, students helped one another think of examples of racist, sexist, classist, or homophobic (all the forms of oppression we had covered at that point in the semester) attitudes and behavior they expected to encounter. The students then strategized ways for interrupting and confronting oppressive comments, jokes, or actions. I let the students know we would have a class conversation when we returned from the holiday to reflect on the opportunities for action we encountered and how we responded. In helping our students prepare for engaging in action, it is crucial that we provide a model for our students about what different types of action might look like in real-life situations. When introducing this activity, I give examples from my own life about instances when I have challenged negative stereotypes held by my own friends and family members. I also acknowledge that many times I have missed opportunities to act. I have found that modeling personal storytelling and allowing myself to be vulnerable in front of students helps them take risks in the stories they are willing to share.

Dre: I completely agree that it is exciting to think about the ways we can learn from one another's experiences and integrate the successful ideas each of us have included in our teaching. The class project you just described is similar in some respects to an opportunity I had to prepare students to take social action through an intergroup dialogue course. While the students interested in dialogue are typically motivated to engage with peers of varying backgrounds, for some this may be the first time they actually work in diverse groups. Consciously and unconsciously some students bring in stereotypes about social identities and may even fall into traditional or historical roles (such as women as note takers, men as dominant leaders, people of color in the background, etc.). As you mentioned, Dave, a similar challenge for me as an intergroup dialogue facilitator is the time constraints we face. Perhaps the most strenuous challenge is attempting to build collective leadership in a short period of time. Collective leadership is a type of group where hierarchy is dismantled, and all group members have a vital role in the group's progress and decision making.

INSIGHTS FOR SOCIAL JUSTICE EDUCATORS

Based on our experiences with facilitating courses and workshops that connect students with opportunities for social action, we believe it is important to continually reflect on the successes and challenges that surface in our practice. Our intersecting identities, our lived experiences, and knowledge of social justice pedagogy shape the choices we make in our facilitation with students. Here are six key suggestions we think may be valuable for social justice educators to consider when designing and facilitating workshops, programs, and courses.

- ◆ Place an emphasis on social action engagement at the beginning of courses or workshops, and maintain this focus throughout the duration of the semester or program. All too often an early focus is placed on sharing information and analyzing content, while time for action planning and reflecting on action is pushed off until the last class meeting or section of a workshop. One opportunity for facilitators to instill a focus on action at the beginning of a learning process is to give examples of their own efforts to create change in the personal introductions when first meeting a group of students. Another way to encourage students to reflect on action over the course of a multiday workshop or semester-long course is to ask them to bring in examples of social action they find in print or online publications. These action examples can also be included in a gallery walk activity.

- Provide current and historical examples of social action and activism, particularly of other students and young people who are engaged in social action. The knowledge that other students are planning and taking meaningful action that creates real change can be a source of empowerment for our students. One source for examples of youth actions can be found in the lists of youth victories that have been published in recent years by *The Nation* magazine, for example King, Rizga, and Palermo (2008).

- Promote leadership opportunities for students and identify creative ways to hold students accountable for the actions they plan on taking. Whether the session is a one-time workshop or semester-long course, some students conclude these sessions looking for guidance and suggestions to continue social action initiatives. One suggestion to help students navigate the next steps they want to take is to offer a listing of student organizations, projects, and additional courses to explore. These opportunities can also be documented on a website, blog, or social media site for students to return to throughout their time on campus. One suggestion for instilling leadership and accountability is to ask students from previous semesters or workshops to return to share their action with current students. While it can be helpful to provide examples of other young people engaging in social action across the country or across the world, it is particularly powerful for students to see what peers on their own campus are capable of accomplishing. Facilitators may want to begin collecting an archive of campus newspaper stories about student activism or video clips showing creative and collaborative approaches to social action.

- Provide frequent and consistent support to your students. It is essential to check in with students who are engaging in social action to listen to their frustrations, provide guidance when requested, and celebrate their victories. In addition, facilitators should take these opportunities to help students make meaning from their experiences by reflecting on their social action.

- Identify sources of support for yourself as a facilitator. As discussed earlier, self-care and striving for some balance between social action work and other life responsibilities is vital to sustain our commitment to social change and avoid burnout. Whether in your family, on your campus, or through a professional organization, seek out other educators who are passionate about facilitating for social action. It is important to find other colleagues with whom you can create a supportive community.

♦ Be courageous and take risks in your facilitation. Many of us may have been encouraged to be guarded with students as it may compromise our leadership as facilitators. However, in many instances sharing insights and experiences from our personal lives can serve as points of connection with our students. While it is important to navigate the fine line where sharing personal fears and challenges may stifle a group's process, these are the moments, when we bring our emotions (joyful and painful) into our facilitation, that get students excited about engaging in action.

CONCLUSION

We are roused and inspired by Cornel West's compelling words about courage and reflection in practice.

> It takes courage to interrogate yourself. It takes courage to look in the mirror and see past your reflection to who you really are when you take off the mask, when you're not performing the same old routines and social roles. It takes courage to ask—how did I become so well adjusted to injustice? It takes courage to cut against the grain and become non-conformist. It takes courage to wake up and stay awake instead of engaging in complacent slumber. It takes courage to shatter conformity and cowardice. (West, 2008, p. 13)

For us, we keep self-reflection central to our work by engaging in the type of ongoing dialogue highlighted earlier in this chapter. Through our ongoing dialogue we have established a trusting and strong partnership that allows us to be open to each other's feedback. Our dialogues are a safe space where we can seek support and advice about the challenges that arise in our work. We are able to provide accountability and allyship for one another, two critical aspects of creating a liberatory consciousness (Love, 2000).

It is courage that we as social justice educators can help to instill in our students. In his reflection on courage, West has drafted a blueprint for how to prepare ourselves and our students for engaging in social action. First, there is the necessity for honest self-reflection, seeing and owning up to the good, bad, and ugly truths about ourselves. And then there is the call to remain awake, living every day in a state of liberatory consciousness as we fight back the urge to nod off, back into the old patterns of oppressor and oppressed. Fortunately, we need not shoulder this burden alone, for courage is both solitary and collective. As allies to one another, as teachers and students, as mentors and mentees, we can gather the courage to enact great change.

REFERENCES

Adams, M., Bell, L. A., & Griffin, P. (2007). *Teaching for diversity and social justice* (2nd ed.). New York, NY: Routledge.

Bell, L. A., & Griffin, P. (2007). Designing social justice education courses. In M. Adams, L. A. Bell, & P. Griffin (Eds.), *Teaching for diversity and social justice* (2nd ed., pp. 67–87). New York, NY: Routledge.

Biddix, J. P., Somers, P. A., & Polman, J. L. (2009). Protest reconsidered: Identifying democratic and civic engagement learning outcomes. *Innovative Higher Education, 34*, 133–147.

Broido, E. M. (2000). The development of social justice allies during college: A phenomenological investigation. *Journal of College Student Development, 41*(1), 3–18.

Chambers, P., & Phelps, C. E. (1993). Student activism as a form of leadership and student development. *Journal of Student Affairs Research and Practice, 31*(1), 19–29.

Chesler, M. (2001). Extending intergroup dialogue: From talk to action. In D. Schoem & S. Hurtado (Eds.), *Intergroup dialogue: Deliberative democracy in school, college, and workplace* (pp. 294–305). Ann Arbor: University of Michigan Press.

Colby, A., Ehrlich, T., Beaumont, E., Rosner, J., & Stephens, J. (2000). Higher education and the development of civic responsibility. In T. Ehrlich (Ed.), *Civic responsibility and higher education* (pp. xxi–xliii). Westport, CT: Oryx Press.

Hamrick, F. A. (1998). Democratic citizenship and social action. *Journal of College Student Development, 39*(5), 449–459.

Hurtado, S., Milem, J. F., Clayton-Pederson, A. R., & Allen, W. (1999). Enacting diverse learning environments: Improving the climate for racial/ethnic diversity in higher education. *ASHE-ERIC Higher Education Report, 26*(8).

King, J., Rizga, K., & Palermo, T. (2008, December 27). Top youth activism victories of 2008. *The Nation*. Retrieved from http://www.thenation.com/article/top-youth-activism-victories-2008

Love, B. J. (2000). Developing a liberatory consciousness. In M. Adams, L. A. Bell, & P. Griffin (Eds.), *Teaching for diversity and social justice* (2nd ed., pp. 470–474). New York, NY: Routledge.

McIntosh, P. (2004). White privilege: Unpacking the invisible knapsack. In P. S. Rothenberg (Ed.), *Race, class, and gender in the United States* (pp. 188–192). New York, NY: Worth.

Schneider, C. G. (2000). Educational missions and civic engagement: Toward the engaged academy. In T. Ehrlich (Ed.), *Civic responsibility and higher education* (pp. 98–123). Westport, CT: Oryx Press.

Schworm, P. (2009, February 3). One year later UMass protesters see injustice in stabbing case. *Boston Globe*. Retrieved from http://www.boston.com/news/local/ breaking_news/2009/02/umass_protestor_1.html

Tatum, B. D., & Ayvazian, A. (2004). Women, race, and racism: A dialogue in Black and White. In J. V. Jordan, M. Walker, & L. M. Hartling (Eds.), *The complexity of connection: Writings from the Stone Center's Jean Baker Miller Training Institute* (pp. 147–163). New York, NY: Guilford Press.

West, C. (2008). *Hope on a tightrope: Words and wisdom*. New York, NY: Smileybooks.

Wijeyesinghe, C., Griffin, P., & Love, B. (1997). Racism curriculum design. In M. Adams, L. A. Bell, & P. Griffin (Eds.), *Teaching for diversity and social justice* (pp. 82–109). New York, NY: Routledge.

Zúñiga, X., Nagda, B. A., Chesler, M., & Cytron-Walker, A. (2007). Intergroup dialogue in higher education: Meaningful learning about social justice. *ASHE Higher Education Report Series, 32*(4).

Zúñiga, X., Williams, E. A., & Berger, J. B. (2005). Action-oriented democratic outcomes: The impact of student involvement with campus diversity. *Journal of College Student Development, 46*(6), 660–678.

About the Editor and Contributors

EDITOR

Lisa M. Landreman is the associate dean of students at Macalester College and an adjunct faculty member at the University of St. Thomas. Lisa received her PhD from the Center for the Study of Higher Education at the University of Michigan, her MS in higher education and student affairs from Indiana University, and her BS in social work from the University of Wisconsin–LaCrosse. Lisa is the author of several publications on social justice topics and has taught and facilitated social justice courses, workshops, and dialogues throughout her career. She currently serves on the ACPA–College Student Educators International equity and inclusion committee; has held directorate body positions on the Commission for Social Justice Educators, the Commission for Housing and Residence Life, and the Commission for Alcohol and Other Drug Issues; and has served on planning teams for the ACPA National Convention, the Social Justice Institute, and the Residential Curriculum Institute. Lisa was recognized in 2011 as an ACPA Diamond Honoree.

EDITORIAL ASSISTANT

Lawrence J. Mrozek is an assistant professor in leadership studies at the University of Central Arkansas. He received his PhD from Ohio State University in higher education and student affairs with a cognate in culture, gender, and sexuality, and his MA from Michigan State University. His research focus is on areas related to understanding and creating inclusive environments on college campuses. Throughout his career Larry has facilitated social justice education workshops across the country. He served on the ACPA–College Student Educators International directorate bodies for the Commission for Social Justice Educators, the Commission for Assessment and Evaluation, and the Commission for Alcohol and Other Drugs.

ACPA–COLLEGE STUDENT EDUCATORS INTERNATIONAL COMMISSION FOR SOCIAL JUSTICE EDUCATORS EDITORIAL BOARD MEMBERS

BRIAN ARAO
STEPHANIE CHANG
MELISSA GILES
MARC LO
HEATHER WILHELM
TANYA O. WILLIAMS

CONTRIBUTORS

BRIAN ARAO is the director of residential programs in the Office of Student Development at the University of California, Berkeley. Brian holds a BA in biology from the University of California, Santa Cruz, and a MEd in higher education and student affairs administration from the University of Vermont. He is pursuing an EdD in international and multicultural education, with an emphasis in human rights education at the University of San Francisco. His dissertation research explores the process by which college students develop the willingness and ability to take risks as participants in social justice education. Brian has been a member of the directorate body for ACPA–College Student Educators International's Commission for Social Justice Educators since 2006 and served as chair from 2011 to 2013.

BRENT L. BILODEAU serves as the assistant vice-chancellor for student affairs at the University of Wisconsin–Whitewater. Brent received a BA from the University of California, Irvine, in psychology and his MA in college and university administration and PhD in higher, adult, and lifelong education from Michigan State University. His research on transgender college students has been recognized with a GLBT Knowledge Community Research Award from the National Association of Student Personnel Administrators and the Scholar-Activist Award from the American Educational Research Association. He is the author of *Genderism: Transgender Students, Binary Systems and Higher Education* (Saarbrücken, Germany: VDM-Verlag, 2009).

Elaine Brigham serves as special assistant to the dean/case manager in the dean of students office at the University of Massachusetts Amherst and co-directs the student Intergroup Dialogue Program at Mount Holyoke College. She is a doctoral student in the Social Justice Education Program at the University of Massachusetts Amherst where she also earned her MEd. Elaine earned undergraduate degrees in history and women studies, with a concentration in African American studies and a minor in education from Guilford College. She has extensive teaching experience at the high school and college levels and spends summers directing a nonprofit diversity and social justice–focused arts and outdoors program for youths.

Kristi Clemens serves as the assistant dean of undergraduate students and director of case management at Dartmouth College. Kristi earned an MEd in higher education and student affairs administration at the University of Vermont and a BS in speech and interpersonal communication from New York University. Kristi served as the chair of ACPA–College Student Educators International's Commission for Social Justice Educators from 2008 to 2011 and has been a member of the commission since its founding in 2006.

Karen Connors worked in residence life at James Madison University. She is currently a doctoral student at the University of Virginia. She received her BA degree from Pennsylvania State University in secondary education and her MA from the University of Miami in higher education administration.

Andrea D. Domingue received her BA in mathematics and sociology from the University of Texas–Austin and her MA in higher education administration from New York University. She is currently pursuing a doctorate at the University of Massachusetts Amherst focusing on social justice education and is an instructor for a diversity course in the School of Education. Her dissertation work is centered on the historical and psychological constructions of college student leadership development among African American women.

Rebecca Heselmeyer is a staff counselor in residence at James Madison University's Counseling and Student Development Center, adjunct instructor in the clinical mental health and school counseling programs, and a member of the Rockingham Memorial Psychiatric Emergency Team. She holds MA and EdS degrees from James Madison University in community counseling and is a doctoral candidate in the counseling and supervision

PhD program. She has given several presentations on intercultural worldview development.

DUSTY M. KRIKAU is the assistant director of international student services at Indiana University South Bend. Dusty received her BS in public communication from the University of Wisconsin–Eau Claire and her MEd with a concentration in college student personnel administration from James Madison University.

TRACY L. LANIER is teaching seventh grade in Charlotte, North Carolina, with Teach for America. Previously she served as the assistant director of multicultural student services at James Madison University. Tracy received a BS in communication studies and her MA in adult education human resource development from James Madison University.

MATTHEW R. LEE received his PhD in clinical/community psychology from the University of Illinois. He serves as cochair of the Asian American Psychological Association annual convention and his honors include the 2011 James Madison University Diversity Enhancement Award and the 2009 American Psychological Association Division 2 Society for the Teaching of Psychology Award for Infusing Diversity in Teaching. Recent publication topics include teaching diversity, privilege, and intersectionality; and Asian American student experiences at predominantly White universities.

CHRISTOPHER MACDONALD-DENNIS is the dean of multicultural life at Macalester College. Christopher received a BA in sociology from Framingham State University, an MS in college student development and counseling from Northeastern University, and an EdD in social justice education from the University of Massachusetts Amherst. Christopher currently serves on the directorate body of ACPA–College Student Educators International's Commission for Social Justice Educators.

KELLY CARTER MERRILL is currently a visiting scholar of communication studies at Randolph-Macon College. Previously she has served as both a student affairs practitioner and higher education faculty member. Kelly received a BA in studio art from Virginia Tech, an MEd in college student personnel from Pennsylvania State University, and a PhD in higher education administration from Loyola University Chicago. Kelly is coauthor, with

Larry Braskamp, David Braskamp, and Mark Engberg, of the global perspective inventory (GPI).

GREGORY I. MEYER served as the assistant director for civic learning in the Office of Judicial Affairs at James Madison University during the writing of this book but now serves as the director of student development at Lafayette College. He received a BA in music composition from Lehigh University and a MEd in college student personnel administration from James Madison University. Greg was the staff recipient of the 2009 Diversity Enhancement Award at James Madison University.

DAVID S. NEELY is a doctoral candidate and a service-learning specialist at the University of Massachusetts Amherst. He received an MA in higher education administration at New York University, a BA in music education at the University of Michigan, and a Social Justice Education Graduate Certificate in Teaching for Diversity at the University of Massachusetts Amherst. His dissertation research is focused on the integration of dialogue pedagogy and community service-learning.

KATHY OBEAR is a founding faculty member of the Social Justice Training Institute and president of Alliance for Change Consulting. Kathy earned a BA in history/secondary education at Washington College, an MA in student personnel administration from Ohio State University, and an EdD in social justice education at the University of Massachusetts Amherst. Kathy was inducted as an ACPA–College Student Educators International Diamond Honoree in 2011 and currently serves on the governing board of ACPA as director-elect for equity and inclusion.

CHRIS D. OREM is the director of institutional effectiveness at Dabney S. Lancaster Community College. He holds a BA in history from Davidson College, an MA in college student personnel from Bowling Green State University, and a PhD in assessment and measurement from James Madison University.

ADAM J. ORTIZ is a house director at Hampshire College. Adam earned a BA in creative writing from Wheaton College and an MEd in higher education and student affairs administration from the University of Vermont. Adam works with ACPA–College Student Educators International's Multiracial Network. Adam has published articles in the University of Vermont's student affairs journal and is a contributing blogger for the Student Affairs Collaborative.

ROBBIE ROUTENBERG is the associate director of the Global Scholars Program at the University of Michigan, a living-learning community focused on social justice in a global context. robbie obtained a BA in sociology with minors in psychology and cognitive science from State University of New York at Geneseo and holds an MA in higher education administration from the University of Michigan. As senior consultant for InciteChange! Consulting, robbie supports colleges and universities in promoting socially just practice. robbie has coordinated ACPA–College Student Educators International's Institute on Social Justice for the past four years as a directorate member for ACPA's Commission for Social Justice Educators.

REBECCA ROPERS-HUILMAN is professor and chair in the Department of Organizational Leadership, Policy, and Development at the University of Minnesota. She received her BA from the University of Wisconsin–Eau Claire in psychology and German and her MA and PhD from the University of Wisconsin–Madison in higher education. She has published five books and more than 40 articles or book chapters related to equity, diversity, and change in higher education contexts. She has served as the editor of *Feminist Formations*, an interdisciplinary journal featuring feminist scholarship on diverse gendered experiences throughout the world.

ELIZABETH THOMPSON works as an area coordinator in residence life at Mount Holyoke College. She holds a BA in sociology with a minor in gender studies from St. Lawrence and an MA in higher education from the University of Michigan. She serves on the directorate body of ACPA–College Student Educators International's Commission for Social Justice Educators.

NANCY TRANTHAM POE is an associate professor of social work and family studies in the Department of Social Work at James Madison University. Nancy holds a BA in sociology from Roanoke College, an MSW with a concentration in child and family welfare from Virginia Commonwealth University, and a PhD in human development specializing in family studies with a graduate certificate in gerontology from Virginia Tech.

ANNEMARIE VACCARO is a faculty member in the college student personnel program at the University of Rhode Island. She earned a PhD in higher education administration and an MA in sociology from the University of Denver and an MA in student affairs from Indiana University of Pennsylvania. Annemarie has published journal articles on a variety of social justice topics and is the coauthor of *Safe Spaces: Making Schools and Communities Welcoming to LGBT Youth* (Santa Barbara, CA: Greenwood, 2011).

RHIAN WATERBERG serves as the program coordinator for the Young Adult Program at Dana-Farber Cancer Institute. Rhian received an MA in higher education from the University of Michigan. Past publications have included pieces in *About Campus* and the newsletter for the ACPA–College Student Educators International Commission for Social Justice Educators.

HEATHER WILHELM is executive director at InciteChange! Consulting, a social justice consulting firm based in Ann Arbor, Michigan. She received her MA in higher education and student affairs administration from the University of Connecticut and dual bachelor's degrees in English and sociology from the State University of New York at Geneseo. Heather has served on the directorate body for ACPA–College Student Educators International's Commission for Social Justice Educators since 2008 as the newsletter editor and publications coordinator.

TANYA WILLIAMS serves the deputy vice president for institutional diversity and community engagement at Union Theological Seminary. She holds an EdD in social justice education from the University of Massachusetts Amherst, BA degrees in journalism and English and an MS in education administration from Texas A&M University. In past administrative and student development roles, she codirected an intergroup dialogue program and developed peer diversity theater and facilitation groups. Her research focuses on internalized racism and a path to liberation for African American women.

Index

ACPA titles available from Stylus

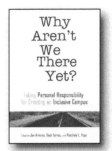

Why Aren't We There Yet?
Taking Personal Responsibility for Creating an Inclusive Campus
Edited by Jan Arminio, Vasti Torres, and Raechele L. Pope

Despite seeming endless debate and public attention given to the issue for several decades, those committed to creating welcoming and engaging campus environments for all students recognize that there is considerably more work to be done, and ask "Why aren't we there yet, and when will we be done?"

This book focuses on guiding individuals and groups through learning how to have difficult conversations that lead us to act to create more just campuses, and provides illustrations of multiple ways to respond to difficult situations. It advocates for engaging in fruitful dialogues regarding differing social identities including race, ethnicity, religion, gender, and sexual orientation, to lead readers through a process that advocates for justice, and for taking personal responsibility for contributing to the solution.

The book is framed around the five elements of the process of engaging in difficult conversations that not only advocate for change but also create change: self-knowledge, knowledge of and experiences with others, understanding historical and institutional contexts, understanding how to change the status quo, and transformative action.

Empowering Women in Higher Education and Student Affairs
Theory, Research, Narratives, and Practice From Feminist Perspectives
Edited by Penny A. Pasque and Shelley Errington Nicholson
Foreword by Linda J. Sax

How do we interrupt the current paradigms of sexism in the academy? How do we construct a new and inclusive gender paradigm that resists the dominant values of the patriarchy? And why are these agendas important not just for women, but for higher education as a whole?

These are the questions that these extensive and rich analyses of the historical and contemporary roles of women in higher education— as administrators, faculty, students, and student affairs professionals—seek constructively to answer. In doing so they address the intersection of gender and women's other social identities, such as of race, ethnicity, sexual orientation, class, and ability.

Multicultural Student Services on Campus
Building Bridges, Re-visioning Community
Edited by Dafina Lazarus Stewart

For new professionals in multicultural student services (MSS), this book constitutes a thorough introduction to the structure, organization, and scope of the services and educational mission of these units. For senior practitioners it offers insights for re-evaluating their strategies, and inspiration to explore new possibilities.

"The authors offer a collective vision of multicultural student services (MSS) that takes the best of what we have learned in the past to move forward in re-visioning the higher education community of the future. This is a bold vision of a newly-fashioned MSS that connects and integrates issues of race and ethnicity with those of sexual orientation, gender identity and religious expression, and takes MSS away from the margins of student and academic affairs units to become a key venue to assist in building transformative and democratic campus communities."—*Laura I. Rendón, Professor at the University of Texas at San Antonio*

22883 Quicksilver Drive
Sterling, VA 20166-2102

Subscribe to our e-mail alerts: www.Styluspub.com